JOHN SIMPSON is the world affairs edito[r ...]
four books about his life and travels, *Stra[...]*
A Mad World, My Masters, News from [...]
Against Saddam. He lives in London with his South African wife,
Dee, and their son, Rafe.

* * *

'If John Simpson's latest volume of autobiography is his most intimate,
it is also delicate and haunting in its remembrance of buried family
matters and their unresolved pain . . . *Days from a Different World* is a
journey back into an almost unrecognisable Britain, a place of stultify-
ing drabness and inhibitions, trapped in post-war rationing and a sort
of toxic fatigue'   *Glasgow Herald*

'This superlative memoir . . . He is blessed as an autobiographer with
an outstandingly strange and only fitfully happy childhood. Further-
more, while we would expect him to have a firm grasp of 20th-century
history and politics, at once authoritative and subversive, what is more
surprising is his tangy, sensuous prose . . . The rationed, soot-black
world of the late 1940s is beautifully evoked . . . Simpson, one senses,
may not be the most demure of men; but with his record – superlative
war reporter, political analyst and now compelling memoirist – he
hasn't a lot to be modest about'   *Sunday Times*

'A superb writer . . . It's a long time since I've enjoyed a personal memoir
so much . . . It's all splendid stuff. Simpson is skilful, clear-eyed, observant, well-informed and compassionate . . . one of the best accounts
I've read of Britain in the post-war years'
                                George Rosie, *Glasgow Sunday Herald*

'A remarkable feat . . . *Days From a Different World* contains a rich
seam of family history . . . It is simultaneously a personal memoir and
an impressionistic history of Britain at the point at which she lost an
empire and much great-power status, though this would not become
fully apparent for several years . . . An unusual and thoughtful book'
                                Tony Gould, *Independent*

ALSO BY JOHN SIMPSON

Strange Places, Questionable People
A Mad World, My Masters
News from No Man's Land
The Wars Against Saddam

JOHN SIMPSON

Days from a Different World

A Memoir of Childhood

PAN BOOKS

First published 2005 by Macmillan

This edition published 2006 by Pan Books
an imprint of Pan Macmillan Ltd
Pan Macmillan, 20 New Wharf Road, London N1 9RR
Basingstoke and Oxford
Associated companies throughout the world
www.panmacmillan.com

ISBN-13: 978-0-330-43562-8
ISBN-10: 0-330-43562-0

1 3 5 7 9 8 6 4 2

A CIP catalogue record for this book is available from
the British Library.

Typeset by SetSystems Ltd, Saffron Walden, Essex
Printed and bound in Great Britain by
Mackays of Chatham plc, Chatham, Kent

All Pan Macmillan titles are available from
www.panmacmillan.com
or from Bookpost by telephoning +44 (0)1624 677237

To my wife, Dee,

with great love and gratitude;

and to my daughters, grandchildren and cousins,

who all share some part in this story.

Contents

Introduction

THIS BOOK, LIKE ME, had its origins in an unprepossessing outer suburb of London. I remember exactly where the idea for writing it came to me: it was in Croydon, close to a little side-street called Kidderminster Place, where my father and mother were nearly killed by the German bombing in July 1944, and I with them, though I was still unborn. My first conscious memory, only a year later, was of being in their flat there. And now, having stayed away from the area for almost sixty years, I paused to take a look at it as I drove back to London from Sussex.

I was returning from the funeral of my father's sister, Daphne. I had loved her, and her death had taken from me the last relative who really knew my father well, and understood the details of so many things that he had done, or that had happened to him, when he was a young man: details that died with her.

It occurred to me that I must be close to Kidderminster Place, and on a whim I flicked the indicator switch, moved across to the middle of the road, and turned right. Until that moment Croydon for me was always somewhere to stay away from, and I had done it pretty successfully for most of my life. Even so, I knew roughly where Kidderminster Place was. I guessed what it would be like, too. This part of Croydon had grown up in the 1860s and 70s, built for people who had striven hard and worked long, but never managed to get anywhere better. During the same period my family, the Simpsons, helped to build an entire suburb of such houses quite close by, in Norwood.

Still, although the approach to it was unchanged, Kidderminster Place itself had disappeared: replaced by an unremarkable little development of houses in the 1980s, I should think. There was a car repair workshop, called Victory Motors, on the corner; which sounded as though it dated from 1945 and was a year younger than me. But the house where my father, my mother and my unborn self were nearly killed by a German bomb as we lay in bed was gone – destroyed not by the Germans but by some particularly unimaginative developer. The same fate, I find, has overcome most of the other places where I spent my childhood: the houses where I and my relatives lived, the school I went to. None of them was worth keeping, I suppose; yet when so many other uninteresting buildings have survived, those associated with my life seem to have fared disproportionately badly.

I sat there for a while, looking at what had become of Kidderminster Place. I didn't get out, and there seemed no point in staying long. Anyway, a man sitting in a car looking at a house always seems suspicious nowadays. I started the engine, and was soon back on the main route to London. But somehow, in the recesses of my mind, a circle had been closed.

Our lives are so short, and all that is left of them after we have gone is a few documents, some photographs, and our fading, increasingly inaccurate memories. After a lifetime's moving and travelling, I have been left with disturbingly little to show for my own and my family's past: half-a-dozen oil portraits of some wealthier ancestors, a few photographs of more recent relatives (not all of them identifiable), and some documents.

The documents are all together, completely unsorted, in an old plastic bag bearing the name of a chain of booksellers which disappeared years ago. It contains a strange mix of things: my old ration-book from my childhood, my father's Army documents, a few letters, some newspaper cuttings about members of the family, a report-card or two from my second school, letters, telegrams, the programme from a concert at my first school. Somehow, all my school caps and some of my school ties have survived. And apart from these, nothing. The rest has vanished for good, scattered by the roadside of my life and the lives of my parents.

Books don't disappear in the same way. They may be fragile, easily torn and burned, yet they have great lasting power; and so the events of my childhood, and the individual characteristics of the members of my family, may have a chance of surviving in this book, instead of evaporating as so much else has.

Not that mine was a particularly eventful childhood, nor a sensational one: no horrors, no mysteries. But it wasn't without its interest either, I hope. The same with my family. They were conventional enough on the surface, yet they were an extraordinary lot in their way; or at least the things that some of them went through were pretty extraordinary.

We are what we are. We cannot choose our families or our countries, though we can, if we so decide, lie about them or move away from them. Yet even if we do, they work away inside us throughout our lives, and if we are really lucky we will come to terms with them eventually, and see them as what they are, not as what we always wanted them to be.

In writing this book, I have tried to be entirely honest about myself, my childhood and my family; and honesty has a certain rarity value, if nothing more. It is an attempt to come to terms with things which are still quite difficult and painful for me. The scope of the book is the course of my parents' troubled marriage, from their first meeting in 1943 to the moment when they parted in 1951, culminating in the difficult choice I eventually had to make between them. It is also a book about the Britain I grew up in, and the way it saw itself: a very different country from what it is now, just as we are all very different from the children we once were. Yet it is still recognizably the same, if only we can stand far enough back from it to see.

I have already written three volumes of autobiography, which is at least two more than anyone should write, and maybe three more than anyone should be invited to read. 'I hope you appreciate,' W. C. Fields once told an interviewer from an American magazine, 'that I am putting myself in serious danger of being arrested for indecent exposure of the personality.' Just so. But then

I am a journalist, and journalists try (or ought to try) to base their work four-square on the things they see and know and can vouch for. And in my case, all I can really vouch for is my own life.

Having said that, I have had to borrow some of the techniques of the Japanese *shishōsetsu*, the I-novel, which is basically autobiographical yet contains episodes which are imagined rather than necessarily experienced. I have, for instance, described the moment my father and mother met for the first time, and their experiences while I was still in the womb, and when I was newly born; and my only evidence for all of this is the stories they both told me at great length when I was a child. Perhaps I misunderstood them, or forgot some of the key elements; perhaps I have drawn entirely the wrong conclusions. Yet they are my memories and conclusions, transcribed as best and as honestly as I could. I chose not to ask anyone else for help or explanation in writing them, because I wanted this to be my version of things, no matter how inadequate it might be.

When I say in this book that I remember something, then that is the case: I do remember it. My memories begin very early, from the time when I was only a little more than a year old. Perhaps that is because my earliest memory, of my mother leaving my father for the first time, was of something so fierce, so strong and so clear that it has stayed with me forcefully for ever.

The other events I remember from my childhood are clarified in the same way: things seem very bright and sharply-edged to me throughout my early years, and I haven't been obliged to invent anything. Except, that is, the dialogue between my parents, and I remember enough of it to be able to reconstruct other conversations with, I hope, reasonable accuracy. But because I wanted this to be more than just my own story, I have tried to open it up, widen it, to take in the experiences of British people in general.

This is the book of someone who has lived much of his life away from his family and his country, and has slowly come round to a deep affection for them both. I can see the failings and shortcomings of them quite clearly, yet long years of watching other people's families and countries have convinced me, not that mine are better than anyone else's, but that they have their good points as well as their bad ones. Because I now understand them both a little better, and to some extent share their characteristics without being blind to their many failings, it is a sense of acceptance, not of pride, which fills this book.

The seventeenth-century poet George Herbert, whose work I have admired since I first read it, at the age of fifteen, hits the tone of affection and understanding perfectly in his poem 'The Son':

> Let foreign nations of their language boast,
> What fine variety each tongue affords:
> I like our language, as our men and coast;
> Who cannot dress it well, want wit, not words.

This is the tone of someone who feels at ease with his fellow-countrymen and women, the language they speak, and the land where they live.

I feel as Herbert does. I have seen for myself the wealth and culture and beauty of other countries, and I understand and admire and respect these things. But I come from one particular place and one particular family, and I belong to both of them, for better and for worse.

My mother's and my father's families were a strange collection of people. In my mother's case a solidly middle-middle-class clan suddenly collided with an extraordinarily déclassé, romantic figure from America who was on friendly terms with royalty and yet committed one of the worst social crimes in pre-First World War society by running off with a married woman and living in sin with her for the remainder of his colourful life.

My father's family were wealthier and grander than my mother's, and dominated the outer London suburb which had partly been constructed by the family business. Yet my grandfather's marriage to my grandmother, forced on them by their own parents for dynastic reasons, was so disastrous that it damaged them and their children socially, financially and emotionally. So while much of the rest of the family continued in their comfortable upper-middle-class way, my father slipped down further and further through the social system until he ended up at last as a factory worker in Croydon; which is what he was when his path intersected with my mother's. I was the result of their not particularly happy union, and was fought over by the two of them until a short time before my seventh birthday.

In this book I have tried to show what happened to one small boy, and one family, and to their world as a whole, on one day per year from 1943 to 1951. I hope my mother and father, and all the rest of my family, will forgive me for the things I have said about them. I may not believe in an afterlife, but I have felt their presence very closely as I wrote. I hope too that my surviving relatives, my half-brother Michael and my half-sister Pat, my cousins Joan and Jane and Peter and Amanda and Suzy, will accept what I have written, even if my view of things differs from their own.

My thanks go to my agent, Julian Alexander, and my editor, George Morley, who both wanted me to write this book even when I was reluctant to do so; to Philippa McEwan and the rest of the people at Macmillan, who have been such a pleasure to work with; to the London Library and its staff; to my cousins Amanda Fidler and Suzy Neate, for entrusting their valuable family photographs to me; to my sister-in-law and assistant, Gina Nelthorpe-Cowne, and her husband Mark, who have made my life so much easier and more enjoyable; and of course to my wife Dee, whose wholehearted support and companionship I have relied on in this, as in everything else.

Paris, April 2005

Sunday 15 July 1951

Sun rises, 4.59 a.m.; sets, 9.11 p.m.
Lighting-up time: 9.41 p.m.
Maximum temperature, 70°F; minimum, 53°F.
Rainfall: nil.
Sunshine: 6.3 hours.
Light southerly winds, occasional cloud thinning
by late morning.

THE ROW HAS gone on all night.

I must have slept through most of it, though I am faintly aware of what has happened when my mother climbs into my little bed with its springs and its flock mattress. The bed is precarious and inclined to tip, yet everything is remarkably satisfactory once we have established a mutually comfortable position, her arm around me, her quiet breathing in my ear. Protection, certainty, peace.

'Is everything all right?'

'Yes, darling, of course it is. Don't wake Daddy.'

'And will we all go to the Festival tomorrow?'

'Everything will be fine.'

That doesn't quite seem to be an answer, but I am too sleepy to divine it.

'Just go back to sleep. I'll sing you a little song.'

She whispers it in my ear:

> Oh, my babby,
> My curly-headed babby,
> Your daddy's in the cotton-fields,
> Workin' hard at noon.
>
> It's toora-loola, toora-loola, babby,
> In your mammy's arms be creepin',
> An' soon you'll be a-sleepin',
> Toora-loora-loora-loora-loora bye.

I drift back to sleep. Everything will be fine.

When I wake, the sun is streaming through the skylight

above the bed and the row has started up again: about things that have happened, things that have been said to other people, about promises made and broken. Every row is the same, and goes over the same ground. And again and again the words are the same too.

'You're just impossible. Impossible.'

'And you're just stupid. I don't know what you're doing here with Johnny and me.'

'Neither do I. I must be crazy to stay with you. Not with Johnny.'

'You're certainly crazy. Why don't you just leave, like you always do?'

'Yes, I'm going to. Directly I can. And don't think I'll come back again.'

'So you always say, but you always bloody come creeping back here. And then you start your screaming set-outs.'

'If it wasn't for Johnny—'

They both hush their voices then, as though to mention me is to usher me into their troubles, while the rest of their shouting has had nothing to do with me whatsoever.

If I spent more time around other kids, I would recognize the pattern with much greater clarity. As it is, these are the only words of anger I regularly hear; and no one is ever angry with me. I am clearly the cause of all this fighting, because my name is always raised at some point, yet they always seem anxious to tell me I am not to blame. I am the onlooker, outside it all and yet horribly, disturbingly involved.

'I'm not going to that stupid Festival with you.'

'Well, that's good at any rate. Johnny and I can have a decent time on our own there in that case.'

'And I'm certainly not coming to that dreadful, absurd church of yours, with all those women in their stupid hats.'

'They look a damned sight better than you do, with or without a hat. And it's not absurd, it's a demonstrable science.'

She snorts with disgust. 'Hocus-pocus, American rubbish. Those people will believe anything.'

They row about the evidences or the phoniness of Christian Science for a few more minutes.

I know I've got to reconcile them so that we can all be together. The trouble is, I don't know how to do it. There must be some formula, some spell, some words I can speak; but it won't come. I lie silently in my camp bed, looking across at them as they stand opposite each other across their double bed, fully dressed now, with their shoes on. If I can only think of the right words, everything will be all right.

Later, as my father is in the kitchen, making his coffee in the kitchen next door, I get out of bed, walk over to my mother, and try out the words I have practised in my head.

'The Festival's going to be so good. Please come with us. You don't have to come to church first – you can meet us after. And it's Daddy's birthday today. Please.'

'No, darling, I don't think I will. Daddy and I aren't getting along too well at the moment, and it's probably better if I don't.'

'But then you'll miss it. The Skylon, you know, and the Shot Tower. And the Dome of Discovery. We could all go.'

'You go and tell me all about it. Then maybe I can go with you later and you can show me.'

'No, please come now. It *is* Daddy's birthday.'

She smiles at me and brushes the hair off my forehead, and I know that I haven't found the formula at all. And as a result of my failure, everything will be spoiled. Perhaps I shouldn't have said that about the Skylon: perhaps I'm the only one who cares about it. I'm so stupid to have mentioned that. If only I could think of something else to say.

She is sitting in the kitchen, elbows on the table, as we leave, Geraldo and his Orchestra on the radio.

''Bye. Have a good time, darling. Give me a kiss.'

'Please.'

'No, darling, it's better if I stay. 'Bye, Roy.'

''Bye.'

He doesn't look at her. I do, but it's no good. The right words haven't come.

Sunday School is at Second Church of Christ, Scientist, in Notting Hill Gate: a grand, sombre building in red brick which some well-known architect based on a Byzantine model in the first years of the twentieth century. There is a dark, rather charming garden with a sundial that talks about recording only the sunny hours; only Sunday mornings at this time never seem sunny.

Inside, in the echoing, low-ceilinged basement where my rubber-soled sandals squeak on the shiny stone floor, we sit around our teacher in little chairs, listening to readings and explanations and sometimes pushing them back to stand up and sing a hymn:

> Shepherd, show me how to go,
> O'er the hillside steep;
> How to gather, how to sow,
> How to feed Thy sheep.

I stopped being a Christian Scientist decades ago, but I certainly bear it no ill-will of any kind. It was just something that happened to me for a time, a gentle, undictatorial religion with a strong emphasis on the metaphysical; no wonder Albert Einstein took a passing interest in it, and commended the writings of its founder, Mary Baker Eddy.

I gave it up because I was characteristically unwilling to accept the word of a single prophet as final on just about anything; and after many years of having no religion at all I went back to the Church of England, which had first encompassed me when I was young. In the Church of England there is very little you are required to believe, which suits me admirably; even the bishops don't always seem absolutely certain whether God exists. I like the medieval buildings and the tombs and hearing the congregation belting out the hymns. It gives me a sense of continuity, which is about as close to godliness as I am likely to get now.

But when I was six, and later, I was very faithful to Mary Baker Eddy; and I soon knew off by heart the Scientific Statement of Being, which is the Christian Scientist's creed:

> There is no life, truth, intelligence nor substance in matter. All is infinite Mind, and its infinite manifestation, for God is All-in-all. Spirit is immortal Truth; matter is mortal error. Spirit is the real and eternal; matter is the unreal and temporal. Spirit is God, and man is His image and likeness. Therefore man is not material, he is spiritual.

You can see why this might have held a passing interest for Einstein. You can see, too, why a six-year-old, hearing words like 'manifestation', 'temporal' and 'material', might quickly grow in comprehension and vocabulary, even if he had missed an entire year of schooling. Christian Science just wasn't really for me, that's all. It wasn't for my father for very long, either; and it certainly wasn't for my mother. Brought up as a Catholic, abused as a child by some disgusting old priest, she had nothing but loathing for all religion.

Now, the Statement of Being having been intoned, the chairs squeak back for the last time and we can run around the garden until it is time to go. I have managed to tell everyone in my class, and several outside it, that we are going to the Festival of Britain today; but being mostly well-to-do kids, with expensive houses in Chelsea and Kensington, they have all been to the Festival already, and are rather superior about my excitement. I keep quiet after that, and go in search of my father, who is surrounded by a group of ladies with hats, all laughing; with one or two husbands on the periphery of the group, who don't seem to be laughing so much. It is some time before the ladies free him and leave us to find our bus.

'Thank God it's not raining. You know what day it is, don't you?'

'Your birthday.'

I've made him a card. He doesn't like people to make a fuss of his birthday, because it reminds him that he is now thirty-seven. But he also doesn't like it if they forget it.

'It's St Swithin's Day. If it rains today, it'll rain for forty days non-stop.'

'No – will it really?'

'That's what they say.'

I am disappointed now that it isn't raining: we could have tested out the theory. But at the same time I don't really want it to rain on his birthday, and I don't want it to rain on our trip to the Festival of Britain.

My father wants to give me London as an experience. I am wearing my best shoes for walking – sandals with a familiar buckle – and light clothes because the day is already warm. At the Houses of Parliament we climb unsteadily down the stairs from the upper deck, like sailors on a three-master out in the open ocean. This is a well-planned event: my father has worked out our entire journey.

His latest job, working for a market research firm, going round and asking people's opinions about different brands of washing-powder, or magazine, or political party, allows him to take time off whenever he wants, so long as he makes it up somehow. Sundays are less special to him, therefore. But this is our day, his and mine, and if only there were three of us I would be remarkably happy. I take his hand, and we walk down towards the Houses of Parliament.

He is an excellent storyteller; that is the secret of his social success. He knows how to make you laugh, but also how to catch your emotions. And he knows a lot about London.

'Can you imagine,' he is saying as we walk past the Houses of Parliament, where the work to repair the ravages of the bombing has stopped because it's Sunday, 'all the things that happened here? Over there somewhere is where Guy Fawkes stored his barrels of gunpowder when he was going to blow up the King and the whole Parliament. That's why we have Guy Fawkes night, to celebrate when he got caught.

'That's the statue of Richard the Lionheart. When Parliament got bombed in the war, it bent his sword, and it took them ages to straighten it again.'

I would quite have liked it if it had stayed curved, like a Saracen's sword, but it looked pretty straight to me now.

'And somewhere round here is where Sir Walter Ralegh had his head chopped off – you know which one he was, don't you? He put his cloak down in a puddle in front of Good Queen Bess to stop her getting her feet wet.'

'So why did he have his head chopped off?'

'Oh, it's a long story. The Queen was dead by then.'

My father is not an historian in any real sense, and no scholar either, but he has a powerful sense of the past as a force that operates on the present. Knowing where great events happened is important to him; it underpins the present. He has made me realize that these great events aren't just things in the pages of books; they have a life of their own, and if you can only summon up enough imagination you can sense their continued existence here in the present, in the place where they happened. My father is an archaeologist of the emotions. He can detect the presence of the past in the humdrum circumstances of the here and now. This is one of his biggest gifts to me.

And what has my mother done for me? Lesser things by comparison, I suppose. Yet she has demonstrated an emotional gentleness, a preparedness to sacrifice herself for my happiness, to fade out when not required. Perhaps that is a negative virtue, but it is a powerful and difficult one all the same. And she is quietly very loving. For the rest of my life I will remember that last night, lying with her in the little camp bed, and turning round when she has finished singing me the lullaby, and seeing her dark eyes watching me. Almost as though she thinks she is seeing me for the last time.

'In the olden days they used to have a fountain just over there, in front of Big Ben, and it used to pump out red wine when there was a coronation.'

And then, because these things are as real to him as his own life, he switches centuries instantly.

'And over there is where Daphne and I stood when the King and Queen came past in their golden coach after they were crowned in 1937.'

Daphne is his younger sister.

'But I thought you liked the Duke of Windsor more than the King.'

'Well, I did, but it's important to go and see these things for yourself. We were standing right there, where the pavement sticks out.'

'And is he a good King?'

'Oh well, I suppose so. It doesn't really matter very much nowadays, you know. He was good during the war. But all that stuff is a bit old-fashioned.'

In the 1930s my father was an anarchist and a fierce republican, and a little of it always lingers.

We aren't here to see the sights, though; we have a different objective altogether. We get another bus, and it takes us past the little street where Clement Attlee, the Prime Minister, still lives, though not for long, and the place where Charles I was executed.

'"King Charles the First walked and talked, two days after his head was cut off."'

'No, did he really, Daddy?'

'No, of course not. You have to look at the words carefully – that's how people can trick you. It means he walked and talked, then they cut his head off two days later.'

'Oh.'

Being of a mistier, less concrete cast of mind than my father, I prefer the first version.

'And a man came to the Parliament and said that if they gave him some money he'd take the statue and melt it down. And he did take it down, but he secretly told all the people who liked the King that he would sell them medals made from the statue, and they all bought them for quite a lot of money. And then when King Charles's son came back to the throne the man went and told him he'd kept Charles I's statue carefully the whole time, and hadn't melted it down at all. And he could put it back there if the King paid him. So he made money off everyone.'

'But weren't all the people who bought the medals very cross?'

'I suppose they were. But they were so glad to have the King back, they didn't really mind.'

'But the man wasn't really very good to say all those things, was he?'

'No, I suppose not.'

There are times when I think my father feels I've missed the point. As someone who has always had to get by in life with the least advantages, he rather sympathizes with the three-way confidence trickster from the seventeenth century.

We pass Nelson's column, and the Eleanor Cross, and head down the Strand; and each has its story, so that I feel I have to grip hold of it all, just as I have to grip hold of the swaying, bucking bus I am riding on, sitting in the front seat on the top deck.

And what lies below us in the streets of London? A black and grey city, with most of its finer architectural details hidden under the grime of centuries of coal-smoke. Shops still gloomy and monochrome and Victorian-looking, though Lyons Corner House, with its friendly cream paint and curly gold lettering, and – just a little farther on – the ABC with orange lettering, are brighter and more inviting. Cars mostly old-fashioned, even by 1951 standards, and very few of them. A few taxis, but they are still rare, and our bus moves fast down the empty Strand. Not many people around this Sunday morning, though on every other day this is still probably the busiest thoroughfare in London.

Every man in a hat and suit and tie, every woman in a dress. Newspaper posters telling us that a cricketing disaster has overtaken England. Plenty of bomb damage up and down its length, with big painted Xs for shelters still clearly visible on the walls. Patches of *Saxifraga urbium*, urban saxifrage, which my father sentimentally calls 'London Pride', forcing their way upwards from the empty walls and open cellars of destroyed buildings, bricks crumbling in the damp. Old torn posters in the breeze, catching the sunlight, looking like fingers waving at us as we pass. A general air of fatigue, of grime, of making do, of just getting by with an effort. Not much pleasure, not much joy, not an awful lot of money. A city going through the motions, in desperate need of something good to happen.

'Let's walk over Waterloo Bridge.'

We walk across the brand new bridge, with the copper-green river moving lazily beneath us, and the ships in dozens unloading or loading at the docks. St Paul's the tallest building on the northern skyline, and on the other side of the river the reason we have come here: the South Bank, and the Festival of Britain.

I recognize it from the pictures, and my heart leaps inside me with excitement. Every day since it was opened on 3 May I have longed to visit it, always afraid that it might suddenly shut before its scheduled end on 30 September. Most of my friends at the Crispin School have already been here too: one, the cleverest and possibly richest kid – her father runs a wine shop – has been here three times. Now my sense of being an unfashionable out-of-towner begins to fall away in admiration of the scope of it all.

I know all the main features, of course. First of all there is the strange Skylon, an immense, slender, cigar-shaped object, silver-coloured and held erect by a network of ropes as delicate as a spider's web, which has no apparent function except to show how clever we all are, and to give some sort of feeling of progress, of upwardness, of non-functional, artificial beauty.

Then the extraordinary dome, a vast mushroom on girders, and the strangely shaped pavilions around it which contain the different exhibitions, and the Festival Hall and the film theatre tucked away under Hungerford Bridge; and at the far end something else which exerts a particular attraction for me, the Shot Tower. This isn't modern in any way: it is made of brick and is more than a century old, and I have read without understanding that once upon a time they dropped molten lead down the tower into a tank of water, and the action of gravity made the drops perfectly spherical, for use as shot in guns. Now, someone at school tells me, the Shot Tower is used to display a range of modern telescopes.

It is all laid out before us, and we have simply to go in and look at it all.

'I wish Mummy was with us,' I murmur, as we stand on the bridge looking at it gleaming in the sunshine, with the river running beneath us; I could show you the exact spot today.

My father says nothing.

'I don't like the screaming set-outs.'

Reluctantly, he says, 'Well, some people can't seem to help having them.'

'But when she says sorry, can't you stop then?'

'Anyone can say sorry, but you've got to mean it.'

'Doesn't Mummy mean it?'

'I don't know. She wouldn't carry on if she did.'

'I wish she was with us.'

'Johnny, for God's sake stop going on about it. She's not, and she's not going to be, so you might as well shut up.'

Now it is my turn to keep quiet.

'Look, I'm sorry, old chap, I didn't mean to fly off the handle like that.'

We stand quietly side by side for a while, and he puts his arm round my shoulder. I think about telling him that anyone can say sorry, but decide against it. Not because I'm scared of his temper, though sometimes I am, but because I would like to have an enjoyable time here and further unpleasantness would wreck everything. And it is his birthday, after all.

'We get in via the entrance in Belvedere Road, apparently.'

'Yes,' I say, knowing that he's right. He's always right.

Friday 8 October 1943

Double British Summer Time.
Sun rises, 7.10 a.m.; sets, 6.25 p.m.
Lighting-up time: 6.55 p.m.
Black-out: 6.55 p.m.–6.42 a.m.
Maximum temperature: 53°F; minimum: 45°F.
Rainfall: showery at times.
Sunshine: 3.4 hours.
Light to moderate north to north-easterly winds.
    Fog patches clearing by morning. Bright
    sunshine at first, but cloudy later.

BY THE TIME I was six, we had moved seven times. Whether my parents happened to be together or separated – something which depended on an explosive mix of temperament and financial circumstance – they always lived in furnished flats. The furniture got better or worse according to our circumstances. Each time we moved, I went backwards and forwards between my parents as though I was a sofa or an armchair. I don't mean they didn't care about me, or didn't love me; but I was part of the things they had to move around, and sometimes I fitted better in one place than another. But when I was three, in the year 1947, something important happened in my life: my father and mother bought me a bed.

It stayed with me for years, often the only piece of furniture we would take with us in yet another move: small, uncomfortable, with a utilitarian curved length of grey steel at its head, and another at its feet. It had a lumpy flock mattress, on which I peed more than once in my earliest years; the stains, scrubbed and deodorized but still as plain as the map of some unknown and menacing land mass, never allowed me to forget my first serious humiliations in life.

Under the mattress were large springs which made a long drawn-out metallic noise when I moved. Depending on what I happened to be reading at the time, this could sound like the sails of a ship, or the shunting of a railway engine. It could even be the low, menacing call of a beast in the jungle. It could also have been a car, of course, but it would be some years before I travelled in a car for the first time: cars were out of our family's range. So of course were sailing ships and jungle beasts, but my imagination was a romantic one, and frigates and tigers came more naturally to me than Armstrong-Siddeleys or Humber Super Snipes.

It was my father's habit to tell me a story each night. Sometimes he would start out on a long, rambling, repetitious tale about two teddy bears, one sharp and bright and somehow reminiscent of my father, and the other slow in the uptake and inclined to do stupid things, into whom I read myself. The two were rivals for the affections of an attractive lady bear, only she always preferred the clever one who was like my father. When he had finished this story, and if he hadn't sent himself off to sleep, I would always say the same thing.

'Now tell me about when I was a little boy.'

Since I was around four at the time, the scope for stories about my past was fairly limited; but he would launch into a long and highly romantic account of bombs and air-raid sirens and the way he met my mother. Sometimes these stories varied utterly, bearing no relation to one another. For although he brought me up to have a great regard for the truth, and was always very angry if he found me out in a lie, he was rather less punctilious himself.

Not that he was a habitual liar, or anything like it; but he loved to tell stories, and couldn't always be bothered to stick to the dull verity of what had happened when a slight tweak or two would make it more entertaining. He was often the butt of his own tales, presenting himself as the fool on whose mistakes everything turned, even when in reality he might only have been a bystander. Yet somehow even as the butt he ran the show. It was as though the ringmaster in the circus was knocked over by the clowns and rolled in the sawdust: you still knew who owned the top hat and carried the whip.

His love of telling funny stories made him a favourite wherever he went. He was the centre of any gathering of people, charming them, bringing them out of themselves, turning the full force of his personality on to them. As something of an adjunct, I would stand to one side and admire him – even when I could see that his version of what had happened to us, say, on our way to the gathering bore little similarity to the truth. For him, reality was something to be pepped up and given a better ending. No wonder my father loved films so much. He had a great deal of the cinema in him.

For a start, a good part of his identity was self-generated, a work of clever and intriguing fiction. He had, I'm sure, done everything he claimed to have done; but his account of his life was like a Hollywood biopic about some famous scientist or soldier or actor. Everything was heightened, coloured, speeded up, edited, so his experiences were much more exciting in the telling than they had been when they actually unfolded. In that sense, his imagination was as romantic as mine; but the chief feature of it was his hatred of everyday dullness.

As he sat on my little creaking bed, and I lay on my right side, my face half-submerged in a pillow that smelt of chicken feathers, he provided me with two main versions of how he met my mother. It never occurred to me to ask why there were differences between them, any more than it occurred to nineteenth-century divines to wonder why there were different accounts of the birth of Jesus in the Gospels. One version was relatively straightforward; he met her at a dance, and trod all over her toes, and made her laugh. Maybe that was the true one, the one with canonical authority; but he seemed to prefer the other one, perhaps because it gave him greater scope for elaboration. Elaboration, I came to realize over the succeeding years, was what my father did best. This story, therefore, is the one he preferred.

PLATFORM TWO at West Croydon station; shortly after nine o'clock on a brilliant autumn morning, of the kind people in these depressing, grey, limited, rationed times associate with the days before the war. The sun slants down through the smoke which still drifts across the station from last night's bombing. There is a sharp, acrid smell, somehow chemical in nature, the insistent, irritating bell of a police car, the sound of digging, an occasional shout: someone is trapped in the rubble. This is all much too commonplace in Croydon for the people who are waiting for the train to bother about. They scarcely even pause to be grateful that it is someone else is who is trapped, someone else whose house or shop has been turned to dust and broken bricks. They have been through it all so many times.

There is the usual mixture of earth-coloured army uniforms, a sprinkling of sailors in dark blues, a few women in drab brown or grey Utility dresses, their hair bundled up on their heads in scarves, a little scarce lipstick enlivening the sallow, strained faces. A few men in civilian clothes, most of them elderly. One man in his late fifties, wearing a cloth cap, has a rakish bandage over one eye and keeps adjusting it. This is a tired country, anxious, stressed, sleepless, too used to bad news to be able to credit the better news which is only just starting to appear.

Through the crowd comes a sprightly, broad, good-looking young man in his late twenties: fairish hair brushed back from his forehead, a brisk, wide-awake look. A bit of a counter-jumper, perhaps: quick-reacting, charming, with an eye always on the main chance, relying on his looks and his quick wit to get him out of any difficulty. His tweed sports jacket is pre-war in cut; his shirt is not entirely of the best or cleanest; his tie is a dullish brown, striped with an equally dullish yellow and green; his shoes are heavy and quite good – pre-war, again; in his hand is a *News Chronicle*. Occasional looks, by no means friendly, from the men in uniform: this is too late in the war for someone to be still waiting for his call-up papers. He must be an idler, a scrimshanker. He might even be a conscientious objector if he weren't so sharp and active-looking.

Farther down the platform, among the uniforms, is a tall, willowy, dark woman in a fawn overcoat. Accompanying her, two children in their wartime best: an eager, interested boy, a pretty girl; nice-looking kids. Accompanying her, too, a distinct air of sadness, resignation. Life, you feel, has dealt unfairly with her and will persist in doing so. Two large, cheap suitcases stand beside her, and a straw bag. The sun, shining across the platform, catches her face, which is turned in the direction of the coming train, emphasizing the gentleness, the resignation, the warmth of colour in her dark hair. A century earlier, Holman Hunt might have hired her as a model, though now she is getting on in years: thirty-seven. In 1943, with the anxiety and shortages of wartime, that is virtually middle-aged.

There is an expectant movement among the uniforms. The huffing of steam, the grind of wheels on rails, the sharp smells of hot metal, oil and coal dust, dull green carriages streaked with dirt, windows smeared and brownish. Only two first-class compartments, all empty. Small green or red triangles on the windows of others: 'Ladies Only', 'Non-Smoking'. Two or three officers head towards the doors marked with a large, curling '2'; the woman with the children goes towards a '3'. The process takes her a little time: the boy has wandered away to look at the town and the rising smoke, and has to be summoned back. It takes a moment to pick up the two cases and the bag as well; and although the girl, tall for her age, her fair hair swinging, does her bit to help, it all takes time. The crowd at the nearest '3' door is much too big for them and their luggage, so she has to hurry further down the platform, panicking slightly, the children following, the cases slowing her down.

The guard's whistle blows from halfway down the platform; she turns to appeal to him, but the still-open doors, leather window-belts bowing out, block her from his sight. The crowd thins, the doors slam. She looks hopelessly up and down, trapped in a band of too-expensive '2's, unable to reach a '3' in time.

A '3' door, just slammed, opens again.

'Oi!' shouts the guard.

Inside the compartment the youngish, fair-haired man looks down at a sailor in the window-seat.

'Just hold the door a second, will you? Lady coming.'

He jumps down on to the platform, and puts his hands out to the woman with the children, as though offering to take her suitcases. She looks at him neutrally: not accepting, not refusing, just unstated. He waves to the guard, who is blowing his whistle again irritably, and gathers the cases from her. She follows him to the carriage where the sailor is now standing up, holding the door open for them all.

'Thanks a lot.'

'Don't worry, mate.'

'Would you like to sit here?' Well-spoken for a man in cheap clothes.

'Thank you. It's very kind of you.' Soft-spoken, timid.

'Are you going far?'

'Victoria. I've got to change. It's so difficult.'

The rest of the carriage looks and nods. His good deed begins to melt their instinctive disapproval of a young, fit civilian.

No more conversation. The young man examines her covertly: good figure, quite a bit older than he is, tastefully but not expensively dressed. Kids well looked after, quiet, nicely behaved. Aware of the inspection, she looks down at the cigarette butts on the floor of the carriage. Other newspapers, a couple of *Mirrors* and a *Sketch*, open to war news. The only *Chronicle* in the carriage stays folded on his lap. Why a *Chronicle*? she thinks. Why the civilian clothes? No sign of injury, weakness, illness. She doesn't care: she finds strident patriotism dull.

The train jerks forward, shrieks, picks up speed. Silence in the compartment. A soldier beside her sinks immediately into sleep, his head drawn down towards her shoulder by some kind of magnetism. She glances across at the young man who has helped her: a mutual half-smile, then a quick turn of the head to the window.

Outside, as they cross the river, utter devastation along both banks. A power-station, a natural target for bombs, rears up, unharmed. How many bricks went into the making of that, she wonders? As many as bombs dropped on London? As many as soldiers killed? How many soldiers on this train? One less, given the young man's civilian clothes. A scar down his cheek: a wound? Or is he too old to have been in the army?

A wedding-ring on her finger, yet she has the air of going somewhere new and final, alone with her children. To her parents? What are the children like, as they sit quietly reading their books? Is the husband dead, or has he abandoned her? Or merely joined the forces? 'Epsom', says the corner of a label on the rack above, clearly written in what seems like an educated hand. To Epsom, or from Epsom?

'And how are you?'

The boy looks up from his book, suddenly wary, almost hostile.

'All right.'

'Well, that's good. You can't be too all right nowadays, you know.'

Grins from behind the *Mirrors*: a pick-up has begun.

The woman looks out of the window some more. The children take refuge in their books again.

The *Mirrors* begin to fold, the train slows and jerks to a halt.

'Victoria! Victoria station! All change here, please, all change.'

'Can I help you?'

She lets him, understanding perfectly well what is going on but prepared to let it run for a while. He pulls the cases down and clambers out on to the platform with them.

'Where to now?'

They flow out with the uniformed crowd, then find themselves in a larger one, milling around under the great glass roof of the station, the panes now criss-crossed with masking tape, forming dozens of Xs overhead.

'It's not here, it's Waterloo.'

'Do you want a bus or a cab?' Knowing that cabs are difficult to get nowadays, and expensive.

'I don't really know. Bus, I suppose.'

'Because I could get you a cab. And I'm going near Waterloo, anyway.'

He does the mental arithmetic, and it almost comes out right.

'Why?'

'To see someone there.'

'No – I find that hard to believe.' Her gentle banter, eyes turned away from him, looking down at the ground, is beguiling. 'Why should you want to help us?'

Because she's attractive and he is sorry for her. Because helping people and feeling better about himself as a result fulfils some quite urgent requirement in him. Because there aren't any other girls he's keen on at present. Because, perhaps, he doesn't quite know who he is, and needs some sort of guide-post: an older woman. Because she appeals to him; or rather, because her situation, lonely and troubled, appeals to him. Unusual for him to be lost for words, but he doesn't answer.

'If you aren't in too much of a hurry, we could have a cup of tea at the buffet.'

The children look at each other and pull faces.

Milky, over-sweet, strongish tea, four hard rock-cakes, the taste of ersatz ingredients.

'So what did you do after your husband died?'

'I stayed on in our flat. But it was much too expensive – the landlord was trying to get us out, and he put the rent up, and we've been trying to get away ever since.'

He is too obvious, she thinks, probing like this. She starts to resent his interest.

'But for now we're going back to my mother. In Epsom.'

The memory of Garden Cottages floats across her mind, like a brief overlay shot in a film: that dreary, narrow, dark place, redolent of girlhood and failure and prohibitions. Then a direct question, perhaps to frighten him off. Or maybe to punish him for being too obvious.

'Why aren't you in the forces?'

'I've had my papers. That's why I've come up to town – I'm trying to get it deferred. Up to now I've been Res. Occ.'

'What's that?'

'Reserved Occupation. I work in a munitions factory.'

'Wouldn't it be safer in the forces?'

'Probably. I just don't fancy all that business of being ordered about and shouted at, and sleeping in dormitories. Like being back at school.'

'So you haven't been excluded on health grounds?'

'I'm as fit as a fiddle. That's what life at sea does for you.'

He grins: strong, confident, maybe a bit too confident.

This is a man who has to take charge, she thinks; and she reflects for an instant on what being with him would be like.

'So are you a sailor?'

No: he was an assistant steward on a series of P&O liners. Just a glorified waiter, really, but he can't stop himself making it sound more glamorous than it was.

'I ran away to sea when I was sixteen.'

'But you don't fancy being a hero now?'

It is meant mischievously, and her dark eyes rest provokingly on his as she looks round at him.

'Can't really say I do.'

'That's a relief.'

And it is; so many people boast about their exploits in wartime, and the dangers they have experienced. She once considered buying one of those lapel-badges you used to see in 1940 and 1941: 'I've Got A Bomb Story Too'. Even though she didn't have any bomb stories.

'Let's go and find a taxi.'

An ancient vehicle with an even more ancient driver is waiting at the stand. The children, quiet up to now, are excited at the prospect of the drive. London is new to them.

The signs of bombing are shocking to people from out of town: great gaps in the grand terraces. Signs everywhere for shelters, and for business as usual. Queues outside some shops. Policemen at all the main street corners. Piles of rubble on the bombed sites. Tidiness, order, peaceableness; the war hasn't even begun to destroy the basis of British society, and it won't now.

Waterloo station, dark and massive.

'So – here we are. I hope everything goes well with you. And the children,' he says, trying not to make it sound like an afterthought.

He looks at them, and they look back. They don't like him, he knows that already. Well, he'll make them like him; that's his everlasting optimism, which usually overrides the understanding.

'It was very kind of you to help us.'

The dark, downcast eyes move up to his, the challenging look, attractive and somehow unsettling, is there again.

'If ever you need someone to lift your suitcases again . . .'

Suddenly he looks very young; too young. She can't decide whether to take this any further.

'I don't even know your name.' He does the deciding.

'Joyce. Joyce – well, Cody, really.'

'Like Colonel Cody.'

'Exactly like that. He was my grandfather.'

She can see he is impressed. Fame, celebrity, means a good deal to him. He is a man who feels he has the instincts, the character, to be famous. But famous for what?

'Mine's Roy. Roy Simpson.'

Nothing in his dull, conventional, middle-middle-class family, he feels, seems worth setting alongside the glamour of a Wild West showman who became the first man to fly in Britain.

'Look, I'll give you my address, in case you're up in town again.'

Norwood is scarcely town, and living with his mother is scarcely glamorous; but he's reluctant to lose his metropolitan advantage.

He writes it down in pencil in large, characteristically bold letters, on the back of an OHMS envelope which he has taken out of his inside pocket: Roy Simpson, 111 Marlow Road, London SE 21.

'We don't have a phone there.'

He regrets the 'we' immediately.

'Nor do we.'

Her look stays with him for a long time: there is a hint of shared experience, even some kind of shared injury: two bits of flotsam from the wrecking process which the twentieth century has exerted on families and their stability. They both recognize it in each other; that, and the need to give and receive help. Perhaps there is nothing more to it; not even a real sexual attraction, in spite of the briefly provocative glances.

'Well, cheerio then. It was very pleasant to meet you.'

Don't say 'nice', she tells herself; and don't let him say it either. If he says 'nice' I won't see him again.

'Cheerio, and it was good to meet you. I do hope we'll see each other again.'

He almost forgets the children, but manages to include them in a last grin. They don't grin back.

'Mummy, I don't like that man.'

'Well, I thought he was very kind. We couldn't possibly have managed without his help.'

'Yes, we could.'

'Oh, nonsense, darling.' Her eyes sparkling again.

'What time will we get to Gran's?'

Gran's. Life as it really is comes flooding depressingly back, after being held at bay for a pleasant moment or two.

'About five o'clock.'

She looks out of the window, not seeing the dullness, the traffic, the policemen, the places where someone's house, someone's business once stood.

Chance rules our lives utterly, and everything flows from it as a result. A few more yards' distance, a ten-second delay, an instinct or two ignored, and all the pain and dullness and boredom and pleasure and duty and failure and happiness which constitute the lives of Joyce and Roy and the rest of us would have been ordered completely differently. No me, no grandchildren, no great-grandchildren. Our small world would have been an entirely unrecognizable place, unpeopled by us and repeopled by others instead. This book in your hand would not have been written; and by the same process of random chance you yourself would not have been reading it at the critical moment if a few extra seconds had elapsed, a few more yards had intervened in your own pre-history.

All chance, all randomness. Remember that, the next time you feel a sense of your own significance, your own inevitability. We are left to make the best of it, and get on with our chance-ridden lives as though there is some sort of fundamental order to them.

WE THINK OF the 1940s in black and white, because that is how we see them on film. The actions are shadowy, jerky, unspecific, the clothes strange and starchy, the faces grinning or serious or vacant yet different from those we see around us. These people are not like us: they are the inhabitants of a darker, poorer, more limited world, remarkably different, even when the photographs you are looking at are those of your own relatives. We are natives of our own time, and other times seem more foreign than other places do.

That is why the occasional close-ups we see in photographs and film of the time often take us with a sudden surprise: 'So they were like us after all,' you feel when you see a picture of a sharp-looking middle-aged man, staring back at you with amusement and understanding, or an attractive young girl walking arm-in-arm with a sailor, with precisely the same look of innocent awareness on her face that you might see today. You and I will one day stare out at our great-great-grand-children from photographs which seem so relevant and up-to-date now, nd they will look at us as though we inhabit some prehistoric age of utter irrelevance. Our only hope is that they, too, will recognize something immediate, present, connected about us.

Everything about the world of 1943 seems foreign to our world. Sixty years of gradually increasing affluence, of vast social and political change, have made everything utterly different. Even walking down the street was different from what it has become after the years of growing affluence. In 1943, 22 per cent of the entire population, more than 8 million people, were in the services, and 33 per cent were doing war work; so the streets were often half empty. The majority of civilian cars were laid up and kept for only the most important journeys. The shops were dull and unattractive, their windows often kept empty for security and the lack of anything much to put in them. The ugly gaps between the buildings (like missing teeth, visitor after visitor to London remarked) were often marked with a perkiness which some people found impressive and others merely tedious: 'More open than usual,' or (on a half-ruined pub) 'Our windows are gone but our spirits are excellent. Come in and try them.'

The greengrocers who plied their trade from barrows in the streets had plenty of apples, pears and plums, but no oranges or bananas and certainly no pineapples; such things had virtually disappeared in Britain. The food, even in expensive restaurants, was dull and unappetizing and very restricted: not only because of the fierce rationing, but also because of a traditional stodgi-ness and lack of imagination on the part of customers as well as restaurateurs. Only two Indian restaurants, and perhaps four Chinese ones, were still operating in London. Many of the owners and waiters from the dozens of pre-war Italian res-taurants had left for home or been interned as enemy aliens. The most popular places to eat, as they had been throughout the 1930s, were J. Lyons' teashops and Corner Houses, where you could still get a decent, filling snack and a cup of milky tea for a shilling.

No British Government had ever taken such sweeping powers over the lives of its citizens, or would ever have them again. Official control over production and the rationing of consumption were stronger than in the post-war Soviet Union. Signs of the extraordinary influence and control of the Govern-ment, and in particular of the Ministry of Information, were everywhere. A report-writer for Mass-Observation, the private agency which monitored attitudes and opinions throughout the country, wrote, with the tartness that makes the MO files so enjoyable to read:

> Taking a short walk from the office where this report is being written, you will see forty-eight official posters as you go, on hoardings, shelters, buildings, including ones telling you
>
> > to eat National Wholemeal Bread
> > not to waste food
> > to keep your children in the country
> > to know where your Rest Centre is
> > how to behave in an air-raid shelter
> > to look out in the blackout
> > to look out for poison gas
> > to carry your gas mask always
> > to join the A[uxiliary] F[ire] S[ervice]
> > to fall in with the fire bomb fighters
> > to register for Civil Defence duties
> > to help build a plane
> > to recruit for the Air Training Corps
> > to save for Victory.

It says something for the nature of British political life that although the country was fighting a war which might well end with its democracy snuffed out and many of its leading citizens executed or sent to concentration camps, the Government merely encouraged people to do these useful things, instead of forcing them by law. But independent-minded people like my father found it all infuriating, and for us nowadays, in freer times, the thought of so much exhortation adds to the feeling that life during the war was a monochrome, dreary business.

Yet my father and mother didn't see the world in black and white at all; their colours were no less bright than ours, and their sounds and tastes were no less sharp. True, the world was a dirtier place, because the use of coal made it so; but the early autumn of 1943 was fine and encouraging, and in south-east England the sun shone almost every day for a month. According to Mass-Observation people still talked about the weather more than any other subject: more than the war itself, more than the bombing, and more even than the rationing.

Almost everything was rationed; every kind of foodstuff, every article of clothing, every form of fuel for heating or cooking or transport, paper. A moderately good suit from Burton's The Tailor (whence, people said, the expression 'Gone for a Burton', though Burton-brewed beer is another possibility) cost £2 10s. 0d.; twice as much as it would have cost in 1939. But as with every other rationed item, it was usually much easier to find the money than the coupons. The points system of rationing meant that you had a certain amount of scope to decide what to use your coupons for; but the choice was often depressingly limited.

The black market thrived as a result. Most people depended on it occasionally, and sometimes much more often; only a moral-minded minority refused to have anything whatever to do with the little luxuries which most private suppliers, from shopkeepers to spivs, were prepared to offer. Yet the Government kept a tight control over these things, and the black market never got out of hand.

To British eyes, used to seeing little else, British clothes were so distinctive that any other kind stood out awkwardly. During the course of 1943 several dozen men were arrested solely on the grounds that their clothes were 'foreign-looking'. The great majority of them proved to be refugees who were wearing their old clothes because they couldn't afford new ones. One senior agent for the Special Operations Executive, just back from France, lost all his clothes when an incendiary bomb burned his flat; all he had to wear was the suit which SOE's French tailor had made for him shortly before he made his first parachute drop into occupied Europe. He was arrested in Marylebone High Street, not far from SOE headquarters in

Baker Street, because a woman told the police he looked foreign and might well be a spy.

Winston Churchill, understanding the effect that dull, mass-produced clothes had on civilian morale, resisted the efforts of his ministers and officials to introduce clothes rationing for some time; but while he was taken up with the operation to sink the *Bismarck* two Cabinet ministers who felt strongly about the issue interrupted him and insisted on talking about it. He told them that if they would only go away they could do whatever they wanted.

Refugees and foreign servicemen and -women aside, the crowds in the streets were mostly pretty homogeneous. Ninety-six per cent of them were white (though the largest per capita proportion of overseas volunteers for the British forces came from the Caribbean). Seventy-five per cent of British people would have described themselves as working-class (by 2002 the figure was only 40 per cent). In 1941 George Orwell described 'the crowds in the big towns, with their mild knobby faces, their bad teeth and gentle manners', and praised 'the *privateness* of English life'. In no European country 'is it easier to shove people off the pavement'. Some years later he wrote about 'the orderly behaviour of English crowds, the lack of pushing and quarrelling, the willingness to form queues, the good temper of harassed, overworked people like bus conductors'. But he also wrote, correctly, 'England is the most class-ridden country under the sun. It is a land of snobbery and privilege, ruled largely by the old and silly.'

My father approved greatly of Orwell, and he enjoyed that when he read it. Yet although the process would take decades, the big class differences between rich and poor were shrinking as a result of the war: being in the same air-raid shelters, suffering the same air-raids, and being restricted in terms of what they could buy and eat and wear brought people closer than they had ever been throughout the country's history. Orwell admitted as much himself.

There are wide gradations of income, but it is the same kind of life that is being lived at different levels, in labour-saving flats or Council houses, along the concrete roads and in the naked democracy of the swimming pools. It is a rather restless, cultureless life, centring round tinned food, *Picture Post*, the radio and the internal combustion engine.

The war years belonged to the young and the classless. A clever twenty-five-year-old could be a colonel or a group captain in the Air Force or the captain of a ship, responsible for the lives of hundreds and the fate, perhaps, of millions. Most people over fifty were onlookers in this war, often suffering as badly as every-one else but of no real consequence: just idle mouths to feed.

Yet the war, although it dominated everyone's attention and thought and conversation, had not become the great killing-machine in Britain that it was in Russia or Germany or Poland or China. In spite of the air-raids, in spite of Dunkirk and the Battle of Britain and the Blitz and North Africa and the Italian campaign, it was not until D-Day that the figure for the number of British people killed as a direct result of enemy action overtook the number who died in road accidents; though the blackout, which led to so many deaths on the road, was itself a consequence of the war.

After 1945, people would talk endlessly about the patriotism and decency of wartime, and compare the behaviour and expe-riences of the wartime generation which those which followed. The wealthy took in evacuees from the poorest areas of the city centres, everyone supported the Churchill Government, people behaved better towards each other, the differences of class and income faded, everyone put their shoulders to the national wheel.

It didn't necessarily seem like that at the time. In October 1944 the Ministry of War announced in the House of Com-mons that 80,000 men had deserted from the armed forces: a huge loss of manpower, and a serious problem for the police when the deserters drifted inevitably into the underworld. Still, although petty crime increased greatly, there was no parallel increase in violent crime. In 1943, only twenty-nine people were found guilty of murder.

To the fury of the men and women serving abroad in the armed services, many people in reserved occupations at home – armaments manufacturing, steel-making, coal-mining – went on strike many times for more money and better conditions. Mass-Observation's researchers registered on a daily basis the resentments and complaints of ordinary people: against the rich, the poor, the Government, the employers. Britain in 1943 was not by any means a band of brothers.

Nor was it necessarily the home of the brave. The American soldiers who had flooded into Britain for the D-Day operation were often scathing about the feebleness of their British counterparts. There was a lack of fighting spirit about them which surprised and angered the Americans. In battle it was commonplace for British soldiers to resist only as long as they had enough ammunition to fight back; directly the ammunition ran out, they would start to surrender. The humiliating fall of Singapore in 1942, perhaps the worst defeat in British military history, was echoed in lesser ways in every other theatre of war.

Until General Orde Wingate showed otherwise, the British forces in the Far East regarded the Japanese as evil superhumans who could never be beaten. El Alamein in 1943 was the first time during the war that a British army had defeated a German one, and victory was achieved only by a supremacy in numbers and tanks of two to one. Until 1943, every time the British fought the Germans or the Japanese on the basis of equality of manpower and firepower, they were defeated.

As individuals and as a nation, the British lacked the kind of confidence the Americans had, and their overwhelming organization and manufacturing abilities, and their sheer physical strength. As the war went on, conscription drew in the kind of undernourished under-class whom many British people had never seen before: small, concave-chested men with wizened faces and thin white limbs who would never have passed the physical examination earlier in the war. They had no notion of personal cleanliness, or the use of a modern lavatory, and could only speak strange dialects. There were Welshmen and Scots who seemed incapable of understanding the most basic commands in English.

The American soldiers who filled London and the towns and cities of the south-east of England could scarcely have been more different: big, beef-and-corn-fed, self-confident fellows, earning much more than the British, full of belief in their country and themselves. They were, perhaps, the finest generation the United States has ever produced. Yet they were often surprisingly unpopular in Britain.

Mass-Observation carefully detailed the hostility to their money and their brawn: the way they handed out chewing-gum, cut out British men by offering the local girls a better time, and represented a life which seemed far more glamorous and wealthy and exciting than anything Britain had to offer. And they were immensely successful. Used condoms issued by the US military littered the ground in the doorways of shops in the vicinity of every American base.

There were other reasons for disliking them. A large proportion of the US troops involved in the D-Day operation came from the southern states, where segregation of black and white was still almost total. Many white American soldiers objected to the presence of non-white troops, American as well as British, in English bars and restaurants; and fights often broke out between them. There was plenty of racial prejudice in Britain, of course, but blacks and Asians in uniform were usually well received, and publicans and other customers resented it when Americans tried to have them thrown out.

If the British lacked the Americans' brawn or fighting spirit, the brain of the Allied effort was theirs. The US forces were completely deficient in many of the key areas required for a great military operation. The British had the only fully effective intelligence service on the Allied side, and it was working superbly: not only had they, together with the help of some of their European allies, broken the German Ultra code system, but they had also captured and turned virtually every single German agent who had been infiltrated into Britain, and were using them to feed highly effective disinformation back to the Germans; particularly about D-Day and its real objective.

And it was, for the most part, British technological and inventive skill which the Allies used on D-Day. The British were in the forefront of research in radio, radar, jet propulsion and atomic energy; it was usually British science that the Americans depended on at this stage in the war, though the balance was already shifting in America's favour.

Now, in the twenty-first century, things have changed again. In terms of training, skills, determination and self-confidence the British Army is superior to the US Army; only its equipment is inferior. The SAS and the SBS outclass the American special forces. At the start of the twenty-first century a senior US officer was forced into retirement for saying that if he had British troops with American equipment he could do anything. Man for man, the British Army is tougher and better physically than the US Army, and is expected to show more initiative.

Other things have changed too. By the year 2000 the average European was slightly taller than the average American, though significantly less heavy. Average incomes were still higher in the US than in the European Union, but there was a much better distribution of wealth and far less poverty in Europe, and its figures for child mortality were noticeably lower than America's. The British and the other Europeans had largely caught up with Americans in their standard of living, and the US economy was no longer greater than Europe's. So Europe, which had been overtaken by the United States after the First World War, and was utterly outclassed by it during and after the Second, had started to restore the balance. Among the many differences between 1943 and our own day, this has been the greatest.

ON 8 OCTOBER 1943, the day when my father first met my mother, the Second World War had already lasted for four years, one month and five days. The war's immensity spread out all around them. Across the face of Europe hundreds of thousands of Soviet troops had been ferried across the River Dniepr in the Ukraine under the cover of darkness, catching the German troops on the west bank of the river entirely by surprise. It was there, rather than against Britain, that the main action of the war was taking place; and many of Hitler's own generals already suspected that the Russian adventure would cost them ultimate victory.

This was to prove a significant day in the conduct of the war. The German Press Agency issued details of speeches by Hitler and other leading Nazis about the disturbing turn the war against Russia had taken. The occasion was a Party conference in Berlin, presided over by Martin Bormann, in which 2,000 senior figures took part. There were clearly long passages of Hitler's speech which were far too sensitive to be made public; especially as the small group of foreign correspondents from neutral countries in Berlin would see to it that the news would reach London and Washington within hours. Yet even the brief agency quotation hinted that Hitler now felt himself to be on the defensive:

We shall strike everywhere, and never tire until our aim is accomplished. Take home in your hearts the unshakeable faith that, if our determination does not falter, this war will end with a great German victory.

For Hitler to suggest that Nazi Germany's determination might be in question must have startled many of his listeners; though privately Hitler had realized as early as 1941 that he was likely to lose the war. The intelligence analysts who listened to it that afternoon in London compiled a report for Churchill which suggested that Hitler was worried about the outcome of the battle in Ukraine. Even more significant was another passage from his speech, which the news agency was told to omit, but which – thanks to some official oversight – was broadcast by radio in Berlin:

> The German people know that their existence is at stake in this struggle. The bridges behind them are burned. The only way left to them is the way forward.

It was an extraordinary admission, and when the details of the speech were published in the British press they reinforced the growing belief that Hitler now felt himself thoroughly on the defensive. All the same, the thought that Germany was becoming desperate, and might use any weapon in order to win, was disturbing.

At the Berlin Party conference Heinrich Himmler, the commander of the SS, also sounded anxious about the way the war was going; characteristically, though, he preferred to react with threats. Only one section of his speech was released to German radio:

> Anybody who does the enemy's job and stabs the German people in the back during its most difficult struggle for existence by spreading defeatism and thus endangering the life of all must die and pay for his deeds as a warning to others.

Elsewhere that day the German Army was displaying its habitual ruthlessness in many parts of Europe. On the island of Crete, shots had been fired at a German patrol from or near the village of Amyra a few days earlier. Now a detachment of soldiers went into Amyra and executed more than a 150 men, women and children. Some were lined up and machine-gunned; others were herded into a building which was then set on fire. Eighty-five people were held as hostages for the good behaviour of the area. They too would be shot, the German military authorities warned with unconscious irony, if there were any further terrorist incidents.

In the afternoon, a British military court in Palestine passed sentence on Eliahu Sacharoff, a supporter of the Hagana, a Jewish underground organization, for being in possession of two rounds of ammunition. For this he received seven years' imprisonment. At a time when the British were fighting a life or death struggle against a country which was committed to exterminating all Jews, some Jews had identified the British as their main enemy. Other Jews from Palestine, many hundreds of them, had volunteered to join the British Army and were fighting in North Africa and elsewhere; including Moshe Dayan, who lost an eye but gained the experience and skills which he brought more than twenty years later to the post of Israel's defence minister in the Six Day War.

In New York that day, another court began hearing the case against Roberto Lanas, who was charged with having passed information to Germany while working as a translator for the US Government's Office of Co-Ordination of Latin American Affairs. There was no question about his guilt. He admitted in court that he had received $2,900 from German agents in Europe for handing over details of American aircraft production. He had, he said, written down the figures on the backs of innocent-seeming letters in invisible ink, but he maintained that he only gave his German handlers information which was freely available in the newspapers. Indeed, that was how he had obtained the figures. The court later found him guilty, but decided not to impose the death penalty.

The Times for 8 October carried a total of forty-two death notices, seventeen of which were a direct result of the war. Twelve people were listed as having died on active service, but it is the entries for civilians which attract our attention. Perhaps it is the combination of conventional phrasing and comfortable surroundings with the sudden intrusion of war:

> ARKELL. – In Oct., 1943, as a result of enemy action, WILLIAM ARKELL, for thirty years the faithful friend and chauffeur of the Glanvill family of The Hill, Bromley, Kent.
>
> FEGAN. – In Oct., 1943, killed suddenly by enemy action, MARY, beloved wife of the late J.W.C. FEGAN of Goudhurst, Stony Stratford, and Yardley, aged 78 years.
>
> LOVELL-KEAYS. – In Oct., 1943, killed suddenly by enemy action, BEATRICE LOVELL-KEAYS, dearly loved niece of Mary Fegan, aged 72 years.

Then there are the private tragedies, whose details we can dimly perceive even after all this time – the fear, the half-hope and the eventual despair – which shattered so many lives.

> CAYZER. – In Sept., 1943, previously reported missing, now reported killed in action, LIEUT. SIR NIGEL JOHN CAYZER, Scots Guards, aged 22, most dearly loved eldest son of Lady Cayzer and of the late Sir Charles William Cayzer, Bt., of Kinpurnie Castle, Angus.
>
> HAWKES REED. – Previously reported missing, now notified as killed, FLIGHT SERGT. JOHN HAWKES REED, beloved son of Olive Hawkes Reed of Tetbury, and darling brother of Prudence, Mary, Ann, and Alan.

That day's personal column is also heavily influenced by the war.

> MACLEOD BAXTER, J.V.E. Card received by his wife in Australia:– 'Safe, in good health and well treated. Japanese prisoner of war.' Mrs Macleod Baxter, 2, Redlands Road, Glasgow, W.2.

> NAVAL Officer's widow, Scottish, thirties, wishes to be in London some months. I would UNDERTAKE EMPLOYMENT aiding war effort; capable and adaptable most circumstances, could relieve, except secretarial or nursing; excellent organizer, manager, driver, &c. – Write Box X.1645, The Times, EC4.

> SHEETS. – Will any householder who can spare one or more pairs of single bed cotton sheets, worn or new, sell to lady running hostel for junior officers and desperately in need of them? Unobtainable in shops. – Address, Caterer, 10, Cheyne Walk, Chelsea, S.W.3. Tel., FLAxman 9961.

> PRISONERS OF WAR. – The perfect present is BOOKS, and we arrange the dispatch of a regular monthly supply. – Write for details of the Overseas Service, The Times Book Club, 42, Wigmore Street, W.1.

Reading all this, we find ourselves left wanting to know so much more. Was Macleod Baxter really being treated well by the Japanese, or did he just say so in order to get his postcard through the Japanese system and keep his wife happy? How much did he suffer in the two years that followed? Did the Scottish widow get a job that matched her qualifications and helped assuage her grief and loneliness? Did the junior officers get their cotton sheets in Cheyne Walk? Reading these things in the files of yellowing, easily torn pages the distance in time slips away, and you find yourself wanting to ring FLAxman 9961 to find out, or write to a box number at a building which no longer exists, in a newspaper which is so changed that no one who knew it in its great days would recognize it any longer. The strange continuum which you enter when you open an ancient newspaper holds you long after you have closed the bound volume and put it away on the library shelf.

Especially, of course, if you are yourself in some way involved in the things you read about. In my case, my parents met with the smoke from the previous night's bombing still hanging in the air, and some of the victims still buried under the rubble. And here, in the news pages, is the account of what happened; though the wartime censorship has blocked out the names of the places which were bombed, in order not to help the enemy's planners. The tone of the information has a studied calm to it, downplaying any excitement or drama.

According to the official British account, a short alert sounded in the London area on Thursday night, 7 October, for the third time in three successive nights. In all, sixty German planes crossed the English coast, of which three were shot down. Only fifteen enemy planes were involved in the raid over Greater London, six of them between 8.15 p.m. and 9.30 p.m., and nine more between 9.45 and 11.00. In all, they dropped thirty tons of bombs. There were, according to the official version, no attacks on places of military significance.

The Ministry of Information, in issuing this information, was very anxious to counter suggestions which had begun to surface in the press that the raid of 7 October was in any way comparable with the big raids of 10 May 1941. This suggestion, the Ministry insisted, was absurd. Then, 450 tons of bombs had been dropped and nearly 1,500 people killed. Nor was this the heaviest raid since that one. The heaviest raid since 1941 had in fact been on 17–18 January 1943, when up to sixty German aircraft had concentrated their attack on London. A number of people had been killed and wounded, but the Ministry was not prepared to say how many.

In one district of London a soldier, back on leave, was out

for the evening with his wife when the raid began. They ran home for safety, but while they were still a couple of streets away the bombs started falling and there was a loud explosion nearby. When they reached their street they saw smoke and flame belching out from the hole in the ground where their house had been. This was the second time the couple had lost everything they owned in an air-raid, with the exception of the clothes they stood up in. Yet on neither occasion had either of them been even slightly injured.

A stick of blast bombs was dropped on a street in a town on the outskirts of south-east London, near a railway station. Among those killed was a girl in the ATS. The aftermath of the bombing was still drifting over West Croydon station when my father met my mother the following morning. If, of course, this really is where he met her, and not at some nightclub or dance-hall where he trod on her toes and made her laugh.

Thursday 20 July 1944

Double British Summer Time.
Sun rises, 6.06 a.m.; sets, 10.06 p.m.
Lighting-up time: 11.06 p.m.
Black-out: 10.51 p.m.–5.22 a.m.
New moon rises: 7.42 a.m.
Maximum temperature: 69°F; minimum: 52°F.
Rainfall: nil.
Sunshine: 11.06 hours.
Moderate south-west wind. Close and humid.

CRUMP.

'Count one-two-three-four.'

Obediently, 'One-two-three-four.'

'They're getting further away.'

CRUMP.

'That's not further away. It sounded quite close.'

'You're always so bloody negative. Everything you say is gloomy. Of course it's getting further away – you can hear. Stands to reason: they're going for central London again.'

CRUMP.

'The picture's gone sideways. Look.'

'Maybe that was after the last one.'

CRUMP.

'Too late to get down to the shelter now.'

A resigned note in her voice, but she's not critical of him. She still looks at him as though he is some kind of improvement on the general run of humanity.

'We could always get under the stairs.'

'As long as you hear it, it's not going to hit you.'

'You don't think, for the sake of – you know?' Looking at her swelling stomach.

'Oh well, maybe.'

CRUMP.

'Do you think it really is safer down here? Don't see how it can be, with just a staircase like this.'

'That's what the ARP always say. I'd rather be in bed, myself. Shall we?'

CRUMP.

'Now that really is further away. Even you must admit that.'

'Of course I do, Roy darling. You're always right.'

'Glad you recognize it at long last.'

He knows she's teasing him, but he is still a little ruffled by his mistake about the bombs.

'Much nicer up here.'

She turns on her side, and he moulds himself to her shape and lays a proprietorial hand over her swelling right breast.

'Much.'

'Fancy those people crammed into Underground stations.'

'All coughing and snoring and farting.'

'Oh, Roy.'

The breast jiggles up and down pleasantly under its night-gown.

'And worse than that.'

'Roy!'

'I tell you, there's going to be a lot more babies born as a result of this bloody war.'

'Only one perfect one.'

'As long as he is perfect. If it's not . . .'

Things can easily happen in the blackout, he was going to say.

'He will be. I know.' Smiling in the darkness.

'Did I tell you about that stupid old Henderson from the factory? Sitting down at home, drinking a cup of tea, when one of those bloody two-tonners went off four streets away and blew the socks and slippers right off his feet. Three people dead, but he didn't care; he's a real ladder-merchant.'

'What's that?'

'You know – "Pull up the ladder, I'm on deck."'

'Oh. What happened to his cup of tea?'

'I didn't ask. He probably drank it before he realized what had happened. And yesterday someone told me an ARP man rushed over to a manikin blown out of Kennard's front window in the High Street and asked it if it was all right.'

The breast shakes agreeably again.

'And was it?'

'Couldn't answer – no head.'

They drift off to sleep for a while. Then the alert sounds again, rising and falling for a couple of minutes. The eldritch noise is taken up further away, and further still: other parts of Croydon, Beckenham, Norwood.

'Oh God, they're coming back again, Roy. I'm really scared this time.'

'Don't worry, my darling. I'll protect you.'

'You can't protect me. Nothing can protect any of us. Not from those.'

The wailing dies away across the face of outer London. Now comes the grim part.

Another wave of bombers, much louder this time, throbbing unevenly in the sky, a nasty sound, dark and angry and full of menace. The anti-aircraft guns bark at them like guard-dogs; people say you can tell the difference between one gun and another if you listen closely.

'Roy, I think we're going to be killed.'

'Do you want to go downstairs, my darling?'

A sudden, immense sadness; the habitual superiority, the assertiveness are gone. If only he was always like this, she thinks in her strangely detached way, things would have been so much better.

'No. I don't think it matters this time.'

She turns over on to her back, her child defenceless against the bombs. There is no point now in defending it. Better a quick death for them all.

Real dogs are howling now, in between the booming of the guard-dog guns. No explosions for the moment: just a clattering sound on the roofs and pavements a little way away. A 'bread-basket' – seventy-two incendiary bombs – has been dropped close by.

'Incendiaries. The swine.'

Incendiaries are the worst, though not the most frightening. More damage is done by fire than by high explosive.

A ringing sound.

'Fire alarm.'

'Not round here, surely.'

This isn't the kind of area where people can afford alarms. Or have enough to protect with them. Kidderminster Place is not exactly a wealthy address.

It's the bells of the fire engines: two of them. They're close, but not in the street.

Another noise, faint still but greedy and disgustingly eager, licking its way up the walls of houses in search of wood and fabric. Roy looks round instinctively to see that there is no light in the room, and lifts the heavy corner of the black-out curtain. The flames light up the room.

'No, Roy, please.'

'Just trying to see where it is. I think we're all right here. It's probably in Windmill Road.'

'Please.'

'It's too interesting to stop looking. Look, some more dropping over there, but they're quite a bit further off.'

'Please, Roy, please. I hate it so much.'

'Oh, for God's sake.'

The flames die down, the ambulance arrives, one of the fire engines is called away.

An hour or so of interrupted sleep, then the wailing again.

'Bastards are back.'

The same sequence: the throbbing in the air, the dogs barking, the guns firing. Then there is a very different sound, like an immense sheet of canvas being torn. Much closer. If it takes ten seconds for the sound to reach you, it's half a mile away. This was no more than six or seven, he thinks.

CRUMP.

'Christ: H. E.'

Heavy explosive is terrifying. The bombers seem to know where you are, to be seeking you out. Just you, no one else.

CRUMP.

Everything shakes. Dust rises from between the floorboards. The electric light flickers, then resumes.

'Roy.'

'Yes, my darling?' He never calls her that usually.

'I'm sorry—' But she couldn't quite think what it was she was sorry for. Not stopping him from marrying her, perhaps.

He is struggling into his clothes.

'Just in case.'

CRUMP.

The house bucks and sways like a frightened colt, and seems to shift in its foundations even though it's part of a terrace. Surely that must give it some support? There is a terrible loose, falling noise, as slates and plaster and bricks shower down. The light flickers, goes out, stays out. Joyce doesn't scream. All she thinks is, this is the third time it's happened to me with him – the baby in her womb. She knows it's a boy; she can tell by the way it kicks. Both times when she was bombed before, the explosion was further away than this one. Suppose there's another? I don't think I could take another, she tells herself, but the thought is interrupted, not so much by an explosion, because she doesn't even hear that, but by a gigantic downward rush which blots out light, sound, sense, memory.

CRUMP.

It feels like the end of everything: of peace, of security, of light, of the world itself – all replaced by a wild, disordered craziness where nothing stays standing, or has any foundation. Only dust to see, dust to smell, dust to breathe. There is a foul chemical stench from the high explosive which makes her cough: the first real indication to herself that she is still alive. But there is a central blankness, an ability to understand exactly what has happened. The bomb has taken two or three seconds out of her life, and left her with a feeling of total bewilderment and loss.

The baby! She puts a hand on her stomach, which is covered an inch thick with brick dust and dry plaster. The baby kicks back irritably, tapping at her hand. God alone knows what effect the shattering noise and the shock will have on him in later life.

'He's alive!'

Silence, then: 'Not sure I am.'

Forgive me, God, for forgetting my husband.

She coughs, her face and body covered with flakes of white paint and white plaster from the fallen ceiling. It is difficult to move, but not impossible. Wonderingly, she begins to think she may not have been badly hurt. Above her, through the gaps in the ceiling and the roof beyond, she can see the searchlights crossing in the sky.

'You're sure you're all right, Joyce?' He scarcely ever uses her name when he speaks to her.

'Of course I'm all right. Someone's got to look after him.'

'And you're sure he is all right.'

'Feel.'

'Thank Christ. My son's alive.'

Not my wife, my son.

CRUMP.

He is standing up now, and even in the semi-darkness she can see he is covered with the whiteness of plaster. He lifts his head like a wolf.

'You fucking swine! You filthy fucking disgusting bastards! I hope your fucking guts fall out, you evil fucking degenerate swine!'

'*Roy.*'

She has never heard the word spoken aloud before, let alone screamed into the night air, though she has seen it written in books by D. H. Lawrence. She knows they use it at the factory, because Roy has told her so. Every second word, he says.

'That filthy fucking Hitler and that disgusting fucking Goering and all the rest of the fucking degenerate bunch. I hope they fucking rot in hell.'

He is so violently angry that he is shaking his fist at the patch of sky visible through the roof: something else she has heard of but never seen before.

'You do look funny.'

'Well, I don't feel bloody funny. This is the third time. Those filthy vicious bastards.'

'It's never been anything like as close as this.'

'You're getting out of here. Out of Croydon altogether. It's a foul place anyway. You're leaving.'

The rescue workers are downstairs, shining torches up as though they are searchlight batteries and Roy and Joyce are enemy aircraft.

'You all right up there?'

'Of course we're all right. What do you think? Would we be still talking if we weren't all right?'

'All right, all right, mate. Keep your hair on. I was only asking.'

'Well, go and ask the people next door. They're the poor bastards who need help.'

'Not any more, they don't.'

'Oh God, Roy. That nice old couple.'

'Well, at least it wasn't us. I'm sorry, but that's all I care about.'

'You should see yourself.'

'Well, you look like a bloody Alp, with all that plaster on your front. Why don't you get up?'

She gets up.

'I've made up my mind, you know: you're leaving here. How far away's the baby now, anyway? Two weeks?'

'Maybe less. Especially after this.'

'Right. I'm taking you to the station tomorrow. I'm not risking my son like this any more.'

His son; she seems to have no say in this at all.

'All right, dear. But for now we could do with a decent cup of tea, and there's nothing I can do here. The ARP will look after us somewhere.'

There is an unholy stench outside in Kidderminster Place, which comes from Kidderminster Road beyond. Smoke is still pouring up into the night sky from the three terraced houses which have vanished. Bricks, glass, bits of metal, bits of things that might be far worse, cover the road. The stench comes from the little chemist's on the corner, also destroyed. It is sickly enough to make you vomit, and it floats up from the cruel hole in the ground. The fire engines are there, the hoses are ready, but there are no flames. The high explosive has merely imploded the buildings it struck, the violent downward rush of air snuffing out the flames like the wick of a candle. Six people are unaccounted for. The rescue-workers are tugging away at the masonry and the wooden beams, bending down and calling into the crevices, shining their powerful torches into them.

'Someone down here!'

An ambulance has arrived and is taking away three or four people, each with serious cuts from flying glass. An officious nurse in her night uniform looks critically at Joyce, then at Roy.

'You two seem all right,' she says grudgingly. 'But you should never be in Croydon with your baby so close. I'm really surprised at you. You're her husband. You should—'

Roy is already starting to bristle when Joyce explains quietly to her that she is leaving that morning.

'Well, I should think so,' the nurse says. 'About time, too.'

One or two undefined figures are faintly visible in the shadows. No one likes to make the accusation, but every month one or two people are prosecuted for looting. It is something you read about occasionally in the papers. People complain that everything they have is stolen while their injuries are being cared for, but no one likes to give it too much publicity: it's bad for the war effort.

The All Clear sounds, and everyone looks at their watch: 1.18 in the morning.

In the dark street, with only the little slits of light from the headlamps on the ambulance to give any indication where you are or what is happening, broken glass crunches and scrapes underfoot, and little bits of shrapnel from the AA guns and the fallen bombs sing across the street as you kick them.

The entire front of the house next door in the terrace has been sheared off, and it looks like a doll's house, with the furniture thrown around on each of the floors. An indecent voyeuristic instinct makes everyone peer up at the open rooms lit by flames: the old-fashioned wallpaper, the brass bedsteads, the furniture burst and leaking horsehair. Who'd have thought the Logans would have such cheap things? Why did they paint their bedroom that awful colour?

Round in St James's Road a mobile stall is offering free cups of tea and some almost inedible cakes.

'Here you are, dear. Hot and strong.'

The ARP man who shone his torch at Roy is telling his colleague how an explosion has thrown an elderly woman into the street in her bath.

'So she climbed out, stark naked, and said, I don't know what you're looking at, young man, but I'd like a towel if you can find one.'

'How old was she, if she thought you was a young man?'

'About a hundred and twenty. Wrinkles everywhere. Completely unhurt.'

'Explosives do funny things. Did I tell you about the head I found round in a street in East Croydon, smiling up at me like my granny?'

'Come on, Roy, please. I don't want to hear any more of this.'

But Roy is already part of the conversation, and the others turn to him with interest and pleasure, as he tells them about a particular horror which happened at the explosives factory where he works.

A FEW HOURS LATER that day, 20 July, a senior German staff officer, Colonel Claus von Stauffenberg, unobtrusively placed his briefcase under a wooden table where Hitler and many leading military and political people were discussing the latest phase in the war: the Allied invasion of Normandy. The bomb in the briefcase exploded a few minutes later, but Hitler, by an unfortunate miracle, was not killed. Josef Goebbels's office rushed out a statement to forestall any rumours:

> An attempt on the life of the Fuehrer was made with high explosives today. Hitler received slight burns and concussion, but no injuries. He at once began to work again. He then received Mussolini for a long meeting, as previously arranged.

At the time this momentous event took place I was still minus twenty days old: a disturbingly restless lump in my mother's womb, with fully developed eyes and hands and fingernails, and a brain which was capable of perception, though not yet of memory or judgement. Sometimes I slept peacefully, sometimes I was tensely awake. I could yawn, though I was not tired, and I could dream; but of what, and on the basis of what experience, no one has yet been able to determine. By the hot summer of 1944 I had ceased to be an excitement for my parents and a cause for congratulation, and had simply become a burden to my unfortunate mother.

Still, she didn't complain about me. She very rarely complained about anything: a sweet-natured, gentle, easy woman, dark-haired, good olive skin, tallish but with a slight stoop to compensate for my father's relative shortness, and a charming way of lowering her head and looking at you. Pregnancy suited her: it emphasized her gentleness, her air of self-sacrifice, her dark, attractive looks.

Joyce Leila Vivien Cody was two days short of her thirty-eighth birthday on 27 July: approaching middle age, by the standards of the time. She had been married once before, and had had two children, Patricia and Michael, and had later been widowed. Then my father had met her and married her within a matter of a few weeks, despite the eight-year difference in their ages.

Getting married hadn't been in anyone's interests – his, hers, theirs, mine. It was just one of those sudden wartime things that people did. If you didn't know whether you would be alive in a week's time, the possibility that you might be making a serious mistake scarcely counted. Nothing seemed to have any permanence. If you wanted to do something, you might as well get on and do it. As for parents and family and other more sensible older people, they scarcely mattered: too busy trying to get their rations and maintain their blackout and avoiding the bombs to care.

In any case, my father was never much of a forward-planner. Life came easily to him, and he had an abiding faith in his ability to charm it and turn it to his purposes. He had always lived for the moment, and he possessed the Simpson family's sharp, self-deprecating humour in large and undiluted quantities. A couple of months before he was killed by a massive heart attack in March 1980, he told me: 'I've just worked out that I've got enough money to live comfortably for the rest of my life. Provided I die next Thursday, that is.'

Roy was only five feet eight inches tall: something which annoyed him. He put it down to having been half-starved at the Anglo-Catholic boarding-school where his mother dumped him at the age of ten. Yet of course he joked about his height too.

'I'm always going back there for my holidays,' he said after spending a fortnight in Sardinia in the 1970s. 'Everyone's so short there that I strode around like a giant among pygmies.'

Like most of his *bon mots*, you had the feeling that he'd used it on others before trying it on you.

It is easy for me to imagine my father working in films, a harassed, short-tempered, melodramatic yet superbly charming director, cajoling an entire angry cast of actors into performing despite dreadful conditions, and persuading the backers to keep their money in the project even when everything was falling about his ears. His entire life, though inevitably far less glamorous, was constructed along these lines.

He was strongly built, with a barrel chest (which, in middle age, I find to my surprise I have inherited) and powerful arms and legs. When I was thirteen and on my way home from school, I found a paperback translation of *The Odyssey* at W. H. Smith's bookshop on Victoria railway station and began reading it on my hour-long daily journeys. Immediately I felt the tough, omni-capable, infinitely resourceful Odysseus was a kind of portrait of my father. No doubt these were just the imaginings of a bookish child without much to compare his father with; yet there was unquestionably something of the subtle sacker of towns about him.

Only something, though. When my father met my mother, in 1943, he was essentially a creation of the first half of the twentieth century: the most disturbed period, perhaps, in the whole of human existence. A generation later, he would have turned the disadvantages of his birth and upbringing into huge advantages; he might indeed have been a film director or a writer, as he wanted. But growing up in the 1920s and 30s, he suffered heavily. His mother had had to bring him up alone, and in the absence of any formal education (the few terms he spent at the Anglo-Catholic school, which according to him resembled a kind of pederastic Auschwitz, taught him nothing except sharp-wittedness) he drifted into the adult world at the age of thirteen.

Now that I have almost reached the age he was when his life ended, I can finally acknowledge to myself what I suppose I guessed decades before: that he was bisexual. He loved women, and they were greatly attracted to his looks and his witty, confident, assertive personality; but there was more than that. He had plenty of affairs with women over the years, which often ended in acute embarrassment ('Oh God, it's Janet. Just say I'm not in, there's a good boy'). On New Year's Eve, 1962, he and I found ourselves in a Norwegian restaurant in Casablanca – it was sheer escapism for both of us, since our vast, ugly red-brick mansion on the Suffolk coast had seized up in the great frost that winter – and he made eye-contact with Zsa Zsa Gabor across the dance-floor.

That effectively ended our holiday together; I took a plane back to London a couple of days later. Yet it wasn't his affair with Zsa Zsa which he talked about later; he seemed quite embarrassed by that. Instead, he told me endless stories about a Brazilian racing-driver he'd met and the trip they'd taken to the ancient city of Medina. There was never any hint from him of any romantic link-up. Maybe I was just too straight for him to be able to talk to me about such things, and he knew I would be deeply shocked. Anyway, homosexuality was illegal at the time, and such liaisons were too dangerous to talk about openly.

Now, as I enter my sixties, I couldn't care less about any of this; it seems to me that in a world of such cruelty and sadness people should be free to find their happiness wherever they can, as long as no one else is damaged, physically or mentally. But in those days I was priggish and fairly fragile, and I had invested a great deal of faith in my father. He probably saw, rightly, that I simply wasn't up to the task of coping with such awkward confessions.

On 20 July 1944, I am nothing more than an unseen, unformed, unborn burden. My parents walk back to their flat, my father's arm protectively round my mother, stepping over the rubble, kicking away the shards of shrapnel, watching out for live electricity cables.

'First thing in the morning, then. I don't care where it is, just as long as there aren't any bombs there. I'm not having fucking Hitler trying to kill my son again.'

Our son, she ought to interpose, or trying to kill *me*. But she is the least assertive person imaginable, and as a result this merely encourages his sense that what really counts is the precious substance he calls Simpson blood.

Which is strange, since his name isn't really Simpson at all; that is his mother's, not his father's surname. More than twenty years after the day his father, a jovial, boastful man called Herbert Fidler, deserted the family, Roy dropped the name of Fidler and became a Simpson. The moment of desertion came in 1922, when my father was eight. The bailiffs − or the police: my grandmother's story sometimes varied − came to arrest my grandfather. He asked them if he could use the lavatory, then climbed through a window and ran across the fields to the nearby railway station with the agility he had once shown as a rugby fly-half. He jumped on a train to London and eventually caught the Holyhead ferry. Ireland had just broken away from the United Kingdom and was still undergoing its ferocious civil war. Using the intelligence contacts he had made during the First World War, Herbert linked up with the successful

Free Staters in their fight against the outright Republicans of Eamonn de Valera. They were happy to take in volunteers.

Herbert was an inveterate boaster. He once told me how he had steadied his rifle against the side of a stone wall outside a village in County Wicklow, and hit a senior figure in the IRA between the eyes. Perhaps it was true; there was plenty of bloodletting at the time. Yet as with all Herbert's stories, its only purpose seemed to be to enhance Herbert's reputation.

After the civil war he opened a small hotel and restaurant – 'A pub, more likely,' my grandmother sniffed when she heard – and lived under the name H. M. Downton with a big raw-boned woman called Grace, until her death long after the end of the Second World War. In 1945 he came back to England and settled on the South Coast. But he no longer had his old athletic figure; instead, he looked like the figure of Mr Punch from the cover of *Punch* magazine: stout, red-faced, his nose and chin in danger of touching. And he was still intensely boastful, as though his behaviour was something to be proud of. My father felt obliged to take him in; and he looked after him remarkably well for the rest of his life.

Still, the fact that my father had long abandoned his surname occasionally made my grandfather fretful, in spite of his own abandonment of it when it suited him. He regarded the Simpsons as a set of priggish, self-righteous snobs, natural prey for the lifelong (though small-time) swindler which he undoubtedly was.

My father was always drawn to success, which is why he preferred the Simpsons – even if it was accompanied by a certain religiose self-approval, as it tended to be with the older generation of Simpsons. He liked wealth and comfort, because he had known so little of it in his early years; and as late as the 1960s, whenever he had a bit of money, he would go out and buy an expensive cigar, light it, and set it on the mantelpiece to burn out. He associated the smell of its smoke, which filled the room, with affluence. During his childhood, he once explained to me, Herbert used to smoke Havanas whenever he was flush with money. As a result my father regarded the smell of cigar-smoke as a sign of affluence and contentment. I, in my turn, though I had never smoked a cigarette in my life, took to smoking Havanas when I reached my fifties – but only when there was something to celebrate, some reason for feeling at ease with the world. In this way we project our comforts and our palliatives from one generation to the next.

So MY FATHER and mother go back to their shattered flat, and for what remains of the night they put the mattress from their bed in the kitchen on the floor and lie there, side by side, with the warm summer air floating through the glassless windows. They sleep till seven, and then my father jumps up with the anger and energy as strong in him as ever, and starts pulling on his clothes.

'But where we going?'

'A long way away from this stinking place, anyway.'

'I don't think you've got any idea where to send me.'

Again, that charming look up at him.

'Of course I do. I've always got a plan.'

That, at least is true: he is one of the most resourceful people on earth.

It takes them a long time to reach Waterloo; but he doesn't want her to catch a train from there. He takes exception to all the available destinations.

'Look, who knows? The Germans can still bomb the south-west. We're going to King's Cross.'

King's Cross station serves the north-west of the country. It is a long journey by tube, and after the adventures of the night, the effort of the journey and my father's continuing excitement and his rage against Field-Marshal Goering, Joyce is pale and inclined to drag her feet as they walk into the ticket office.

There is a long, patient queue; but my father, impressive despite his civilian clothes, the energy still radiating from him, pushes her in front of him to the very front of it.

'Here,' one or two people protest as he elbows them out of the way; but, since the British are an essentially unaggressive people, they go quiet when they see my mother and the burden she is carrying.

'I'm so sorry,' she whispers.

'Don't worry, dear. You can't stand around in your condition.'

'Hope you're not going far,' says a wag at the back, but several people turn round angrily and he looks away.

'Well, then?' asks the ticket-clerk, who has watched my father push his next customer aside. 'Where's it to?'

'Wherever this will take her.'

With a conjuror's timing he produces a handful of silver coins and a pound note from his pocket, and slams it all down on the curved brass tray under the glass of the ticket-desk.

Sighing, the clerk counts it out.

'One pound, eighteen and ninepence. Let me see.'

He consults a chart on the wall beside him.

'First-class, that will take you to Stratford-on-Avon. Second-class, it'll take you to Stoke-on-Trent.'

'Not far enough. Where will it take her in third class?'

The clerk frowns and consults his chart again.

'Looks like Blackpool. Change at Preston.'

Behind my father there is a little sigh of pleasure. Blackpool seems to represent everything the war has taken away.

'No illuminations,' someone jokes.

My mother turns and smiles, and the joker, abashed, is entirely won over by her.

'Blackpool it shall be,' my father says grandly.

She travels alone, and the journey, when it finally begins, takes more than thirty hours. In the daytime it is unbearably hot, and the train often stands for long periods, stranded in the sun, while other trains work their way round the damaged section of track.

The compartment is full, as all compartments are nowadays,

and the corridor is blocked by dozens of soldiers and their kitbags.

'I could see if one of the officers in second-class will swap with you, miss,' says a soldier at their second halt, sticking his head in through the door.

'No, please don't trouble,' my mother answers. 'It'll be just as hot there, and besides, these gentlemen are being so kind to me.'

Though they aren't used to hearing themselves referred to as gentlemen, the soldiers have shown the greatest courtesy and good manners towards her. They have lifted her worn leather suitcase on to the rack, they have shuffled themselves around so she can have the window-seat facing the direction of the train, and what little air there is can cool her face. They have brought her rust-tasting water from the lavatory down the corridor, and they have interrupted her reading a dozen times to ask about the baby, and her feelings, and where her family comes from. When she does an imitation of my father dancing with rage and shaking his fist at Goering the entire compartment erupts with laughter, and the soldiers in the corridor look at each other enviously, left out of the general amusement.

The hot, airless summer night finds them stopped in a siding somewhere near Crewe. Someone makes a pillow for her out of a rough grey Army blanket, so she won't have to rest her head on her neighbour's shoulder. It rests on the window instead, and when the engine starts up and the carriages jerk forward at around three o'clock she feels every motion of it.

Yet she isn't unhappy or worried. She knows everything will work out; even if she has to have the baby right here in the compartment, it will all pass off well. Nothing troubles her. In the darkness and the heat of the train she holds herself tightly and smiles. The birth will be fine, and the boy will be something special. If she could possibly have known, that July night, how divisive I would be between her husband and her, and how little she would ever see me or know me, her secret confidence in the dark might have faded a little.

Yet it's the fact of coming motherhood which pleases her that night, not the distant future. She can really focus only upon the immediate, and anything further off will have to take care of itself.

She wakes to the noise of excited conversation. The men in the compartment look across at her guiltily, but she can see that something important has happened, and smiles at them.

'Hitler's nearly been killed, miss.'

'How? Was he bombed?'

'Well, yes, but one of his own lot put it there. A general. Took in a bomb in a briefcase and it went off under the table. Hitler was badly hurt, they think, but he's still going.'

'More's the pity,' calls out someone from the corridor.

In her present mood, Joyce doesn't even wish any harm to Hitler.

'How did you find this out?'

'Someone came out from the village in the night to tell the train driver. Seems to have happened yesterday afternoon.'

'Hitler's trousers got blown off,' shouts one of the soldiers.

The men in the compartment look across at Joyce, checking to see whether this kind of talk might upset her.

Instead, she laughs. Her laughter, full-throated, deep-toned, is one of the finest things about her, though it is rare enough. The other people grin with the pleasure of hearing it.

'Seems old Mussolini was due to arrive, and Hitler had to find another pair to put on, sharpish. Couldn't have his arse hanging out of his trousers for Musso, could he?'

'Not so much of that,' says the corporal in the far corner. 'Ladies.'

Joyce looks down at the carriage floor; she isn't shocked in the slightest, of course, but she feels she has to comply with the expectations of these men, who think that middle-class women cannot take such language.

'Pity he wasn't blown up by one of his own Flying Bombs. That'd show him what it's like.'

Everyone nods. I do want Hitler to die, of course I do, Joyce tells herself; but just at the moment there is so much to be glad about, that I can't concentrate on it.

'When that man is dead and gone, What a day to wake up on,' someone is singing in the corridor, and a soldier in the carriage takes up the tune on his mouth-organ.

The train jerks, then slowly starts to move again.

THE BROWNISH WATER is unpleasantly cold, even for an English summer, but Roy doesn't mind. All those years of bathing in unheated sea-water on board ship have acclimatized him to this kind of thing. It strikes his thickish white body across the stomach, and he stands on tiptoe on the sharp stones, gasping. Then he throws himself forward, splashing and ducking his head into its brownish depths. He has finally made it to Blackpool, and then on to the Queen's Hydro, on the sea-front at Cleveleys. Blackpool is too working-class for him to want his son to be born there, but Cleveleys is different: a pleasant, comfortable spa town just outside. In a country where people know their place, they also know that Cleveleys is a cut above the seaside-landlady, amusement-arcade, fish-and-chips atmosphere of Blackpool; even though for the past five years the arcades have been closed, the fish hard to get, and the landladies have had to take in evacuees and the Home Guard.

Roy stops splashing and looks back at the beach to see if his clothes are all right. He can see the little pile above the heaped-up sand and pebbles farther up the beach. He treads water for a while. No one wanted him at the Hydro: the nurses made it clear that a father's place at the birth of his child was out in the waiting-room, smoking.

'Have I got time for a swim, do you think?' he asked

'Yes, of course you have,' the midwife said absently.

If he swam off to Ireland it wouldn't matter to anyone, her tone seemed to say.

The red-brick mass of the Hydro hangs over the beach like

a cliff. Treading water again, Roy looks back at it. Third floor, three windows from the right, he tells himself, counting. There is a brief flash of white behind the glass, then another. Now someone is lifting the window-sash. A white figure, a nurse or a midwife, holds something up for him to see. Roy leaps up, his feet just finding sand and pebbles, and runs out of the water and up the beach to his pile of clothes.

They still chafe his damp body as he stands in the delivery room, looking at the baby's ugly little face, purple and red and screwed up with anger and fear, as it lies in the midwife's arms. The early afternoon sun shines into the workaday ward and makes everything gleam.

'What a lovely little stranger.'

The midwife is angular and sandy-haired, and her face has some of the same angry tints as the baby's; but even her features have softened as she looks down at it.

Roy stares at the lick of black hair across the baby's fragile cranium. For the first time the midwife acknowledges him.

'So ye're here.'

'I did ask you if there would be time for me to have a swim.'

The midwife sniffs, and looks across at the nurse. 'Some people,' her look seems to say. This is a woman's realm, and he is here on sufferance. It is an article of faith among the women in this ward that men are clumsy, selfish and unnecessary.

Roy sits down on the bed. The springs groan faintly under his weight. Everything else seems extraordinarily quiet.

'Thank you, darling.'

It is strange to him to feel such a flow of kindness and approval for her, as she lies propped up on the pillow, her face still damp with the sweat of labour. She squeezes his hand, exhausted and happy that she should have succeeded so well.

'He's perfect,' she breathes, knowing how important it is to him to have a son, without defects.

She herself would have been happy whatever the baby was like; in some ways she might even have felt closer to it if there had been something wrong with it, for then it would have relied on her even more. But she knows that Roy would have cut himself off from the baby completely if it had been mentally or physically deficient in some way.

'Better to put a pillow over his face quietly and sort him out,' he told her during the pregnancy.

Now she reaches across and opens the white towelling in which the baby is wrapped. He lies exposed in the midwife's arms, the extraordinary colours of the womb only now starting to fade, an occasional wipe of blood on his body, the cut umbilical cord still hanging loosely from his stomach. He starts to cry with a sound like an ancient door closing, and raises his red fists to his tightly closed eyes, like a boxer expecting a blow. Roy looks at him with a certain approval.

'Nothing wrong there.'

The midwife is affronted.

'And why should there be something wrong?'

She wraps up the baby again, like a present which has been criticized and won't be handed out now, after all.

'Never mind, my little darling. You're fine, no matter what the man says.'

Joyce smiles faintly, and Roy smiles back at her. They are closer and more affectionate than at any other moment in their entire relationship. But everything depends on her success; there would have been no understanding of failure, no forgiveness. She knows that now.

The midwife puts the white bundle in her arms, and she looks at the ugly little red face. Who will he be? What might he achieve? Will he love her unconditionally, or will he be hard and demanding, like his father? The baby turns and seems to nestle against her, though experience tells her he is just trying to accustom himself to the greater freedom outside the womb, and will soon want the breast.

Although this child is myself, I am as much an observer of the baby as my mother and father were. The potentiality is there, certainly, but it is essentially neutral, as unformed as the child's nature. At this stage it is as reasonable to assume that I could be an Einstein, an Attila, a Leonardo, a Shakespeare, as to think that I would turn out like everyone else. I have never, as an adult, been able to think of that pleasant scene in the Queen's Hydro without remembering the words of the Scottish folksong:

> Oh, little did my mother think,
> When first she cradled me,
> The lands I was to travel in,
> And the death I was to dee.

As I lie there in my mother's arms, I seem capable of virtually anything; capable even of being a close and loving son to her. Surely the last thing she can think at such a time is that I will be so alienated from her in the years to come.

All of us are wrapped up in guilt, as closely as the child in my mother's arms was wrapped in its white blanket. We wrap ourselves in it, and are wrapped in it by others. Those who seem outwardly to experience no guilt whatever – my father, for example – simply carry it at a different level of consciousness. They have screwed up their eyes against it, and balled their fists to ward it off.

But at this precise moment, 3.30 in the afternoon of Wednesday 9 August 1944, my father and mother are perfectly content. My father is delighted that he has a son, and my mother is delighted that she has finally given him what he wanted. The three of us will never be quite so happy together again.

AT THAT STAGE, EVEN if they had had the money, my mother and father were not the kind of people who would have thought for an instant of announcing my birth in *The Times*. For a start, neither of them knew anyone who read it; they didn't have the kind of money that would have encouraged them to make a purely empty gesture; and anyway *The Times* probably wouldn't want advertisements from people whose address was 2 Kidderminster Place, West Croydon. *The Times* carries notices of eleven births for 9 August 1944, all of them with distinctly upper-middle-class names: Anthea Priscilla Barber, Jeremy John Bright, Rosemary Mackenzie Inkson, Julia Victoria Sandifer. The most attention I will receive from the great world is a birth certificate, on which my father is registered as a factory store-keeper. The registrar, a feeble-looking man in his forties, looks at him critically.

'Most men are in the Army now, aren't they?'

'You're not.'

'There's no call to be personal.'

Everything had changed since the moment my father met my mother. On 2 August, a week before I was born, Churchill told the House of Commons, 'On every battle front all over the world the arms of Germany and Japan are recoiling ... The losses by U-boats since the start of 1944 have been almost negligible ... I no longer feel bound to deny that victory may come perhaps soon.'

It seemed closer than it really was. The attempted assassination of Hitler on 20 July made it seem as though Germany itself was turning against its Fuehrer. Shortly before my mother went into labour with me at the Queen's Hydro, a court 1,000 miles away was trying eight German officers who had been part of the plot. The Berlin press reported a key section of the trial; in particular the evidence of Col.-Gen. Hoeppner, commander-in-chief of the Home Army.

> *President of the court:* Why did you not commit suicide after the failure of this despicable plot?
> *Hoeppner:* I did not commit suicide because I did not feel as though I had acted like a swine.
> *President:* What class of animal do you think you belong to, then?
> *Hoeppner:* Asses.
> *President:* No, sir, you are and you remain a swine.

By the end of the day Hoeppner and the other seven defendants had been sentenced to death.

They had been very courageous, but they were neither clever nor lucky. The thickness of Hitler's oak table had ruined everything. 'There was only one spot in the room which remained untouched by the explosion,' his propaganda chief Goebbels declared on Berlin Radio, with only a little exaggeration, 'and that was the very spot where the Fuehrer stood. Never again will the Almighty reveal Himself to us as he has just done in saving the Fuehrer. His intention was to let us know that it is for us now to work for victory.'

But Goebbels was a less effective spokesman for God than he was for Hitler. God's plans seemed rather different. In the previous thirty days, the Allied forces had taken 52,000 prisoners in Normandy and Italy, including two generals and an admiral. During the same period the RAF had dropped 57,500 tons of bombs over Germany. Farther to the east the Poles of the Underground Army were fighting to capture Warsaw. It was not yet clear that Stalin would betray them by refusing to help them, nor that the bloodshed would be terrible. Soviet troops were advancing into Latvia, and some units were encouraged by their officers to loot the houses and rape the women.

Hitler's only hope lay in the introduction of new and more terrible weapons. Churchill had told the House of Commons a few days earlier that Germany had developed a type of rocket-gun, firing a much heavier explosive missile.

'This means,' he said, 'that Londoners might yet have to face even sterner trials.'

This public announcement brought a measure of relief to Barbara, a quiet, artistic woman whom my father took under his wing in later years, as he looked after several other slightly damaged people. She worked in a branch of British intelligence, and saw the secret information which was coming in from Resistance groups on the Continent about the new weapons which were being developed. The strain of so much secrecy and such long hours affected her badly, and she found herself wandering around London like some cloak-clad Cassandra, knowing all about the destructive power which would shortly be unleashed against London in the form of V2 rockets, yet unable to warn even those closest to her. Once Churchill himself had hinted publicly at the danger, the pressure on Barbara subsided; yet she remained strange and somehow absent for the rest of her life, occasionally wandering in her mind and inclined to paint embarrassing canvases covered with twee, sexless fairies and maidens as a kind of therapy.

On the day of my birth Herbert Morrison, the Home Secretary, gave the House of Commons even more disturbing details of these new, extraordinarily fast V2 rockets.

'It is regretted that no more than a minute and a half's warning is possible. The danger warning will be three two-second blasts on a klaxon. The "release" will be a continuous six-second blast. It is to be regretted that these measures will be admittedly imperfect.'

London was already used to the slower, older, yet sometimes equally destructive V1s. At around one o'clock on the afternoon of 9 August, just as my mother's labour was approaching its end, one fell on a building in central London which was used as a canteen for office workers. The building was crowded, and many people were killed or injured. Another destroyed five houses on an estate in the southern outskirts of London; four people died there. A third fell on a row of houses, killing four neighbours.

Some hours before my birth, in the heat of a Bombay morning, Mahatma Gandhi had agreed to accept an official restriction on the size of a demonstration to celebrate the anniversary of the founding of the Congress Party. Twenty-five people were given permission to picket schools and colleges in the city, and the day passed off quietly. One of the arguments used by the local officials (who were, as it happens, all Indians) was that with so many Indian soldiers fighting the Japanese in Burma, there would be no back-up for the police if the demonstration got out of hand. While registering his moral disapproval of war of any kind, Gandhi accepted the argument and agreed with it.

Three hours earlier, after a brief gun battle, a black Citroën crammed with men wearing large black berets and carrying an array of weapons, from Sten guns to an old blunderbuss, drove into the centre of Quimper, in Brittany. They were the advance guard of the Resistance. They were met with near-hysteria, as the local people competed with each other to give them information and show their patriotism; and soon the now defenceless collaborators were brought out, spat at, threatened with lynching, their clothes torn, their heads shaven. These people had openly backed the wrong side, and those who had not committed themselves that far, or (in a few cases) had actively supported the Resistance, now assuaged their guilt and anxiety with acts of gratuitous cruelty. For the most part the men and women of the Resistance stayed apart from these demonstrations of good faith. They themselves had chosen the patriotic

side, the right side, the winning side; what more did they have
to prove?

In Normandy, the Allies were making good progress.
General Dwight Eisenhower chose this day to establish his
headquarters in France. American troops, full of confidence
and drive, captured the port of St Malo during the morning.
To the south-east the Canadians were getting close to the town
of Falaise, the birthplace of William the Conqueror, which was
still held by the Germans.

At around midday, a small detachment of men from the
XII SS reconnaissance battalion attached to the 12th Panzer
Division marched a group of nineteen captured Canadian
soldiers down a small country road to the village of Pavie, in
the Calvados area of Normandy. Under interrogation the nineteen men had refused to give away the positions and relative
strengths of their units, and their senior officer had protested
that it was contrary to the Geneva Convention for the Germans
to demand this kind of information.

The Panzer officer who was escorting the nineteen Canadians ordered them to leave the road and head into a meadow.
Larks hovered above them in the clear summer air, butterflies
flew up around their feet. The officer shouted to them to halt.
Five or six German soldiers knelt down and took aim at their
backs. An order, a crackle of fire, the sound of a few individual
pistol shots, then the larks started singing again. No one would
ever be brought to trial for these murders.

All that day the British Eighth Army was engaged in a heavy
artillery battle outside Florence. More than twenty British soldiers were killed, and 118 were wounded. By pre-arrangement
with the British commander, groups of Italian partisans spent
the day hunting down German snipers within Florence itself.
The lucky ones were those who were killed instantly; though by
the end of the day each of the eleven snipers who were found
was dead, and no doubt glad to die.

The newspapers of the day reported a race riot in Philadelphia, which came about as the result of a widely supported transport strike. A black boy, thirteen years old, was killed by a bullet to the chest, fired from a passing car which contained white men.

At Liverpool police court the Recorder, Mr E. G. Hemmerde, KC, ordered a West Indian, George Alexander McGuire Roberts, to pay a fine of a farthing – a quarter of a penny, for those unfamiliar with the old pre-decimal coinage – for failing to turn up for his Home Guard duties. The usual fine was five pounds, but Roberts explained that people had insulted him because of his colour and he felt intimidated from attending his local ARP post. The Recorder replied that he was sorry to have to fine Roberts at all, but this was because he had pleaded guilty.

'People come over here to risk their lives on behalf of what they proudly call "The Mother Country",' Mr Hemmerde said, 'and I consider it an impertinence for any country to accept the aid of coloured people from any part of the world, and then to say, "Our laws do not enable us to deal with you on terms of complete equality."'

The British Colour Council, which had nothing to do with race but was one of the dreary state agencies which the Government had set up to oversee the rationing system, announced the colours for women's clothes for the autumn season. There would be coats, suits and dresses in a darkish red, and in a dull blue. A third colour, newly introduced, was called 'crottle', a warmish brown as boring as its name. 'Stockings,' said the official announcement made on 9 August, in a determinedly cheerful aside, 'are still restricted to the present four useful colours.'

On the evening of my first day of independent existence, some people in London did their best to forget the war and its restrictions for a couple of hours. Given the shortages of everything from clothes to electricity, the West End was still able to put on a surprisingly large number of shows: eleven theatres in all were open for business that evening, most of them showing comedies or light entertainment of some kind. At the Ambassadors, Hermione Gingold was starring in *Sweeter and Lower*, the Apollo was showing J. B. Priestley's topical (that is, wartime) comedy *How Are They at Home?*; Sonia Dresdel was in *This Was a Woman* at the Comedy Theatre; the Duchess was showing *Blithe Spirit*, the Duke of York's *Is Your Honeymoon Really Necessary?*, the Globe *While the Sun Shines*, the Savoy *The Last of Mrs Cheyney* with Jack Buchanan, Coral Browne and Athene Seyler. At Wyndhams, *A Quiet Weekend* was playing.

Lilian Braithwaite and Naunton Wayne were in *Arsenic and Old Lace* at the Strand ('The biggest laugh of the Wartime theatre,' the *Daily Herald* said). Phyllis Dixey appeared from 2 p.m. to 9 p.m. daily at the Whitehall: 'England's popular pin-up Girl in her show, *Peek-A-Boo*, and a galaxy of beauty.' The stalls were packed with men in uniform for this essentially innocent parade of girls wearing a minimum of clothes, just as they were at the Windmill in Piccadilly Circus for *Revudeville* – '176th edition, 13th year, second week, continuous daily, 12.15–9.30; last performance 7.50.' The advertisement ends with the final, proud, entirely justifiable boast: 'We never closed.'

At the cinema, the Carlton was showing *For Whom the Bell Tolls* (A) with Gary Cooper and Ingrid Bergman. Betty Grable was in *Pin-Up Girl* (colour, U), at the Gaumont, Haymarket, Humphrey Bogart was in *Passage to Marseille* (A) at the Warner, Leicester Square, and Rita Hayworth and Gene Kelly were in *Cover Girl* (Technicolor, U). 'U' stood for universal entry, 'A' for adults only.

The radio was the only other form of mass entertainment, and the BBC was the sole licensed broadcaster in the United Kingdom. It had reduced its services to a single station, the Home Service, which had to fit in news, talks, drama, religious programmes, classical music and light music, in a way which managed to irritate almost everybody. Broadcasting on 203.5 metres, 391.1 metres and 449.1 metres medium wave, these were the programmes for the day I was born:

7.00: News
7.15: Physical exercises
7.30: Records
7.55: Morning prayers
8.00: News
8.15: Radio Doctor
8.20: Harry Fryer and his Orchestra
9.00: Records
9.55: Al Bollington (organ)
10.15: Daily service
10.30: Jack Payne with his Orchestra
11.00: Records
11.50: Marjorie Hayward string quartet, Henny Cummings (baritone)
12.30: Works concert
1.00: News
1.15: Interlude
1.20: BBC Scottish Orchestra
2.15: BBC Variety Orchestra
3.00: Victor Silvester and his Orchestra
3.30: Fred Hartley and his Music
4.00: Wednesday Matinee: *Mr Watson's Vacation* and *The Quiet Moor*
5.00: News. Eistedfodd news and interviews in Welsh
5.20: Children's Hour
6.00: News and announcements
6.30: Command Performance (musical variety)
7.00: Can I Help You?
7.15: BBC Symphony Orchestra
7.55: This Is the Law – Slander
8.15: *The Voice of Michael Vane* – a play by James Dyrenforth

9.00: Big Ben. A Minute for Reflection.
       News and War Report
9.35: Esmé Percy in *At the Cross-in-Hand*
10.10: Record Cabaret
10.40: Short Story: *Time Out For Lunch*
10.55: Emelie Hooke (soprano)
11.25: Records
12.00: News
12.10: Close down

There was something almost desperately reassuring about the BBC's programming: an attempt, perhaps, to persuade people that at a time when much of the world was involved in a war which was unlike anything human beings had ever seen before, there was still such a thing as stability and decency, even when the evidence was starting to emerge of death camps, mass murder, and cruelty on an unthinkable scale. The BBC could of course be suffocatingly cosy, wilfully turning away from the horrors that could strike randomly at almost anyone; yet that was what people most wanted, just as they wanted to watch light social comedies and chorus-girls who showed off their legs. And those who were stationed abroad with the armed forces most wanted the comfort of knowing that home was still the same quiet place they carried around with them in their minds. A BBC pamphlet, published shortly before I was born to counter criticisms of the expense involved in broadcasting the Empire Service, contained several stories to show how it was linking the forces abroad with their families at home:

Not long ago a man climbed into a captured enemy tank. He switched on the radio set – and received a message from his wife. A mother from Britain was sending a message to her soldier son in India – but how could she reach her other son in the Merchant Navy? The son in India was told in advance and was ready at the loudspeaker. The sailor son reached Malta in a convoy an hour before the broadcast, sat down in the canteen, and both sons heard the message at the same time. An Australian introduced his English bride to his parents in Australia over the microphone.

The BBC deliberately appealed to the peaceable side of the British, the comfortable, inward-looking, unimaginative side, the side which made them unwilling to believe that the worst might happen, and encouraged them to look for a quiet life. These were the attitudes which made the Munich Agreement with Hitler possible; but heroism and self-sacrifice are rare qualities in human beings, and can only be supported in relatively short bursts. Even at their most heroic and self-sacrificing, the British thought mostly of peaceful days at home. And the BBC, for all the awkwardness of its efforts to satisfy the demands of everyone, reflected that.

We get the entertainment we deserve, just as much as we get the politicians we deserve. The British like their entertainment, and their politicians, to be comfortable; too much seriousness, too much stress, upsets them. Their tastes, like their politics, are essentially middle-brow, and it is unwise to unsettle them too much; even at a time of national sacrifice.

Wednesday 10 October 1945

Double British Summer Time.
Sun rises, 6.14 a.m.; sets, 5.19 p.m.
Lighting-up time: 5.49 p.m.
Black-out: discontinued.
Maximum temperature: 52°F; minimum: 48°F.
Fair at first, with occasional rain showers later.

I RECALL THE ENTIRE SCENE with great precision. My mother and I are in front of the empty fireplace, over which is a large mirror; the mirror, hanging from a chain, is tipped at a slight angle towards her. My mother is standing on tiptoe, looking up into it and putting on lipstick. She has some kind of coat on, which is brown. Perhaps it is camel-coloured, or a little darker, and the collar is of some kind of fur; imitation, it seems safe to assume. Because I am much closer to her feet than to her face, I am particularly aware of her shoes. They are dark brown and clumpy, and she is wearing thickish stockings which give her legs an unnatural colour, quite different from the rest of her. Her skirt comes down to mid-calf under the coat. I suppose I am observing this as I sit on the floor, since I doubt if I could stand up for long without swaying and falling over.

Light is coming in from two large windows side by side in the room, where the heavy, dark curtains have been drawn. I have other faint memories of this room, too: of my half-brother Michael making a tent for me with a sheet over the chairs and table, and of being left alone in the tent, frightened for a moment until I hear voices coming back into the room. But that is in the past, when I was even younger; and if something hadn't happened to fix these very early, blurred memories like a Victorian photographer would fix his images, they would have vanished.

I can see now that my mother is crying as she applies the lipstick, and they are not quiet, gentle tears. They come in great gusts of misery, and her face is wet with them. I understand tears, because I am used to shedding them myself; but I also understand that these particular tears are something altogether out of my experience. They mix with the lipstick, and she has to turn away to get a handkerchief or perhaps a cloth to rub the mixture off her lips and start again, talking as she does so. I remember the act of talking clearly, though I have no idea what she is saying. Presumably I can't understand most of the words she uses anyway. But she must be saying something about going to Epsom to live with her family, and about everything turning out all right. We will, I'm certain she is saying, be very happy. The tears, which I can understand better than the words, tell a different story.

She goes up on tiptoe once more, staring into the mirror as though it can tell her something; for years afterwards, when I think about the fairy story where the wicked stepmother says, 'Mirror, mirror on the wall,' I will remember that mirror, with its inch-wide scalloped edges and its strange curves, hanging heavily forward with a kind of menace.

It must, I assume, contain some sort of secret: the secret of why my mother is crying with such abandon. Yet I can't see the reason. I shift my position on the floor. Perhaps I am frustrated at not being able to speak properly and ask her what is happening. I doubt it, though; at this age I have not entirely appreciated that I will soon be able to talk and communicate like adults do. I accept that I am altogether separate from my parents, a different species altogether.

My mother is talking to me now, but I have no understanding of what she is saying. I do not recognize any of the words she uses; she is talking to express herself, not to communicate with me in the limited terms of love or annoyance which parents mostly use towards babies. All I can see when she turns her head away from the mirror is that she is still crying as much as ever. The tears make marks on the front of her camel coat. She puts her lipstick away in her small dark brown handbag –

could it perhaps be crocodile? – and sits down with me on the floor.

This is usually the start of a game of some sort, and perhaps I grin in the middle of my perplexity. It makes no difference to her mood. There is more talk, another flow of undecipherable words. All I can understand is that we seem to be about to go somewhere: I too am being prepared for the outside world. I am turned and bundled into a coat whose colour I cannot any longer remember: perhaps pale blue, though that may be a conflicting memory from a later time. My mother isn't rough with me, because she never is; but there is an urgency about her movements which I find somehow painful. And all the time those terrible, puzzling tears, as her face comes close to mine and she holds me closely in her arms. Have I done something bad? What is wrong? The entire world seems to have been turned upside down.

I am fourteen months old: this is October 1945. I accept that it is unusual for children to be able to remember things at such an early age, but certainly not impossible. My younger daughter, Eleanor, has memories of lying in a creaky little cot on a holiday we took in the West of Ireland a year and a month after she was born. Perhaps our memory is a brain function which, if left to itself, will switch on at around the age of two or two and a half, but in cases of particularly strong events can start earlier. For most of my life I have assumed that this scene with the mirror took place when I was older than eighteen months; but having gone through all the available documents, it is now clear to me that it happened even earlier. And I assume that none of this would have stayed with me, if something of such major, incomprehensible importance had not been taking place in front of me.

We leave the flat. There are stairs, a door, then a blast of cold air: and, after that, nothing more for a while. I suppose my mother controlled her tears, and as a result the sharp urgency of my child's memory faded. But there is one other brief flash of recall, a couple of hours or more later. I am sitting beside my mother on a bus, at the front of the lower deck, looking straight ahead at the road in front. There are still buses in London which follow the same design, with the driver's cab projecting on the right hand side of the vehicle, and the upper deck overhanging the seat where we were sitting.

My mother is her usual quiet self now, yet just occasionally when I look round at her I can see she is crying again. I lean forward and grasp the shiny metal rail that runs under the window, and the cold of it instantly strikes my hands with a new and previously unknown sensation. I have a distinct feeling that I should do something to show my affection for my mother, but I have no idea if I do, if anything. Then this smaller window on my earliest past closes too.

I feel certain that the feelings I have described were those which I experienced at the time; in other words, that I haven't invented them or added to them, merely allowed them to have the force and meaning they had for me then. My father appears only rarely in these memories, because he was in the Army for part of my first year of existence. I have a sense of being lifted up and held against his rough Army blouse, with its softer lining showing at the collar. But there is (or was) a photograph of the two of us from the winter of 1944/5 which shows me as a baby in his arms, and I assume it is the photograph, rather than the experience, which has fixed this in my mind.

I never went back to the flat with the mirror and the dark, heavy curtains; my father lived there alone for a short while, then gave it up and went back to stay at his mother's house. What I was observing was the start of the break-up of my parents' marriage. Much later, speaking of this time, my mother said, 'Your father was quite impossible.' Several other people were to say the same thing about him in the years to come; I would be one of them. Yet he was charming, funny, and immensely persuasive, too, and all of us who stormed away from him at one point or another found ourselves going back and, mysteriously and without intending to, asking his forgiveness; which he would never quite give.

My mother, like all the rest, will return to him quite soon. But for the time being she is on her own. My father's return from the Army has not brought her the happiness she hoped. How could it, when their natures are so different and their emotions so little in accord? He is still hugely relieved at not having to go and fight in Japan, and surprised at having been released from the Army so quickly, but because he was still based in England, and had had so little training, he was demobilized fast.

And so at the end of September he comes back, wearing his brown demob suit, his flannel demob shirt, its collar-ends curling up, his brown checked demob tie short and hanging out of his jacket because of his long, brisk walk from the station, a brown paper parcel of possessions under his arm like a prisoner. My mother (she told me later) is preparing my feed when he knocks briskly and heavily at the front door, then knocks again. She thinks it could be the postman, perhaps with a telegram, so she is flustered when she runs down, with me in her arms, and opens the door. She is wearing a kind of wrap with pale blue and yellow flowers on it, slightly faded: her pre-war clothes for doing her chores. She has no make-up on, and her hair needs brushing. She looks remarkably vulnerable.

'Oh,' she says.

His responses are always so quick, that his entire expression alters at once.

'That's a nice way to say hello.'

'Oh, I'm sorry, darling, I just wasn't expecting you.'

'No, I can see that.'

He imagined her much warmer, much better-looking.

She kisses him awkwardly, her lips pursed. Her responses are rarely quick, and she is still coming to terms with the fact that he is here.

'Well, you could always let me in and give me a cup of tea.'

He looks closely into my face and kisses me on the forehead; and because I have inherited my quick responses from him, I burst into tears.

'I'm beginning to wish I hadn't hurried home.'

They are sitting in the little kitchen of the flat, with its scullery-like appearance. Joyce is a good housekeeper, but she has not had a chance to tidy up today. She puts the powdered milk in his tea, and loads the precious sugar from my ration into his cup. He sits down and sighs with pleasure – not necessarily at being home, but at being finished with the Army. He has a great many stories to tell her, and he begins now.

Joyce listens carefully as she moves round the kitchen, preparing a meal for him. She takes much longer than he does to make up her mind, but her judgements are often truer and more clear than his. She is a listener, rather than a talker, and she analyses what she hears.

'So this chap Fleming picks up his Sten gun and lets fly with it.'

She is already starting to detect a new coarseness, a new brutality about him, that she has never noticed before. The months of living cheek-by-jowl with men from every kind of background have not made him gentler or kinder, she can see. His stories used to be funny because they were rueful and self-deprecating; he was always the one who came off worse, even when in reality he probably hadn't. Now he is the hero of his own anecdotes. Everything revolves around him; he comes up with the solution to the problem which has stumped everyone else. Everyone, officers and men alike, turn to him for advice; and if only they would follow it, everything would be all right.

'We were still on the bloody mountainside, and the fucking mortar landed just close to us. Poor old Thee-and-thou caught it properly in the stomach – you should have seen his face! I was laughing so much I could scarcely find the bandages – and they weren't sure they could save him, though they did, the lucky bastard.'

'And why did you call him Thee-and-thou?'

She asks a question at random because she doesn't like him to use that kind of language in front of the baby. For his part, he is annoyed that she hasn't followed the thread of his narrative with sufficient care.

'I told you, he comes from Lancashire and it's hard to understand a word he says. Even harder now.'

His usual full-chested laugh, which she always enjoyed, now sounds overpowering and a little false; as though he's using it to impose himself on her.

So many things she used to love in him have somehow become coarsened. When he talks about not having to fight in Japan there is a crude selfishness to his words. Let other idiots fight the battles, he seems to be saying; anything, so long as I don't have to go. Maybe, she tells herself, I've just been listening to too many patriotic speeches; but although she's very happy that he hasn't had to fight anyone, she would somehow prefer it if he showed he was even slightly sorry. He isn't, and it sounds like crowing.

'So my tactics worked – staying on at that fucking awful factory until it was too late to go to Normandy or the Far East. Not bad, eh?'

He can see the resistance in her eyes, but he can't quite work out its cause. Is she glad not to have him around? Is she sorry now that he's back? Might there be some reason for that – some other person? What about Reggie, that horrible little swine who once got drunk and started on at her? 'Go on, a slice off a cut cake'll never be missed,' he said.

'Seen any of the old crowd? You know, Reggie and the others?'

'Not since I saw you last.'

He knows how hard it is for her to lie, and is satisfied; but only for a moment.

'So have you been spending a lot of time down there with your awful old mother?'

'Oh, she's not been that bad. She's been quite helpful since Johnny came along.'

'Glad she's got some uses.'

'Though it was quite hard for her to get up here from Epsom through the blackout.'

'I bet you had to keep going down there.'

'Well, once or twice, yes. They were all very nice to me.'

The old battleground is being staked out again. Nothing has really changed, except Roy himself.

And of course the baby. I am the one thing that keeps my parents' arguments with one another from getting out of hand, and my mother is adept at introducing me into the conversation at the key moment.

'I just can't understand why you haven't been—'

'Look, he's so sweet, and he's got your family's eyes all right. You should see how well he sleeps now.'

But the worship of me can't last very long, and Joyce knows that. She also knows that there will be other problems.

'I didn't know you'd be coming so soon, or I wouldn't have asked Pat and Mike to come here for a few days.'

'Isn't there any way to put them off?'

'Oh Roy, they're my children too, you know. I can't leave them down there forever.'

'But just when I need a bit of time to see you and the baby again. I really think that's a bit much. Can't they come when I've fixed myself up with a job?'

'Yes, of course, dear, but how long will that take? There must be a lot of men coming out of the forces just now.'

'Well, with a bit of luck I'll just get in there before them, and be able to give them the old V-sign from inside.'

'You won't go back to the factory, will you?'

'Good Christ, no. I'm going to do a damn sight better than that for myself.'

'You sound a bit like a ladder-merchant.'

She says it to make him smile, but somehow it comes out wrongly. He stares at her, then turns his attention to the meal she has rustled up for him. The Army has done nothing to improve his eating habits, she notices fastidiously.

Afterwards they – we – go out for a stroll. There has been no money for a pram for me, so they take turns to hold me as they walk down the seedy avenue and out by the giant gas-holders, breathing in the chemical smell which, mysteriously, is always said to be good for you if you have asthma.

'Can't go to the bloody flicks with him, I suppose; pity. But anyway I'd rather be at home, tucked up in bed with you.'

She no longer responds to that as she once would have, and the evening is a poor, gloomy affair, enlivened only by every mention of me. She knows that Roy is immensely proud of me, and she is happy to have given him the son he wanted. Yet she knows he already sees me as belonging on his side of the divide in their marriage.

WHAT THE PRECISE CAUSE of the first big rupture between my parents was, I cannot say; and in later years, neither of them seemed very clear about it themselves. Perhaps it was simply a case of irreconcilable differences. Or maybe they simply didn't want to tell me. We have persuaded ourselves that major problems like this must always have a sexual cause, yet the trigger for some powerfully destructive outbreak of anger can often be less deep-seated: a sharp word, a feeling of hurt or pain, something simply misunderstood. In that case it is the reaction, not the initial difficulty, which determines the scope and significance of the argument that follows.

By this time, 21 October 1945, my parents, never close even in the few months they lived together before my father went into the Army, have grown even farther apart. Whatever briefly brought them together and persuaded them that they should marry has long since evaporated. Now, having been apart for many months, they see each other as they really are, with no light of attraction playing about them.

My father sees a weak, ageing woman without the drive and spark he admires in people. To him, her quiet sadness now means little more than an absence of character, a feebleness which is not what he wants for his son. My mother sees a young man coarsened by his experiences in the Army, a bully, noisy and over-demanding of attention. Sometimes love and commitment can help people overcome the distance between them, and they find it possible to overlook these big faults of character to the point where they eventually fade from sight. Not in the case of my parents.

My mother isn't really weak at all. Her gentleness is based on early discouragement and a lack of wider scope, but she is clear-minded and disciplined, and perfectly capable of running her own life and the lives of her children. My father's mistake is a characteristic one. Assertive and infuriatingly articulate himself, he can argue and hector and out-think almost everyone he comes into contact with; and it is very hard indeed to get through his armoured self-assurance. As a result, he is able to dominate almost everyone around him; and he has little respect for anyone he can dominate.

Now, after a night which may or may not have been difficult and frustrating, they are facing each other across the table. A truce exists between them: since they woke up, nothing has been said on either side to cause any difficulties. I am in my high-chair, which I can faintly remember, playing with the loose wooden beads, descending and ascending in size, on the front of it. My mother is feeding me with a spoon. My father has decided to take a day or two off before going to look for a job, in order to get over the tiredness and stress of the previous weeks. An air of lassitude lies over everything. The day is a dreary one, and the rain lashes at the windows. I can never seem to get those windows out of my memory.

So we are all sitting together in the kitchen, with its square, shallow, yellowish sink and its single tap, and the heavy kettle on the gas stove, which supplies the only form of hot water we have. On the floor stands a large galvanized iron bucket, into which the dirty dishes go, and on the wall beside the sink there is a wooden rack where the clean dishes dry.

Even wealthier people (and it wouldn't be hard to be better off than we are) do not live much differently, unless they are in a modern block of flats with hot water piped though them. In older houses, the only difference between the classes is that better-off people have servants to cope with boiling the water and doing the dishes and the laundry. We don't. All we have is my father's Army pay, which is two pounds per week, and the occasional help of wealthier relatives when times are really hard.

I gulp from the spoon my mother proffers me, and my father eats the unappetizing breakfast he has created for himself from powdered eggs, thin flavourless white bread, and a scraping of margarine, so pale that it is almost white. Food rationing is tighter than ever now, although the war has been over for two months. The radio plays dance music in the background: Harry Engleman and his Players, a slightly condescending BBC announcer says.

And at that point something goes wrong. Maybe it is a word out of place, a look, a reference. Maybe it's just a general feeling of awkwardness, an absence of sympathy. A small thing leads to a greater thing, and the unspecific anger which has been waiting only a little way below the surface ever since my father arrived home flares up. In themselves, these sudden eruptions are trivial enough, and a little humour and affection can usually sort them out sooner or later. But in that ugly, cold flat, with the rain running down the windows, there is no humour and not much affection.

Since I cannot understand the words that are spoken, I can only look on in bewilderment. My father starts it with some aggressive remark, which my mother responds to uncharacteristically. His sharpness turns to anger, and he comes back with something which is clearly savage. Then he puts the dishes down heavily in the sink, and storms out, slamming the door. After a few seconds, the outer door slams too.

We spend the morning alone, my mother and I, not leaving the flat once. Sometimes she cries; sometimes she picks me up and speaks to me with great earnestness; sometimes she stands by the window, looking out at the rain. In the early afternoon the outer door slams again. My mother looks up: this time she is both angry and relieved that he has returned.

He throws the kitchen door open, and it is clear that

nothing has changed for the better. There are more loud words, more angry looks, more references to me and to the flat. The time when the right word or gesture could change the mood has long passed. Both of them are stubborn and surprisingly unforgiving; their anger is long-smouldering. It is the one thing they really have in common.

That, and love for me. But since they have decided to live separately, my father will have to give me up. There is further anger, and more accusations about the uselessness of my mother's family. That mysterious and sacred substance, Simpson blood, is invoked again. And then the doors are slammed for the last time, and we are on our own in the darkening room.

So now my mother stands on tiptoe at the hanging mirror, her tears mixing with her lipstick, and we are leaving our home. I must be able to understand something of the significance of all this emotion, or I would never have remembered it all with such clarity. I don't feel at all lonely or abandoned, because I am with my mother, who is the most important person in my life. But I do know that something of immense significance is happening around me.

And I cannot for the life of me understand what it is.

SUDDENLY, BRITAIN WAS an entirely different country. The war in Europe was over, and so was the war with Japan. The man who had steered the nation through it all had been turned out of office and was back at Chartwell, drinking more brandy and champagne than was good for him, getting his first consistent rest since the war started, thinking about bricklaying again, and trying to work out what had happened.

The new men in power were still, for the most part, as surprised as Churchill. Among them, only Emanuel Shinwell and Aneurin Bevan had foreseen the possibility that Labour might win the election which took place on 5 July 1945, and neither of them had realized it would be such a landslide. The King told everyone that when Clement Attlee came round to Buckingham Palace to kiss hands on 26 July, when the much-delayed election result was announced, he looked very surprised indeed.

The crowds weren't. Winston Churchill received a friendly reception from them when he went to the Palace earlier in his chauffeur-driven Rolls-Royce to hand back his seals of office to the King, but when Attlee arrived at the wheel of his elderly Standard Vanguard, with his wife sitting beside him, the Mall was full of ecstatic Labour supporters, greeting him, someone said, as though he were a bald, middle-aged and rather dazed Messiah.

With some important exceptions, his ministers were largely unknown. Years later, when Shinwell was a very old man, he told me a story which may or may not have been entirely accurate about having dinner with Hugh Dalton, the new Chancellor of the Exchequer, and Arthur Greenwood, the new Lord Privy Seal, responsible for co-ordinating government policy. They sat in the restaurant of the Royal Court Hotel in Sloane Square a couple of days after the election, and stayed late talking about what they planned to do. When the bill came, none of them had any means of payment. Shinwell went over to the head waiter and explained the position.

'We'll make sure you get the money first thing tomorrow. You see, that's the Chancellor of the Exchequer and that's the Lord Privy Seal, and I'm the Minister of Fuel and Power.'

'Oh, yes, and I'm the Archbishop of Canterbury. Now clear off out of here before I call the police.'

The country was still getting used to the extraordinary change that had come over it. The election represented a complete social revolution, a sense that it was impossible to go back to the old, slumbering, Conservative Britain of the 1930s, where there was poverty and profiteering and a determination not to think about the evil things that were happening on the Continent. It wasn't a personal rejection of Winston Churchill, but it was a rejection of Conservative habits and ideas.

New people were needed, new ideas, new energy. It might have been better if Attlee had not felt obliged to fill his Cabinet with the mostly elderly figures who had worked their way to the top of the Labour Party years before – the average age of his Cabinet was over sixty – but that was a realization which came afterwards. For now, it seemed like a clean sweep and an extraordinary new start.

It was certainly the greatest victory in British politics since the Liberals had swept the Conservatives out of power in 1906. Labour gained 227 seats, the Tories lost 203. Of the 393 Labour MPs, the great majority had never seen the inside of the House of Commons in their lives. There weren't enough places on the Government benches to seat them all. Anything, it seemed, was possible, any change could be made; and the first time they all assembled in the chamber, the Labour ranks broke into 'The Red Flag'. When the Conservatives replied by greeting Churchill with 'For He's a Jolly Good Fellow', the new Speaker said he hoped he hadn't been elected as the director of a musical chorus.

But the promised revolution never quite happened. Much was nationalized, yet nationalization was a process which plenty of Conservatives thought was necessary. Eventually, the National Health system was introduced, there was social legislation on quite a respectable scale, and even steel was taken into public ownership. But it wasn't the wholehearted change everyone had expected in July 1945. It probably couldn't have been, given the terrible economic position of the country, the shortages which were to grow even worse in the years following the war than they had been during it, and the desperate, failing attempt to maintain Britain's place as one of the world's three main powers. At the next election, Labour lost almost all the seats it had won so spectacularly five years earlier, and there seemed remarkably little for the party to boast about.

'We are the masters at the moment,' said the Attorney-General, Sir Hartley Shawcross, as the victorious Labour members gathered in Parliament in July 1945 – though his words were not as boastful as the Conservative press made out – 'and not only for the moment but for a very long time to come.'

In fact, after the losses of 1950 Attlee was forced to call another election a year later, and was defeated. Labour remained out of power until 1964, dogged by the reputation it had earned from 1945–51 of being the party of austerity, of shortage, of decline.

1945 represented the start of a new world in other, more troubling ways. On the day Attlee announced his Cabinet, Monday 6 August, the United States bombed Hiroshima with horrifying results; and Nagasaki followed soon afterwards. The world had entered the atomic age, and destruction was possible on a scale which hadn't been achieved during the rest of the Second World War.

But the bombing of Hiroshima and Nagasaki brought immediate victory over Japan; and my father was only one of large numbers of young men who were glad about the bombing, because it meant they wouldn't have to face the prospect of invading Japan and fighting their way through its islands.

By October, many people were at last starting to come home from the war; among them, my father's younger brother Alan, who had been in Burma. It was something of a surprise to me, a few years later, to find that Alan's war had been so distinguished, and that he had risen to great heights in the Malayan police afterwards. The reason it was a surprise was that I had always thought of him as an inadequate, ugly little shrimp who was permanently in trouble with more sensible people; the sensible people being my father, his elder brother, who was five years older than he was. As a result of my father's many stories about him, I visualized Alan clearly, from the chilblains on his fingers' ends to the permanent line of snot down his upper lip.

And then, when I was six, Uncle Alan came home on leave, and I met him for the first time. He looked like everyone's ideal image of the empire-builder: handsome, immensely confident, with the kind of moustache that all colonial officers seemed to have in those day, broad-shouldered, dressed in an excellent pin-striped suit. He had a blonde woman on his arm who seemed to me (because even at that age I was susceptible to the beauty of women) to be dazzlingly glamorous. The only way I could tell that he and my father were related was that they were the same size and general build, and their feet stuck out at an identical angle as they walked down the street laughing. And instead of ticking Alan off for his incredible stupidity and ugliness, my father even seemed to defer to him a little.

As for me, I was almost speechless with admiration.

'Hello, youngster, and how are you then?'

'I'm quite well, thank you.'

'Oh, quite well, eh? I can see you've been properly brought up. In spite of everything.'

He went off into fits of loud, confident, empire-building laughter, and after a moment or two my father joined in. I did too, though I couldn't quite see the joke. But I could see that my Uncle Alan was a tremendous figure; and I wondered where the chilblains and the snot could have gone.

Alan always called himself by his correct family name, Fidler. Maybe it was a reaction against his mother, who seemed to have more Simpson blood than was feasible, and who had never really liked him. While she was lying semi-conscious in hospital after giving birth to him in 1919, a nurse carelessly put a newly filled stone hot water bottle into the bed against her leg, and burned her quite badly. This, somehow, became Alan's fault, and things never got much better between them. He joined the Royal Air Force at the minimum age of fourteen, in order to get away from her.

'You can't hit me now,' he shouted defiantly a few weeks later, 'I'm in the Air Force.'

'You're only a boy-entrant,' his mother answered haughtily, and she did hit him. For a long time, 'only a boy-entrant' was a term of joking abuse in our family.

Nevertheless Alan's war record was something that everyone, even my father with his brotherly scorn and his instinctive dislike of armies and organization and heroism, could be proud of. He was posted to India in the late 1930s, and did a certain amount of flying. But his real expertise was as a wireless operator, and when Col. Orde Wingate began to build up his force of Chindits to operate behind Japanese lines in the Burmese jungle – the name derives from 'Chinthé', the mythological half-lions, half-dragons which guard so many Burmese temples – he needed more wireless operators than the Army alone could provide. A notice went up at RAF stations in India and Ceylon, asking anyone with knowledge of ground to air communications to volunteer for a special mission. Alan, walking past one such noticeboard at his base in Sind, was intrigued, and put his name forward.

Wingate was an extraordinary man, and Alan came to hero-worship him. The son of ultra-evangelical Plymouth Brethren, Wingate was brought up to believe, as many Americans and some British people still do, that in order for the Second Coming of Christ to take place the Children of Israel had to occupy the holy places of the Bible. As a result, when he found himself based in Palestine under the British mandate before the war broke out, Wingate was a passionate supporter of Zionism and used teams of Jewish volunteers to hunt down Palestinians who had attacked Jewish settlers. Then he was posted to Burma.

Until Wingate arrived, the British were seriously intimidated by the Japanese forces. The relative feebleness which British soldiers often showed against the Germans was mild compared with their outright fear of the Japanese, who seemed to be both more and less than human. Their dedication to their Emperor and to their code of honour had the appearance of utter fanaticism, and their vicious treatment of their prisoners soon became infamous. The surprise was that British soldiers were so often willing to surrender to the Japanese, rather than to fight them to the death.

They were, after all, usually former civilians, brought up with the memory of the terrible casualties of the First World War. The feeling had grown within the British Army that the Japanese could not be defeated by ordinary mortals. By the start of 1942 the British had lost most of their Far Eastern empire to the Japanese within a matter of three months: Malaya, Singapore, Hong Kong, and a good half of Burma. Sir Alan Brooke, chief of the Imperial General Staff, wrote in his diary: 'If the army cannot fight better than it is doing at present we shall deserve to lose our Empire.' As the British retreated, half-beaten, towards the western borders of Burma, it suddenly began to look as though India itself might be Japan's next objective.

At that point – February 1942 – Wingate, strangely obsessive, surprisingly short, and distinctly unworldly, arrived with a completely different gospel.

> If the British soldier is allowed to get the notion that he cannot take hardships that men of other nations can, he had better reconcile himself to being a member of a third rate nation ... I personally am quite satisfied the British soldier has a better body and a better mind than average humanity. He can not only equal but beat the Japanese.

The raw materials were unpromising enough to make Wingate's boast seem unrealistic. Most of the soldiers serving in India and the Far East were conscripts from the industrial towns and cities of Britain: poorly educated, unused to heavy exercise, ill-equipped for any sort of warfare, and nervous about what lay ahead. Fewer than half the NCOs and men under Wingate's command could swim, and in the unfamiliar, hostile climate of eastern India and Burma they went sick with great regularity.

Wingate changed all this. He made everyone, including his officers, run everywhere instead of walk; and although this made them feel stupid, it emphasized the new doctrine of fitness before everything else. In a period when almost everyone smoked, Wingate discouraged the cigarette habit. As 1942 wore on, the thoroughgoing exercise, the emphasis on aggressive operations against the Japanese, and the extraordinary new tactics Wingate was proposing had their effect. His men grew confident and tough, and looked forward to putting their training to the test.

His vision of how to use the terrain, particularly in dense forest, was revolutionary for the British Army. He taught his men how to move through the forest, using streams and ridges as their guides. They learned to reverse their shoes on paths, in

order to confuse the enemy's trackers, and to make their way
through undergrowth without being heard. They learned how
to regroup after being caught in an ambush: to melt away fast
into the jungle, then search for the nearest stream and wade up
its course until they found a meeting-point, deeper behind
enemy lines.

My uncle Alan delighted in the training. He had always
been a strong swimmer, and his difficult upbringing had made
him resilient and self-reliant. Now he pushed himself harder
and harder, making do with even less than the very limited
food-rations which Wingate recommended them to take. Alan's
job was particularly demanding. The RAF wireless teams con-
sisted of two men, equipped with an enormous radio set like a
barrel organ, known as the 1082/83, which had to be carried by
three mules. The batteries and their charger required even more
mules. It was a problem; but with this equipment they could
put out a signal which could to be picked up at an RAF station
across the Indian border in Assam.

Alan carried enough morphine in his medical kit to kill
himself if necessary; all the Chindits did. They knew that if
they were too injured to walk they were dead men anyway.
Wingate tried to encourage local villagers to see that it was in
their interest to help the British wounded, rather than hand
them over to the Japanese, but everyone knew this was unlikely
to happen. The Chindits wore Australian-style Digger hats,
with the left brim clipped up – Alan's sat in a cupboard of mine
for years, until I finally handed it over to his daughters – and
they dressed in the lightest of uniforms with no signs of rank
on them.

Wingate shook up the normal structure of his brigade, and
divided it into columns. The traditionalists were affronted,
but few of the Chindits set much store by tradition; they were
fighting a very different kind of war. Some were from the
Indian Army, some from the British Army, and there was a

strong contingent of Gurkhas. There were also Burmese, from the Karin, Kachin and Chin tribes, which have as a result been persecuted in Burma ever since. Once across the River Irrawaddy the Chindits' mission was essentially to shock the Japanese and raid their communications.

In the jungle, some of the radio operators became fond of their mules, and were unhappy when the food began to run out and Wingate gave the order for the mules to be killed. One man even disobeyed, and brought his mule back to India with him at the end of the mission. Alan found his particular mules a serious nuisance. One of them tended to get excited in the claustrophobic conditions of the forest, and when a Japanese patrol passed close by it almost gave Alan's position away by braying noisily.

There were other traps: bamboo stakes smeared with excrement and sticking out of camouflaged holes in the pathway, for instance. Again and again Alan was grateful for Wingate's warning that they should avoid paths wherever possible. Sometimes the Japanese would dress the dead bodies of Burmese villagers in Japanese uniforms and tie them to the upper branches of trees in the firing position, as if they were snipers. Late one afternoon, as they were looking for a convenient place to set up their transmitting equipment, Alan and his partner spotted one of the supposed snipers and fired.

A six-man Japanese patrol, hiding close by, heard the shots and burst through the undergrowth, trapping them. Alan and his companion were seized and knocked to the ground. The Japanese tied their hands, then marched them triumphantly along the jungle path towards their base. Both men were determined to escape, and they walked slowly, so that a short gap built up between them and the Japanese soldiers in front. Choosing his moment, Alan threw himself into the thick jungle to his left, and the other man followed him. Wingate had always taught them to move independently through the forest, and they headed off separately for the stream they knew would be somewhere ahead of them. The Japanese fired at random into the thick vegetation, but were reluctant to follow.

Alan reached the stream, then walked down through the cool water to a convenient little beach on a bend. Within a couple of minutes his companion found him. They cut each other's ropes, and decided to hide out until the hunt had died down.

In telling the story during the years to come, Alan didn't try to present himself as the hero of the adventure; but he disliked his partner intensely. 'A real know-it-all', he described him, 'a line-shooter'. They decided to wait until dark, and then head back to the place where they had hidden their mules and their equipment; they believed, rightly as it turned out, that the Japanese hadn't discovered these things. As they were walking silently through the trees they heard voices close by and saw lights. A dozen or so men were walking in line along a pathway, carrying lanterns.

'They're Burmese,' whispered the other man. 'Must be a funeral party. We should just slip out behind them and follow them. That way we can get closer to the village and save a bit of time.'

Alan agreed. They waited till the last man had passed, then stepped on to the path behind him. Fifty yards farther down, the man ahead of Alan turned round and his lantern shone full on his face and uniform. They weren't following a Burmese funeral party; it was a Japanese patrol searching for them.

Alan was always quick-tempered. He said later he shouted at his companion, 'You bloody idiot – these aren't Burmese, they're bloody Japs.'

He probably didn't shout at all; but the Japanese were alerted anyway. Both men had to throw themselves off the path into the jungle once again, with more bullets cutting through the foliage about their heads, and they had to find the same stream all over again. They got away successfully, and duly reached their mules and their equipment; but Alan couldn't stop belabouring the know-it-all for making such a mistake.

After they rejoined the main column Wingate made Alan his personal wireless operator, and in spite of the difference in rank the difficult jungle conditions brought them close together. Alan shared more than one snake with his commander ('horrible, slithery white meat, like raw wet chicken', uncooked because it was too dangerous to light a fire). They were often reduced to eating banana leaves.

The last of the Chindits returned to India at the start of June 1943. Their long and daring raid behind Japanese lines had destroyed the myth of Japan's inevitable superiority in jungle warfare, for the Japanese as well as the British.

The Allies needed some good news from South-East Asia, after a series of dismal British failures, and Wingate and his Chindits provided it. A press conference was held in Delhi to trumpet their successful return, and the newspapers duly gave it the full treatment. The *Daily Mail* called Wingate 'Clive of Burma', and the rest of the press devoted large quantities of space to what was called 'the British Ghost Army'. On Wednesday 7 July the *Mail* ran a series of photographs of five Chindits, under the heading 'Wingate's Follies – A Long Way from Aldershot':

> The bearded, grinning men may not bear the Aldershot stamp, but they are soldiers – and good ones. They are men of Wingate's Follies, the expedition which spent three months behind the Jap lines in Burma, shooting up Japs and blowing up communications. Here they are back.

Underneath the photographs the caption reads:

> Five of Wingate's Follies shown above are (left to right) Tony Aubrey, of Handsworth, Birmingham; Flight Sgt. Alan Fidler, of London (Wingate's communications man);

Lce-Cpl. Fred Nightingale, of Lancaster; Private Jack Wilson, of Preston, Lancashire; and Major Bernard Fergusson, of the Black Watch, who led one of the Chindit (Jungle Penetration Force) columns.

The news of Wingate's success was received ecstatically in Britain, and the Americans, who felt that Britain had not been pulling its weight properly in the Far East, were duly impressed. Still, the cost of the operation was high: of the 3,000 men who had gone into Burma, only 2,182 returned, and of those only 600 would be fit for active service in future.

Alan was one of those who wouldn't be able to fight again. In the bag of old documents which is all I seem to have left after my father's death there is a fragile telegram from October 1943:

OHMS Priority. Mrs E. A. Fidler, 111 Marlow Road, Anerley SE 20.

KWY 25/25 important from A.M. Kingsway PC 675 25/10/43

Your son Warrant Officer Alan Montague Fidler (550693) was removed from the seriously ill list on 23rd Oct.

On the back, in my grandmother's elegant, spidery writing, is the draft of her answering cable:

Thankful better news stop always thinking of you darling stop Mother and Daphne's best love

Alan stayed in India with the RAF, but he was to suffer from recurrent bouts of malaria for the rest of his life.

Less than a year later, Major-General Orde Wingate, who received the Distinguished Service Order, the second highest medal for the armed forces, three times, and was perhaps the most unorthodox soldier in the British Army, was dead. A plane taking him over Burma suffered engine failure, and hit a mountainside; everyone on board was killed. Wingate, with his Old Testament beard and his habitual solar topee, was a familiar and greatly admired figure; and for people like my uncle Alan, his loss was devastating. He was only forty-one, and his wife Lorna was fifteen years younger. Their son was born three months after Wingate's death.

THE MEN AND WOMEN who had been caught up in the war in the Far East were starting, like my uncle Alan, to sort their lives out and start again. On 10 October 1945 the personal columns in the newspapers were full of messages about them, sometimes reassuring, sometimes wistful:

> Danberry, Maj. W. G. (TIKKA), Royal Signals, late prisoner of war in Siam, arrived safely home. In good health.

> Capt. D.G. Russell-Roberts, 11th Sikh Regiment, has returned to England from Singapore. Address Bath Club, 76 St James's Street, W1. His wife, Ruth, died on January 20, 1945, in the Women's Internment Camp at Muntok, Banka Island, off Sumatra.

> Jack Findon, 'Daily Express' War Correspondent, last heard of, 7th March 1942, Bandoeng, Java. – Any news gratefully received by his wife at 36, Great Thrift, Petts Wood, Kent. 'Phone, Orpington 3716.

'The fighting is over,' reads a determinedly jolly advertisement which appeared that day in the British press, 'but there is a gigantic tidying-up job to be done in Europe and the Far East, and for thousands of Service men and women the order is "carry on". NAAFI, the official canteen organization for HM Forces in war and in peace, will also carry on – amplifying its service with additional clubs and other amenities for the Occupational Forces in Europe, and, once the position in the Far East has been stabilised, canteens and garrison clubs wherever British troops are operating.'

The situation in the Far East had certainly not been stabilized yet. In the Dutch East Indies, which would soon become Indonesia, there was continuing violence. The independence movement led by Dr Soekarno had supported the Japanese, and now that Japan had surrendered the Dutch had been unable to restore an effective colonial government. There was no government, and no law and order. Thirty thousand former prisoners and internees, mostly women and children and predominantly European or Eurasian, were still in the camps in Java because no one had been able to arrange their release or their return home.

In Japan itself, though the British press scarcely mentioned it, the scale of the disaster created by the two atomic bombs on Hiroshima and Nagasaki had still not been fully understood by the occupying powers. People were dying every day from the immediate effects of the explosion, and increasingly the hospitals, most of which had been damaged by the Allied bombing, were having to deal with injuries caused by radiation: something which was scarcely understood at the time.

In Europe the overwhelming problem was the huge displacement of people: prisoners returning home from the Nazi labour camps, German-speaking people forced to leave their homes in Poland, Russia, Czechoslovakia, Hungary and Romania because of the inevitable ethnic cleansing that followed the collapse of Hitler's Reich. That day the harassed general commanding the British Zone in Germany told a reporter he was expecting two million German-speaking refugees to reach his area over the next few weeks.

With the winter coming closer, there was serious anxiety about the effects of all this displacement. On this day there was a discussion of the situation in the House of Commons, which was still coming to terms with its unexpectedly overwhelming Labour majority.

'We now have to face the serious prospect that millions may die from starvation and cold in Europe this year,' a Labour backbencher intervened during a speech by Ernest Bevin, the Foreign Secretary; and Bevin didn't deny it.

On the evening of 10 October Dr Chaim Weizmann, one of the founding fathers of the future state of Israel, addressed a meeting in the Palace of Westminster which was attended by 150 Labour MPs.

'Given the terrible conditions in Europe at the present time,' he told them, 'it is essential that His Majesty's Government should permit a far greater level of immigration of European Jews into Palestine.'

The MPs showed their agreement by thumping their desks.

A few of those who had been responsible for putting Hitler's genocidal policies into effect were already being brought before military courts. At Lüneburg that day, a British tribunal cross-examined the former commandant of one death camp, Josef Kramer. The chief prosecutor, Col. Backhouse, was unable to shake Kramer's composure when he insisted that everything he had done was through obedience to his superior officers, and to the Nazi hierarchy.

Backhouse: But it is surely true, is it not, that you were
 chosen by them to do the dirtiest and most evil jobs.
Kramer: No, your honour, this is not true.

But he agreed that he had personally gone down and helped to force his victims into the gas chamber.

One of the specific charges against him was that on Himmler's orders he had gassed a group of eighty people and sent their bodies to the medical faculty at Strasbourg University. He didn't deny it.

It was an order of the highest military authority. I cannot
 imagine what they would have done with me in war if
 I had refused to obey.

This seems to have been the earliest use of a defence which was soon to become commonplace: 'I was only obeying orders.' Kramer was later sentenced to death and hanged.

In Paris that day, the former Prime Minister in Pétain's Government, Pierre Laval, also received a death sentence. Refusing to be present in court, he was found guilty *in absentia* of conspiring against the security of the State. The public prosecutor told the court that Laval had provided Pétain with the kind of extra-constitutional powers which enabled the two of them to carry out the wishes of the Nazi occupiers. Laval had used these powers to send French men and women to work for the Nazi war effort in Germany. He had deprived French Jews of their rights as citizens of France, and two years later he had ordered that they should have the word 'Jew' stamped in their passports. 'This ensured the deaths of many men, women and children,' the prosecutor said.

When Laval was told in his prison cell that he had been sentenced to death, he answered, 'I expected it. I will not sign a petition for mercy.' He was executed not long afterwards.

At a court martial held in the afternoon of 10 October at Chelsea Barracks in London, William Humphrey Griffiths of the Welsh Guards was charged with voluntarily aiding the King's enemies by taking part in Nazi radio propaganda. The court was told that he had been taken to Poland as a prisoner of war and offered the chance of easier conditions if he would agree to work for the German cause. Although the work wasn't specified, Griffiths agreed and was taken to Berlin where he met William Joyce, the Irishman who was known as 'Lord Haw-Haw'.

Joyce warned him that he would be sent to a concentration camp, or perhaps even executed, if he refused to read out a series of radio scripts on the air. Two other prisoners, Macdonald and Beasley, refused and were taken away; Griffiths had no idea what became of them. The scripts were written, he said, by a mysterious British man named Brown, who had lived in

Germany for many years before the war. Griffiths duly read them out, in a broadcast which scarcely anyone seems to have heard. In court, his behaviour was contrite.

> I had a wonderful welcome when I returned home, and I
> was hurt because I knew I was not worth it.

Griffiths was very small fry indeed: weak and alone, he had not had the strength of character to resist the threats of his captors. The court listened to the story of a sad, inadequate man, and found him not guilty.

There was a good deal of anxiety that day about the direction the relationship of the wartime Allies was taking. Britain, Russia and the United States had always managed, during the war years, to keep up the outward appearance of unity and agreement, despite the most ferocious private disputes about the way the war should be fought. Now there was no further need to appear united, and the fundamental disagreements were coming to the surface.

For the first time, the United Nations Council of Foreign Ministers had met without agreeing a communiqué on the most basic issues; there was not even a statement to say that they had disagreed. The meeting, which was held in New York, had broken up on 2 October after three weeks, but details of the dispute were only now starting to emerge. The particular cause, it seemed, was the future of Romania, which Stalin was determined to incorporate into his new, Soviet-dominated Eastern Europe; but this was only one symptom of a much more disturbing division. Even now the full extent of the division was not made public. The American diplomat John Foster Dulles, an anti-Soviet hawk who later became US Secretary of State, merely announced in a radio broadcast: 'The American proposals, which, in the main, were supported by Great Britain, France, and China, cut across certain political ends which the Soviet Union sought.'

The true Cold War was still a little way off, and senior politicians in Britain and the United States found it hard to rid themselves of the feeling that, for all its difficulty and toughness, the Soviet Union was still basically friendly. The British foreign secretary, Ernest Bevin, assured the House of Commons that even though there had been differences of opinion over the future of Romania and Bulgaria, he had had a cordial exchange of letters with his Soviet opposite number, Viatoslav Molotov. President Truman insisted in a speech that he didn't regard the meeting as a failure. 'Russia is as much misunderstood in America as the United States is in Russia,' he said. His Secretary of State, James Byrnes, not one of America's brighter politicians, was also bewilderingly generous about a system which would very soon be regarded as America's greatest challenge in the world.

> Russia is frankly incorporating into its Communist system of government the best features of the capitalist system, while the United States is tending to put into our democracy some of the worst features of Communism which have now been discarded in Russia.

He seemed to be referring to some elements of President Roosevelt's New Deal. Which features of the capitalist system he thought Stalin was introducing, it is hard to say; though there was some talk in the West that the Soviet Union might start to ease some of its tougher planning controls and allow greater freedom to local Party bosses to run their economies in a way that might suit their own conditions better. It came to nothing.

On this day, when Bevin was speaking about cordial exchanges with Molotov and Byrnes was babbling about the positive side of Soviet government, several hundred thousand Soviet citizens who had had the misfortune to be taken as prisoners of war by the Germans were being put into cattle-trucks and sent off to labour camps in the eastern part of the Soviet Union. Stalin was affronted that they should have surrendered rather than died for him, and worried that they might have been contaminated by Western ideas in their German camps. Soviet prisoners of war had been treated with the utmost cruelty by the Germans, and were systematically starved, often to death. Now, for the survivors, another seven or more years of ill-treatment awaited them; this time at the hands of their fellow-countrymen.

President Truman showed his anxiety at a press conference that day in the White House that Stalin would soon be able to manufacture an atomic device of his own. In fact, thanks to the efforts of a series of British and American traitors, the Soviet Union was already acquiring the secrets of the process, and Russia would soon test an atomic bomb. Truman wanted to make sure that Britain and Canada, which had helped America to build the bombs which had been used against Hiroshima and Nagasaki, kept the details to themselves.

> The United States will keep secret the way the atom bomb is made. Foreign scientists are certain to fathom the secrets of atomic energy, but the engineering know-how is something else. The United States will not give this away to anyone.

Slowly, the British were starting to turn their thoughts to the future. The newspapers were worried that day about the lack of an airport for London. Three American airlines had announced that they would soon be reopening their services to Europe, but 'Heath Row, the proposed terminal on the Bath Road, near Hounslow, will not be ready for eighteen months or two years.' There were plenty of airfields around London, but the RAF was anxious to hold on to all of them. 'British Overseas Airways' nearest land plane base to London,' *The Times* pointed out gloomily, 'is at Hurn, near Bournemouth.'

The dock strike in the north of England had spread to London. The dockers, it emerged when the KGB's files were opened fifty years later, were a particular target for Soviet infiltrators. On this day the Cabinet agreed to use troops to unload essential food supplies at Merseyside, Manchester, Hull, Grimsby, Hartlepool, Sunderland and the Royal Docks in London.

The Cabinet also decided to let the BBC start up its television service again in the spring of 1946. 'The transmitting apparatus at Alexandra Palace is undamaged,' said *The Times*, 'but it has been used for war purposes and a certain amount of reconversion is necessary. There has been no radiation for the public since September 1939.' After Hiroshima, the word 'radiation' was already taking on an altogether different connotation, and soon 'broadcasting' would be applied to television as well as radio programmes.

Other things were returning to normal, too: including the tedious tradition of the tongue-in-cheek letter to the newspapers. On this day *The Times* published a typical example.

Sir – If pedestrian crossings are to be made compulsory, may it now be suggested that clear directions should now be given to pedestrians, telling them whether they are to pass each other in the streets on the left or the right? The present situation is chaotic, causing inconvenience and danger.
    Yours etc., W. Reeve Wallace
        Savile Club, 69, Brook Street W1.

And there were all sorts of cheery advertisements in the press from companies which had not been able to produce their well-known goods during the war because of rationing and the problem of getting the necessary raw materials. They gave the pleasant but entirely false impression that things would shortly be back to normal.

The lads are coming home again, the Weather report is 'news' again, cars are on the road again, and the day draws nearer for the return of Kia-Ora fruit drinks.

But as it turned out, that day wasn't particularly close after all.

Friday 17 May 1946

Sun rises, 5.09 a.m.; sets, 8.44 p.m.
Lighting-up time: 9.14 p.m.
Maximum temperature: 52°F; minimum: 41°F.
Rainfall: trace.
Sunshine: 3.2 hours.
Light to moderate northerly winds, cloudy with
    bright periods. Chilly.

I INHABIT A WORLD without time, unaware even of seasons, let alone of months with identifiable names and characters of their own. At the age of a year and three-quarters, I have little notion of anything outside myself and my immediate sensations. I may perhaps have noticed that there is such a thing as morning; it's possible I may have come to expect that an afternoon and an evening will follow immediately after it, and that darkness rounds off every passing day. But for the most part I simply occupy a sphere of time which is *now*, the continuous present. This shifts from second to second and from hour to hour, but I'm not conscious that it is developing in any way, or that it is even slightly different from what was *now* until a short time ago. I live in a continuum, without reflecting that there could be such a thing as a past or a future.

Like an animal, I am conscious, certainly, and aware of cold and heat and the immediate sensations of hunger and tiredness, warmth and comfort. I have an understanding that there are people around me who know and love me, and I know and love them back. Since I will be able to recall it so clearly decades later, I demonstrably have the capacity to remember things that are painful and frightening: the circumstances of our move away from my father and our old flat, for instance, and something of the emotional uneasiness and uncertainty that has been aroused in me; but those feelings have been soothed and assuaged by the fact that I have lived for many months now in a quiet, stable atmosphere. And beyond them, there is nothing but an all-encompassing mistiness, in which it is very hard to discern anything at all.

Yet for a long instant on this May morning, the mist has cleared. I am sitting in a pool of sunlight, in front of a bank of wallflowers, rich, yellow and reddish-brown, and dusted with pollen which comes off in my fingers and tastes strangely bitter on my tongue. Everything is sharply defined. To my brand-new faculty of smell the wallflowers are so gloriously and powerfully scented that I can remember them as sharply today as if I were down on my hands and knees again in my small white frock with the blue stitching on the front, burying my nose in them. We all know the importance of taste and smell in recreating our childhood experiences from the madeleines Proust dipped in his cup of herbal tea; but long before I had read any Proust, or understood the notion of the Proustian moment, I felt the sharp attraction of the flowers in the pathway.

And so at the age of sixty, a towering, paunchy grandee in a baggy suit and a much-cleaned Garrick tie, trailing a string of failures and successes and experiences and relationships and wives and children and grandchildren and honorific titles behind me through the late afternoon of my life and on towards its evening, all I have to do each May is to walk past a flowerbed stocked with wallflowers, and I feel myself to be a year and nine months old once again, sitting on the ground at Garden Cottages, Epsom, and staring with inquisitive intensity at the yellow and red glory blazing in front of me.

Throughout my life that particular deep chrome yellow, that particular russet red and that particular scent will remain my favourites; because, I suppose, they are the first colours and the first smells I have ever admired. I shall not turn out to be a gardener, alas, but for the rest of my life the look and smell of wallflowers will represent a kind of sensual perfection for me, my ideal of lush richness. For something of the same reason, perhaps, some men are deeply attracted all their lives to women who look like their mothers and have become their ideal of beauty and comfort.

So here I am, sitting on the pathway to the back door in my strange little white dress, because even at this stage the British hadn't altogether given up the pre-Victorian habit of dressing up baby boys as baby girls, looking up at the wallflowers. I am becoming aware of ordinary things as they are, and not because they represent some major upheaval in my small universe. I can feel the grit of the path under me, yet I am not aware of any great discomfort or any need to shift my position until the gravel has dug deeply into my fat leg. I dig an experimental finger into the thin grey crumbling earth, and feel its harshness; and all these years later I am confident that this is an authentic memory rather than an imaginative recreation, since if I were making it up I would presumably envisage the soil as being rich and black and satisfying.

There are dozens of things for me to examine: the half-bricks which line the flowerbeds, with their corners uppermost, the old, abandoned spider's web hanging limply above the pail of soapy water by the door, the hard little segments of white dog-turd by the back gate. These things possess no aesthetic qualities, either positive or negative: they are simply objects of interest to me, now that my eyes are in the process of being opened. I have become a sentient being, and these are the first things that have come to hand.

Soon, of course, someone will come out of the house and tell me to stop whatever it is that I am doing, that it is dirty, or dangerous, or stupid; but for the moment I am able to exercise complete control over my brand-new senses. They have been issued to me like a quartermaster issues a new recruit with his kit. Brain, one; eyes, pair; nose, one; mouth and tongue, one each. And don't come back to me complaining you've lost them, son, because these are the only ones you're ever going to get.

Adults imagine that the discovery of new powers should be an exciting experience, like finding a new species or a new world or a new lover. That is not at all how I find it, here on the gritty garden path. I suppose I must have some sense of wonderment, but I can't be absolutely certain that I haven't unconsciously added this afterwards, simply because as an adult I assume it must have been there. Einstein spoke of life as a movement away from childish wonder, a process we have a duty to halt and reverse. Quite right; it's just that I'm not certain that by May 1946 I have yet acquired my full share of childish wonder.

For the most part, I suspect, my overriding emotions are of inadequacy and stupidity. All the huge people around me, whose knees I can still only just reach when I stand up uneasily on my fat legs, understand these things and do them so much better than I could; while I am scarcely able even to walk, let alone discover things for myself. I am like some medieval figure reflecting on the lost arts of the classical world. I know I have an enormous amount to learn, even though I cannot understand the subjects or even the direction of my learning. Life is bewildering rather than exciting, and the adults around me make it more bewildering still.

They are a strange lot, anyway. My mother and Pat and Michael are fine: I understand them, and expect them to be around. They are also loving to me, and I am very aware of affection, and grateful for it, even at this early stage in my life. But there are other people in this tiny, cramped little workman's cottage, which seems so vast and cavernous in my memory, and they are rather less affectionate: so much so that I do my best to keep out of their way. At a year and nine months I am already perfectly capable of detecting impatience and irritability, and know to avoid it. That's why I prefer being in the garden: no one bothers about me here.

Garden Cottages were knocked down during the 1970s, and all that exists from my time there is a white clapboard house on the corner, and the remains in the roadway of the kerb that marked the turning to the little lane where the cottages stood. I have a strong memory of a wall, and the sensation of old mortar crumbling under my fingers, and a feeling that it led directly to the cottages themselves. That is all.

In a photograph that has survived from this time, my mother stands by the back gate at Garden Cottages in her navy blue dress with the buttons down the front and her best peep-toe shoes. I am wearing a little buff-coloured coat and my sandals which have to be buttoned up, though I can't yet manage the job myself. The photographer has told me to smile, but that is something I find hard to do artificially; so I am pulling in the corners of my mouth in the hope that this will look like the same thing. It doesn't.

My mother looks tired and prematurely old – she was only forty in 1946 – but she has kept her figure very well, and I still think she looks charming, if a little melancholy. Behind us is a fence on the other side of the path, whose precise splintery feel and creosoty smell I recall very clearly. You can also see the corner of a locked tool-shed which I always longed to enter. Close to me there is a lupin; I remember its blueish, pinkish colours and the stiffness of its petals well, as though we were at school together and the lupin was one of the other pupils who had befriended me.

There must have been five or six little houses in the terrace called Garden Cottages, and ours was near the farther end; so perhaps it was number four. Of course, I could easily check these things with someone who remembers them better: my half-sister Pat or my half-brother Michael, for instance. But that would be interfering with my own childhood memory, and I prefer not to do it.

For me, Garden Cottages contains everything I want or need. Yet for reasons I cannot possibly understand, being here represents a humiliation for everyone else who lives in the little house: a sense of failure, of poverty, of abandonment and loss.

My mother wouldn't be here if it weren't for the breakdown of her marriage to my entirely unsuitable father. Pat and Michael wouldn't be here if their own father had lived. And the two older people in the cottage, whose presence is vaguer and fainter and much less personable to me, are also here as the direct result of worldly failure.

I have no real sense of my grandmother at all; no image of her in my mind, no photograph of her in my files. I suspect that no picture of her exists, by her own wish, because she was utterly convinced of her own ugliness. To me she is simply an absence of everything: no face, no figure, no emotion. She is a kind of presence at Garden Cottages, often spoken about, but that is as much as I know about her.

Uncle Charles is altogether different: noisy, smelly, sleepy, cross, and inclined to be objectionable, particularly to my mother, in ways I can't possibly understand. What I think of, when I summon him to mind, is his moustache: immensely long, and waxed so that the ends curl round in little circles on either side of his nostrils. It's synecdochal: for me, the moustache is Uncle Charles, Uncle Charles the moustache.

In addition, he is represented, like a candidate in an election in some pre-literate society, by another symbol: a large, strangely curved, much charred and unpleasantly reeking pipe. Sometimes it lies beside his armchair, cold but still smelling crudely of the shag tobacco he smokes; sometimes it is in his hand, or between his teeth, so that his words come out in a strange, denatured fashion, like meat from a mincer. I only seem to see Uncle Charles through a cloud of tobacco smoke, and he is always accompanied by a deep and liquid cough, very unpleasant even to the ear of a twenty-one-month-old child. He cannot be as immensely ancient as he seems to me, but I doubt if he will last much longer at Garden Cottages than I will.

He is never to be disturbed or annoyed in any way; and for his sake I am better off in the back garden. Someone, I see now, must have troubled to plant out the wallflowers and dig the flower-beds, and it may have been that Uncle Charles wasn't as ancient and immobile as I thought at the time.

Yet both my grandmother and Uncle Charles are interesting people in their own right. And although they are dull, unaffectionate complainants, they haven't necessarily been like this always. In fact my early childhood is lived out in the faint afterglow of the glamour which once surrounded their lives. It is difficult to spot nowadays, yet it is part of our entire existence as a family, like the faint hiss which radio telescopes pick up from the original Big Bang.

In Garden Cottages, my grandmother is known as Liese Phillips. She was born Elizabeth (whence Lizzie, and after that the more exotic Liese) King, and she married a man called Arthur Whittall; the little house contains a couple of books with his signature on the front end-paper, which at some date in the future I will inherit, and will manage eventually to lose. These two books are all that is left of him, except for the genes he passed down to his children, to me, and eventually to my children and grandchildren. Liese, Whittall and his children were all, I think, Catholics; including my distinctly anti-Catholic mother.

Liese had four children by Whittall. Not long after my mother was born on 29 July 1906, Whittall, an officer in the newly-established Territorial Army, left home and went off with his regiment for their annual manoeuvres on Salisbury Plain. Thirsty after marching along the dusty roads, his men drank some water from a nearby stream. Arthur Whittall drank from it too. They all contracted typhoid fever, and most of them died, including Arthur. Liese was left without money or even a home, since the Whittalls had rented their house, and she had no money of her own now that he was dead. She gathered up her four children and went to live with her mother.

In most families this would be normal enough. But there was nothing remotely normal about Liese's mother. Lela

Cody – Madame Cody, as she liked to be called – had been a bareback rider, a circus performer, a balloonist and (on 14 August 1909) the first woman to fly in an English-speaking country; indeed, she was only the second woman to fly in the entire world. Her marital life was as unorthodox as her professional life; and as a result she detested her daughter Liese, seeing her and perhaps her children as a living reproach. She too was a devout Catholic.

Madame Cody's father, John Blackburne Davis, was a wealthy bloodstock agent who owned a large stables in Sloane Square that supplied horses to Buckingham Palace and provided riding lessons for Queen Victoria's children. Davis used to get his horses from America, and during one of his visits there he hired a young cowboy to escort the horses he had bought across the United States to an East Coast port, and thence across the Atlantic Ocean.

The cowboy called himself Samuel Franklin Cody. He was deeply inventive about his own past, and with some reason. For years, out of family loyalty, I used to stick to the family's official version of Cody's personal history, but the evidence has now built up to the point where it is impossible to ignore it any longer.

It seems that he was born Franklin Samuel Cowdery in the town of Davenport, Iowa, on 6 March 1867, the fourth of five children whose father, a wagoner, could trace his family history back to the Pilgrim Fathers. Sam left home at the age of fourteen and headed further west to Montana, where he broke in horses for stockmen and soon became a fully-fledged cowboy. His skills in roping cattle and firing a gun were so impressive that by 1888 he had joined the roadshow which the famous Annie Oakley had set up, after she had broken away from a much bigger show run by Buffalo Bill Cody. At the age of twenty-one Cowdery married a seventeen-year-old girl called Maud Lee, giving his name as Samuel Franklin Cody and his place of birth as Birdville, Texas. Romancing as ever about his origins, he encouraged people to think that he was related to Buffalo Bill.

Maud's father was English, and this may be the reason they travelled to London. They toured Britain as 'Captain Cody and Miss Cody: Buffalo Bill's son and daughter'; Maud would hold small glass balls in the air and Cody would shoot them out of her hand. But Buffalo Bill spent a good deal of time in Britain too, and he sued them. Sam left 'Miss Cody', and went back to transporting American horses across the Atlantic to Britain. Maud accepted her rejection and joined another circus group. Eventually she injured herself badly in a parachute jump, and ended up in the United States in a home for the insane.

Sam Cody cut a remarkable figure, riding along the King's Road in Chelsea to John Blackburne Davis's stables. He habitually wore buckskins, high boots and a huge cowboy hat, he was big and remarkably handsome, and he knew how to make himself pleasant to everyone he came across. And in spite of all the lies and romances about his past, he was a decent, generous and courageous man. In later years, when he turned to aviation, he was the most popular of all the pioneer airmen, known affectionately to his much younger rivals as 'Papa Cody'.

Tiny, beautiful, tempestuous and an excellent horsewoman, Davis's daughter Lela had been married for nearly twenty years to a licensed victualler in Chelsea, a man called Edward King: decent, but something of a bore. She had given him four children, of whom my grandmother Liese, born in 1873, was the eldest. By 1891, Lela was thirty-nine: no longer a young woman by the standards of the time. That was when she came across Sam, who was a foot taller and fifteen years younger than she was.

Cody once told a newspaper interviewer he had first met Lela in Montana, and was challenged to fight a two-way duel for her by a couple of admirers. Instead of fighting, he said, he had eloped with her, and they rode off into the sunrise while his two rivals were getting ready to fight him. But many of his stories about their early days were invented, because of the awkwardness about Edward King and poor Maud, and this one seems even wilder than the rest. We can assume, I think, that they met first in Chelsea.

Despite the various problems and disparities, it was a *coup de foudre* on both sides. They adored each other, and remained devoted for the entire twenty-two years they spent together; except possibly for the time when Cody, who was often absent-minded, sent Lela up in a man-carrying kite and forgot all about her for several hours while she dangled 200 feet in the air. But she soon forgave him. 'Make your husband your king and your home your world,' she advised my mother decades later. Lela brought two of her three sons to live with him, and they worshipped Cody too. Though Cody and Lela could never marry, they were accepted as man and wife almost everywhere over the years – except at Buckingham Palace during Queen Victoria's lifetime. But Edward VII was fond of Cody – he had an instinctive liking for men with irregular backgrounds – and his son, later George V, first met him at a flying display and took to him immediately. By saying 'Good afternoon, Colonel Cody,' the Prince of Wales confirmed Cody's honorary title to everyone's satisfaction; including that of the newspapers who had habitually plagued Cody with their barbs and criticism. And he addressed Lela as 'Madame Cody', which was felt to regularize their relationship.

But despite this success, Lela's daughter Liese still seems to have reminded her too much of her real husband, Edward King. Liese was, anyway, only six years younger than Cody himself: another reproach. Madame Cody rarely lost an opportunity to humiliate her over her ugliness and lack of skill in the Wild West shows which the rest of the family put on. Liese, big, clumsy, unattractive and apparently unable to ride a horse well, was left out of the excitement and glamour of the Cody roadshow. Her mother, who rode superbly and had nerves of steel, continued to play the part of Cody's heroine in his elaborate melodramas until her late forties, with her son Leon as the hero and Cody as the villain.

They toured the United States, France, Belgium, Switzerland, Germany, Austria, and went all over England and Scotland. Once, on an Internet site, I found a playbill for their most famous production and bought it at once:

THEATRE ROYAL
ROCHDALE

MONDAY, AUGUST 6th, 1900
AND EVERY EVENING DURING THE WEEK

Mr EDWARD LEROY's Powerful Company,
including the Famous Western American Actor,

MR. S. F. CODY

(THE KING OF COWBOYS), also
Horses and Mules, and the Alaska Brass Band;
All under the Management of Edward Fletcher,
in the New Sensational Drama in Five Acts,
entitled – The

KLONDYKE
NUGGET

By S. F. CODY.

Sam Deats, alias George Exelby .... Mr S. F. Cody
Joe Smith, in love with Rosie .... Mr Fred Lester
Waco, true as steel .... Mr Edward Leroy
Tom Lee, and old Trapper and Guide .. Mr W. H. Burton
Bill Sykes, Sam Deats' Pal .... Mr Graydon Garth

Ted Lee .... Mr Leon Cody
{Sons of Trapper.}
{Dead shots}
Vivian Lee .... Mr Vivian Cody
Dr Paddy O'Donoghue .... Mr Ern Clifton
Nellie, a Bar Girl .... Miss Pritchard
Jim Wilson, Sheriff of Klondyke District .... Mr Geo. West
Judge Matherson, of Dawson City .... Mr Arthur Moreton
Captain of the Emigrant Train .... Mr Harry Gibson
Steve Gray, a Clerk .... Mr George Leigh
Raven, an Indian Chief .... Mr. F. Wickenden
Usher, Dawson City Court House .... Mr Clive Cody
Henry Garcon, a French Emigrant .... Mr. Doc Horsfal
Rosie, Tom Lee's Daughter .... Madame Lela Cody
Indians, Miners, Emigrants &c

Act 1 – HOME OF THE LEE FAMILY, ALASKA
Scene – Wooden Bridge on the Road to the Chilcoot Pass,
fifty miles from the Coast of Norton Sound.
In this Grand Scene the Bridge is severed by the Villain. The
Hero attempts to cross with his horse, which is precipitated
into the Ravine below, a distance of fifteen feet. The Most
Sensational Stage Picture ever presented to the Public.

Act 2 – SNOWY SUMMIT OF THE CHILCOOT
PASS AT NIGHT
In this Grand Scene is presented a faithful representation
of Aurora Borealis, commonly known to the natives as the
Northern Lights.
Scene 2 – Sunrise on the Eastern Slopes of the Chilcoot
Pass.
Scene 3 – Quartz Mining in full swing in the Heart of
Klondyke.

Act 3 – ELDORADO SALOON IN DAWSON CITY
Specialities by Messrs. CLIFTON and GIBSON, the
Klondyke Kids.

Act 4 – INTERIOR OF DAWSON CITY COURT HOUSE

In this scene, Waco the Indian Chief (Mr. Edward Leroy) dashes through a real plate glass window, and produces evidence just in time to save the Hero's life. A most daring feat and must be seen to be believed.

Act 5 – JOE SMITH'S RANCH

Don't miss the Destruction of the Ranch, and the most realistic and exciting Knife Fight ever seen on the Stage.

Mr. S. F. Cody (King of the Cowboys) and his Family
WILL EACH EVENING GIVE AN
Exhibition of their skill in Rifle and Revolver Shooting.
NEW SCENERY by Mr. S. F. Cody, and the whole
produced under his Personal Supervision.

POPULAR PRICES OF ADMISSION.
PRIVATE BOXES £1 10s and £1 5s. SINGLE SEATS 5s.
Dress Circle 3/- Orchestra Stalls 2s IF BOOKED 2s.6d.
Upper Circle 1/6 Pit Stalls 1/-
Second Tier 1/- Pit 6d. Gallery 4d.

Half-price at 9 o'clock to all parts except Pit & Gallery.
Children under 12 Half-price to all parts except Pit & Gallery.
Doors open at 7-0, Performance to commence at 7-30.
Early Doors at 6-30, 6d. extra to all parts, Gallery 4d. extra.
Seats may be secured at
Edmund Wrigley's Music Warehouse, 25, Drake Street.
Children in arms not admitted.
Seats not Guaranteed. No Money returned.
Tradesmen are cautioned not to supply goods to the Theatre
without a written order from Mr. C. Lucas.
The Refreshment Saloons of the Theatre are open.
Minerals, Cigars, and Cigarettes of the best quality
may be had at ordinary prices.

The Klondyke Nugget was a remarkable spectacle, requiring a cast of at least thirty and a particularly large stage so the horses could be ridden across it at full tilt. During the climax in Joe Smith's ranch, Cody, as the villainous George Exelby, tied Lela to a small but very real barrel of gunpowder, and lit the fuse. On the other side of the stage, Leon had to work his way loose from the shackles with which Cody had chained him to a tree, jump on to a nearby horse, race across the arena, cut Lela's bonds, throw her across his crupper and ride to safety before the barrel of gunpowder exploded; which it duly did, night after night, in the most satisfactory way, even though at their slower moments Lela, Leon and the horse were often only a couple of yards or so away from disaster.

Lela wore blood-red tights when she stood in front of Cody's target, in case of accidents. In the depths of a cupboard somewhere I still have the sequinned costume she was wearing at a show in the United States on the night when her husband galloped at full tilt across the arena, firing at a series of glass balls which were fixed into a steel backing around her body. (Afterwards, any of the glass balls which survived would be sold off to the highest bidder.) Most unusually, the horse stumbled at a key moment, and Cody shot Lela in the thigh. She stayed exactly where she was for the rest of the performance, the blood staining her red tights. She was determined not to let herself fall down and so ruin Cody's reputation for first-class marksmanship. Only when the show was finished and she had taken all the required bows did she leave the stage and allow herself to be treated by a doctor.

Cody's other show-stopping trick was to put apples on the heads of Frank and Leon, and ride away from them fast with two rifles pointing backwards over his shoulders. He aimed them at the apples with the aid of rear-view mirrors attached to his saddle, and fired them simultaneously. Fortunately he always hit the apples; but since all these acts were entirely genuine, each performance held its very considerable anxieties.

By this stage, my grandmother Liese, keen to free herself of her mother's control, was married to Arthur Whittall and had four children of her own: Leon, Viva, Joyce and Leonie. Whittall was a surprisingly dashing young man from London, who had come to see Cody's show and was so captivated by it that he insisted on meeting not just the cast but the entire family as well. Maybe, by courting Liese, he felt he was sharing a little in the Cody family's glamour.

After Whittall's early death, Cody insisted that Liese and her children should come to live with them near Farnborough. The Codys had now settled down, and Sam had given up his Wild West shows. Instead he was concentrating on designing and building man-carrying balloons and kites for the War Office, which paid him the handsome salary of £1,000 a year. On 5 October 1907 Cody established a world record by making the longest flight in an airship. His *Nulli Secundus* – 'second to none' – flew for three hours and twenty-five minutes from Aldershot to London, circled St Paul's Cathedral, and landed at the Crystal Palace. For the great majority of Londoners, it was the first flying machine they had ever seen. This success encouraged him to design and develop an aeroplane along lines pioneered by the Wright brothers in America.

The newspapers, particularly the *Daily Mail* with its instinctive dislike of foreigners and immigrants, were often scornful about Cody's strange ideas and American ways, but although Lela was furious and more than once urged him to leave the country, Cody affably ignored the newspapers' attacks on him. He kept working on the principle of manned flight. After their first success in 1903, the Wright brothers had had little idea how to develop and promote their aircraft. A few weeks after their famous flight, British military intelligence sent one of its most senior agents to Kittyhawk in South Carolina to recruit the brothers and buy their idea. Agreement was reached in principle, but in the end the Wright brothers demanded too much money and the deal fell through. The intelligence agent recommended instead that the War Office should support the work of pioneers like Cody in Britain.

While he designed and built his aircraft, getting closer and closer to making the first manned flight in Britain, my grandmother Liese, newly widowed, found life with her four children increasingly difficult. At some stage she began a relationship with Charles Phillips, one of Cody's most faithful grooms and all-round handymen, who had made the transition with him from show business to the manufacture of man-carrying kites and, eventually, to powered aircraft. Charles was a gruff, uneducated man who adored Cody and for the rest of his life wore a carefully waxed and tended moustache in homage to him. Cody had himself adopted the moustache, together with a little Imperial beard, as a sign of his respect for the former Emperor of France, Napoleon III. The Empress Eugénie had become a faithful supporter of Cody's ventures during her long exile in Britain.

Cody was forty-one by the time of his best-known achievement, the first recorded powered flight in Britain at Farnborough, Hampshire, on 23 October 1908: too old, many people thought, to be doing such dangerous things. But he was becoming genuinely popular with the British public, in spite of the original hostility of much of the British press, and gradually established himself as the best-known and certainly the most recognizable pioneer of the air. Not long afterwards he became a naturalized British subject. A *Vanity Fair* cartoon, published a week or so later, shows Cody in his flying gear and carries the caption 'All British'.

'Papa Cody' was a clever and resourceful engineer, but his many successes in flying competitions owed more to his courage and tenacity than to his abilities as a designer. His aircraft lacked the technical flair of those built by men like A. V. Roe or Claude Grahame-Whyte, and in terms of design he quickly fell behind. But he drove himself and his machines harder than any of the other pioneers, and was never intimidated by his frequent accidents and narrow escapes. As a result he won several of the biggest competitions of the time, including two Michelin trophies in successive months in 1909 which were contested by the most famous aviators of the time, and in 1912 was awarded the £5,000 prize offered by the War Office for the best international aircraft. This was a particularly satisfying success, since officials at the War Office had earlier tried to hold Cody back in order to favour British-born aviators.

Only a year later, on 7 August 1913, Cody was trying out a new hydroplane in which he intended to compete for the *Daily Mail* prize for the Coastal Circuit of Great Britain. He had promised to take his stepson Leon with him as a passenger, but instead agreed to give a ride to W. H. B. Evans, a well-known cricketer who now worked for the Egyptian civil service. The hydroplane took off normally and completed the first part of the flight. Then Cody turned back. He always enjoyed skimming over the tree-tops; but just as he started to descend the body of the hydroplane was seen to collapse, and the wings folded in on one another. The aircraft had no seatbelts, and Evans and Cody, who was wearing his familiar white coat, fell to the ground. Both were killed instantly.

Cody was given a huge official funeral in Aldershot, paid for by the War Office, which had once treated him so meanly but had then benefited hugely from his skill and foresight. George V, now King, sent Lela a message which showed his strong personal liking for Cody.

He was such a dominant figure, ebullient, kind, amusing, daring, that the light seemed to go out of the family altogether with his death. Forty years later, in the early 1950s, I went to his house: the one where Lela had received the King's message on the day of Cody's funeral. Ash Croft was a pleasant, large, late Victorian villa, standing separate from the other houses in the street. All the curtains were closed, and sheets lay over everything in the main rooms of the house. Every time I looked underneath them, it seemed to me, there would be some extraordinary treasure: a model of one of Cody's planes done in silver, a propeller mounted and edged in brass, a flying helmet, a rifle or a hand-gun. These things would glimmer briefly in the dim light, and then be covered over again.

The family underwent something of the same change. The excitement and glamour of the past was completely obscured, and nothing seemed to have moved on since the day Cody fell from his plane. Mrs Cody survived for several decades, grander and gloomier than ever, and more spiteful towards her daughter and many of her grandchildren. I came to know her son by Edward King, Uncle Ted, who was the Edward Leroy who had staged *The Klondyke Nugget* and played the part of Waco, the Indian chief, true as steel. He used to tell me stories of Cody's cowboy feats, and his own: I rather had the impression that, wonderful though Cody was, Edward Leroy was the one the crowds came to see. Yet he became intensely gloomy in later life, and wrote some notably depressing poetry. 'Sleep on, sleep on, sweet death is peace,' one of his poems concluded.

Charles Phillips and my grandmother reached the point where they lived together as husband and wife. The family knew they weren't married, of course, but such unconventional unions were now so familiar in the Cody family that nobody seemed to mind. With little work and no savings, Charles and Liese slipped further and further down the social scale until they ended up in Epsom, at Garden Cottages.

And now my mother, her two older children and I had joined them as well, jammed into this tiny place, with failed marriages and failed lives all around us. No one knew how long we would stay, but there seemed no reason to doubt that it would be a very long time. I might even grow up here. For now, though, we seemed happy enough. Having been so aware of my mother's tears earlier, I would certainly have noticed if she shed more. But, free of my father, she seemed to smile again, and sang songs all day long.

Over the next few months I started to become conscious of the world outside our little lane: the street at the end of it, the railway bridge, the buses, the occasional cars. I convinced myself that I had seen a car without a driver heading down the road, and tried very hard for some time to convince everyone else as well. I was introduced to another and much wider world, too. Michael and some of his friends decided to take me into the local cinema – still there, I noticed when I passed through Epsom not long ago. I was entranced when I saw the screen: great figures walking around, vastly bigger than ordinary human beings.

I was frightened, too. They took me to see a Bob Hope film, a comedy which must have been *Monsieur Beaucaire*. The costume scenes passed me by – I suppose I couldn't understand them – but when a group of revolutionaries chased Hope through New York firing at him, I was simply terrified by the gunshots and the business of hiding in cupboards and behind furniture. And although Michael and the others promised me that it was just a comedy and there was nothing to be afraid of, I ducked my head down so I wouldn't have to see the screen, and stuck my fingers in my ears. After that they took me to other films, which frightened me even more. It was a long time before I could watch actors like James Mason and Edward G. Robinson without being scared.

I had no appreciation whatsoever of the things that were happening on the screen, and came to assume that even the gentlest and lightest of comedies would erupt in gunfire and sudden death at some point. I found one film particularly frightening. It was in colour, and I scanned the screen the whole time, anxiously on watch for any sign of an unexpected attack. When the hero and heroine sang songs, I felt they were in particular danger; they were concentrating on the words and on each other so much, they couldn't spare the time to look out for the gangsters who, I felt certain, were stalking them. Even now, to my ear, the most famous song from this film has a sinister tone to it. I associate it with gunfire and sudden death:

> Blue skies, shining on me,
> Nothing but blue skies do I see.
> Never saw the sun shining so bright,
> Never saw things going so right.

I had not the remotest idea that *Blue Skies*, with Bing Crosby and Fred Astaire, was intended to be a romantic comedy. The only purpose of films, as far as I could see, was to terrify me.

Over the next few years I came to regard these faintly illicit trips to the cinema as being responsible for the growing sense of sexuality which slowly stole over me. Looking back from the age of five or six, I imagined that I must have picked up this sense of concupiscence at the pictures, from watching all those attractive blondes and brunettes kissing Bob Hope and James Mason (and, now I come to think of it, a third person; could it possibly have been Red Skelton?).

By the time I reached the age of twelve I was, if anything, grateful for my early glimpses of the sexual life, and had come to terms with the whole idea; but until then the faint sense of wrong-doing which I felt as a result of watching films intended for older people merged imperceptibly with the growing child's sense of his own body, and of the bodies of others. And maybe the exciting, nerve-racking darkness of the cinema did indeed have something to do with it as well.

Yet at Garden Cottages my overwhelming sense was of my own inadequacies. I watched my mother write a letter in her precise, smallish, rather spiky handwriting, and was filled with a sense of longing. If only I could make myself understood by these strange marks: I would take the pen from her and make squiggles on the page, willing them to mean something. Then everyone would laugh and pretend they could read what I had done, while I knew perfectly well that my squiggles were meaningless and illegible.

It was the same with speech. I could say quite a few words now, and had done for several months. And after my father finally turned up at Garden Cottages and asked my mother to come back to him, they took me to South Norwood and showed me, among other things, a church near my grandmother's house which had been bombed a few years earlier.

'That's the steeple,' my father said, pointing at an ugly blunt object, pointing up to the sky. 'It's been partly knocked down.'

'Boken dee-dole', I said, meaning that the steeple was broken; and my parents were inordinately proud of me as a result.

I don't remember this myself, though. I learned about it because they both insisted on telling me the story again and again afterwards, as a sign of my amazing, preternatural intelligence, and a portent of the remarkable future which lay ahead of me; whereas all it really showed was that I was a good mimic.

I was virtually all they could agree on. My mother had brought me back, but had left her other two children at Garden Cottages; and the inevitable rows started up again. My mother said my father was just as impossible as he had been before; he warned her that even if she wanted to go back to Epsom she couldn't take me with her.

'He can't be allowed to grow up there,' he said. It didn't seem to worry him that Pat and Michael were still there, but of course they didn't have Simpson blood.

I did, and the quality of my blood won the day. Instead of living with Uncle Charles, his moustache and his pipe in the fug of Garden Cottages, I would now live with my father. My mother was to come and stay with us at frequent intervals, so that I wouldn't miss her.

Did she realize, even at this stage, that by agreeing to this she was starting to surrender her rights to me? I'm sure she did. But she was a gentle woman, easily defeated, and my father, when he was determined about something, usually got his way. If charm didn't work, ferocity would. After that, I don't think I ever went back to Garden Cottages, even for a day. My father would never have allowed it. As he saw it, I had left all these Codys and Kings and Whittalls for good, together with the atmosphere of muddle and gloom and decline which they seemed to breathe. I was going to be upwardly mobile; my father had decreed it. It wasn't very nicely done, but it was settled.

I trotted up the slight cobbled slope of Garden Cottages between my father and mother, holding on to their hands, sometimes trying playfully to drag them down. It was the last time I would smell the tobacco and the overcrowded house and wallflowers, the last time I would see the long wall, the garden gate, the street where the car without a driver had passed me, the cinema where I shouldn't have been allowed to go. The others must have waved us goodbye, though I don't remember that part. All I remember is looking up at the faces of the two people who had brought me into the world, but couldn't get along with each other.

'Where are we going now?' I asked brightly. I was buttoned into my little tan-coloured coat, so it may have been early autumn. In fact, now I come to think of it, the surviving photograph of my mother and me by the garden gate may well have been taken on this day by my father, as a way of commemorating the big change that was taking place. He was a good photographer, and someone has gone to the trouble of ensuring that my little buttoned sandals and my mother's fashionable peep-toed shoes are properly in the shot.

'You'll see,' said my mother, who was probably trying not to cry.

'You'll like it very much,' said my father, who was full of jubilation.

'Will I?' I asked.

I knew I would. To the mind of a two-year-old, everything is bound to work out well. And parents invariably stay together.

THE DOCUMENTS WHICH I inherited from my father are a strange lot. There are invitations, notices of births and marriages and deaths, letters, postcards, newspaper clippings. And theatre programmes, including one for a Crazy Gang show at the Victoria Palace in 1950, in which someone called Monsewer Eddie Gray appeared with his Performing Dogs; these, it immediately became clear even to me, as my father and mother and I sat in the stalls, were completely untrained, and may well have been picked up at random in the streets before the performance. Instead of doing the tricks which he kept announcing with increasing frustration, the dogs simply scattered across the stage in their excitement, barking, mounting each other, and relieving themselves at random. I laughed so much, my parents discussed in whispers whether to take me out of the theatre.

Among the rest of the things is a small brown booklet, printed in black, dominated by a black circle with a crown and the inscription 'M of F' in it. Underneath are the words 'Ration Book', with my name and address set out in my mother's handwriting. The address is Garden Cottages, Epsom. One page has been cut out, and there are various arcane crossings out and stamps and signatures, but the all-important coupons are still intact. Presumably my Epsom ration book was no longer valid once I had left there, and I was given a new one for my father's flat in Upper Norwood.

Ration books were the one central part of everyone's lives during and after the war. Virtually everything was controlled, and the book was your key to obtaining your ration of everything from cigarettes and tea to furniture. It was part of the command economy, and there are a great many commands in it, many of them impenetrably difficult to understand:

> Fill In The Spaces Below If You Deposit With Your
>   Retailer Any Of The Pages 13–18;
> Do Nothing With This Page Until Instructed;
> Do Not Cut out Coupons.
> The Retailer Will Do This For You.

One section is printed on cheaper paper than the rest, yellowing and coarse. These are the points themselves, with the names of the main commodities alongside: Sugar, Bacon, Cheese, Fats, Eggs, Meat. There are two entire pages dedicated to tea, and other pages with boxes which are unexplained and are marked arcanely A, B, C or X. Four pages carry the words 'Personal Points (Sweets)'.

Rationing was, of course, a bureaucrat's paradise, and the complexity of it must have flummoxed millions of people over the years. This is the text of a government advertisement in a women's magazine:

> Take care of your 1947–8 clothing book.
> To save paper it will have to last you two years.
> The 20 yellow coupons on page iii of the General,
>   Child's and Junior Clothing Books become valid
>   on 1 October for the first five months ending
>   29 February next.
> This is how they are made up: 16 coupons 'E' – value
>   1 = 16
> 1 set of ¼ coupons – value 1 = 1
> 2 token 'F' – value 1½ = 3
>
> Do not cut any of the invalid coupons from the
> 1947–8 books. They will be needed later.

As the bureaucracy built up and flourished, intruding every-where, it sometimes seemed like deliberate persecution. The Ministry of Food appeared to relish its ability to reach down into the lives of the most obscure and ordinary people, and make them a misery. Examples could be found everywhere, every day:

> The owner of a small confectionery shop, keen to provide his customers with something a little better than the usual, put his own personal ration of sugar into a batch of home-made sweets; fined £5.
>
> A Devonshire farmer's wife welcomed a Ministry inspector with tea and scones, and added in a bit of her own cream as a treat for him; fined £5.
>
> A greengrocer sold six pounds of potatoes more than his limit, while making it clear to his customers that they were frost-bitten and would have to be thrown away if they weren't cooked immediately; fined £6.
>
> A pig-farmer brought in a butcher to kill a pig on the day his licence specified, but because the approved shed was being rebuilt they had to use the shed next door; fined £6.

It would be thirty years before the Labour Party began to throw off the reputation for heavy, intrusive regulation which it gained during the immediate post-war years.

The pettiness of the rules and the mindlessness with which they were imposed created the kind of climate where everyone, even the most honest, was in danger of breaking the law. As a result, people were tempted to feel that small things scarcely mattered. If you were to feed your family properly, you had to pay the shopkeeper a bit extra, and he would let you have something under the counter. Small-time dishonesty was every-where. People took towels from hotels, and cups and spoons from the railways. If you were one of the very few people able to go abroad for business or pleasure, it was virtually impossible to keep within the currency limit of £5 which was all you were able to take out. Three hundred and twenty-two people were prosecuted for currency offences in 1946; by 1948 it was 4,583. A single interview carried out by Mass-Observation during an investigation of the change in personal honesty speaks for the great mass of people:

> I've taken toilet paper from women's lavatories I've been to. There was a shortage of it a little while ago. When I was working in a pub part-time, I used occasionally to take packets of cigarettes – I gave them to my husband. Everyone else used to take them, so I thought I might as well.

In 1938, the figure for the value of stolen property was £2,500,000. In 1947, it was £13,000,000.

The most representative figure in post-war Britain, after the Ministry snooper, was the spiv. Spivs sprang up in London from nowhere during the summer of 1946, like the weeds on bombed sites, their shallow roots spreading in the general chaos and destruction. No one could even agree where the name had come from: one or two of the more erudite linked it to a word used by Welsh gypsies, 'spilav', which apparently meant 'to push'; yet even that didn't sound very convincing.

You knew exactly who they were, though: you could tell them from the unfeasibly wide lapels of their double-breasted suits, their narrow waists, their thick-soled suede shoes, their pencil-thin moustaches, the remaining stubs of cigarettes attached to their lower lips, the hats crushed down on their duck's-arse haircuts. And, usually, the wad of notes in their hand. I don't really think I ever saw a spiv in all his glory, and my ideas were probably created for me by newspaper and magazine cartoonists, who depicted them constantly. But everybody talked about them, with an apparent disapproval which seemed to cover a certain sneaking admiration.

Spivs represented a relief from the dreariness of the war and the years which followed it. They were part of the post-war relaxation process, the return to the ordinary, selfish, often ignoble nature of ordinary life. And they could get you anything, from a tankful of petrol so you could take your girlfriend out for a weekend in the country, to nylon stockings or a bottle of whisky. In the surrounding greyness, they provided a splash of illicit colour. And they were the best way round the ludicrous, mean-minded regulators employed by Government ministries, and the endless, depressing shortages.

These shortages infected every imaginable area of daily life. In 1946, as I was leaving Garden Cottages, the Ministry of Health warned brides-to-be that they should book a bed in a maternity ward, not when they became pregnant, but on the day they were married. Even powdered egg, a horrible substance whose rubbery texture and faintly acidic taste I remember faintly to this day, and which seemed to embody the essence of wartime shortage and austerity, disappeared for months at the end of 1945: and it was only then that people realized how dependent they had become on it.

Rationing ended finally in 1954, and the great majority of British people have known nothing since then but growing affluence and a range of choice unthinkable in the 1940s or early 50s. The very concept of rationing is hard for us to grasp today, and even at the time it seemed inexplicable that the supply of food should be more carefully controlled after the war than during it. The fuel cuts were worse than they had been when U-boats were sinking the tankers which brought Britain's oil supplies across the Atlantic or through the Mediterranean; soap was in shorter supply than it had been during the Blitz. The food ration generally was even smaller than it had been at the worst moments of 1941–2. In 1946 the average woman spent more than an hour queuing every day: 20 per cent longer than she had during the war itself.

Oranges, which had occasionally begun to appear in the shops in twos and threes during 1945, and required far too many coupons for most people to be able to afford them, abruptly vanished again. By 1948, the weekly food allowance for the average adult male had dropped to one egg, thirteen ounces of meat, six ounces of butter or margarine, an ounce of cooking fat, eight ounces of sugar, two pints of milk, and one tin of dried milk every eight weeks. There was an all-pervading, debilitating gloom about the daily business of staying alive, a dreariness which, an elderly gentleman told me years afterwards, was always summed up for him whenever he heard Sir Stafford Cripps, the presiding genius of rationing and austerity, pronounce the word 'coupon' as 'coupong'.

Yet it wasn't, as many Conservatives believed, the result of Labour's instinctive desire to control the details of everyday life. The basic reason for the austerity was simple: the war had cost the British economy so much, so many investments had been lost or sold, that there was far less for everyone to manage on. Britain's net income from its foreign investments in 1938 was £175 million; by 1940 it had fallen to £73 million, and would soon drop even further; and at the same time the value of Britain's imports had quadrupled. Overall, the economy was something like a fifth of its pre-war size.

If it hadn't been for Marshall Aid, the rations of most basic foodstuffs would have been cut by an extra third, and shortages of timber would have cut the house-building programme from 200,000 a year to 50,000. Unemployment would have shot up to 1.5 million. Yet Marshall Aid for Britain was brief. A new American loan was to take its place, and the terms which the US demanded would ensure that rationing in Britain would be fiercer than ever, and would last for years.

The wartime generosity of large numbers of individual Americans had rarely been matched by the US government, even when the personal friendship between Churchill and Roosevelt was at its closest. The Roosevelt and Truman administrations, and American political opinion generally, saw Britain and its still vast overseas empire as standing in the way of American power and progress; and during the profoundly important series of negotiations between the US, Russia and Britain about the future of the world, from Tehran to Yalta and Potsdam, the Americans often sided with Stalin against the British in order to diminish Britain's already fading power. On more than one occasion Churchill found himself close to tears as he tried to persuade Roosevelt of the damage he was doing to British interests by agreeing with Stalin.

In economic terms, the US was determined to extract full payment for every loan it had made to the British during the Second World War. Lend Lease, which had helped to keep Britain afloat during the war itself, was cut off almost without warning directly the Japanese surrendered in August 1945. For a time, Marshall Aid helped to plug the gap between Britain's huge outgoings and its relatively small earnings. But the atmosphere during the negotiations for a vast new American loan to the Attlee government shocked the British officials who took part in them; it was, one civil servant said publicly, as though the Americans were being deliberately vindictive. 'They seem to be looking for ways to do us down,' another minuted. Individual American politicians were often outspokenly hostile. 'Not one dollar for Britain,' said Rep. James Short during a discussion in the House of Representatives, 'so long as they have the Crown Jewels in London.'

The negotiations ended in agreement – they had to, since Britain would otherwise have been bankrupt; there was no alternative to accepting most of the American terms. But the stress of it killed the economist John Maynard Keynes, who headed the British negotiating team. And the result was clear: the British people would have to pay through the nose for the American help they had received.

Britain, full of pre-war pretension yet scarcely able to afford to send its troops where they were needed, and often too poor to be able to finance its beleaguered friends, began to fade fast as a great power. In 1949 the Labour MP Ian Mikardo compared the British Government to 'people who do without their Sunday dinner or give up smoking cigarettes, but nevertheless buy a new set of plush curtains to impress their neighbours'. The empire was dissipating, and Britain's efforts to hold on to it, in Kenya and elsewhere, would sometimes result in brutality and outright cruelty. By the mid-1950s Britain had effectively ceased to be a world power at all; and when Sir Anthony Eden, as Prime Minister, took the disastrous step of invading Egypt with France and Israel in 1956, the last self-delusion fell away.

But for now, in the late 1940s, the exhausting efforts of the war and the rapacity of the Truman administration helped to ensure that couples like my father and mother had two eggs and twenty-six ounces of meat a week. I, as a child, on the other hand, benefited greatly from the rationing and the shortages. I can still taste the thick, sweet, pungent orange juice which was ladled out of a medicine bottle for me every morning. There was also compulsory halibut liver oil, from another bottle: disgusting stuff, which used to coat the tongue and the palate long afterwards. There were also little quarter-pint bottles of milk. I was obliged to drink one every morning, and another at nursery school when I started going there in 1948.

Children of my age were unaware that there was anything to miss. Sweets were rarities, chocolate almost unknown. A Cadbury's advertisement of 1947 read:

> Our milk chocolate is wonderful. Unfortunately,
> Cadbury's are only allowed the milk to make an
> extremely small quantity, so if you are lucky enough
> to get some, do save it for the children.

When my father used to take me around London with him, we would walk along the dark platforms of the Underground, and I would ask him again and again to tell me about the tall, upright machines that stood and rusted against the wall. 'Before-the-war,' he would say, knowing how much I loved that mysterious, incantatory expression, which was second only to the even more exciting 'In-the-olden-days', 'you put a penny in the slot there, and a bar of chocolate would come out.'

What an extraordinary world, I used to think to myself, where magical substances like chocolate were obtainable for a single penny on every Underground platform! How rich, how privileged, how perfect life before-the-war must have been! And how shrunken and decayed and poverty-stricken our own life was, by comparison! I felt, I suppose, like a young Roman after the barbarians had captured the city. Once there had been wealth and scope and glamour and chocolate; now it had all vanished. My world, full of darkness and restriction, was very slow to change. Rationing would last until 1954, when I was ten.

Yet every Christmas from 1946 onwards my stocking would always contain some rare and magical hint of a world beyond food rationing and restriction: an orange or a tangerine, a pomegranate, and in 1948 a pineapple: things I had never even heard of before. I disappointed my father, who must have gone to the most extraordinary and probably illegal lengths, by disliking the pomegranate intensely; and when I bit into the tough thorny outer skin of my pineapple at five o'clock on Christmas morning, not knowing how else to attack it, I cut my mouth and needed comforting. But I liked the pineapple when it was cut up for me.

So we children had no sweets, little fat of any kind, and we were force-fed with supplements rich in vitamins and nutrients. I was often hungry in the late 40s, but that was probably just a child's natural appetite making itself felt. We filled up, where possible, on vegetables, which for the most part weren't rationed. There were probably very few households like the Waughs', where – if Auberon is to be believed – his father Evelyn used to insist on sitting down in front of the entire family and eating the eggs which his children received as part of their ration. He had to work, he said, and they didn't.

Most children, even the poorest, thrived. Perhaps it isn't

surprising that my generation, given a diet which was compulsorily frugal and excellent, should have grown up to think of ourselves as different, as stronger, livelier, healthier, more individualistic, and longer-living than our elders. Our teeth were safe from sugar, and our waistlines and cholesterol levels were unpolluted by hamburgers, chips and sweet fizzy drinks. We have mostly stayed healthy and active. As a result, we now think it is absurdly wasteful to retire at sixty, and many of us expect to keep working until late into our seventies.

But there was always something about us which looked with longing to another world, another time: a sense that things should be better than they were. How could it not be, when our parents endlessly dwelt on the life they had lost? The newspapers and hoardings were full of reminders; and with no raw materials and no labour force to create the goods of the past, the companies which produced them could only summon up their memory, like ghostly presences.

> Won't it be nice when we have lovely lingerie, *and*
> Lux to look after our pretty things? Remember how
> pure, safe Lux preserved the beauty of delicate fabrics?
> And how easily it rinsed out! But while there is still
> no Lux, and you have to wash treasured things with
> the soap or flakes available, do take extra care . . .

I remember the smell and the harshness of those available soapflakes to this day, so resistant to water, so reluctant to foam, and, as the advertisement suggests, so unwilling to let themselves be washed away later. I remember too the redness of my mother's hands when she used it; and the rough feel of the strange, alien flecks that appeared in the yellow soap we had to wash our hands and faces with.

One morning over breakfast, on one of the days in, I think, 1947, when my parents were together, my father read out a story from the *News Chronicle* about a war crimes trial somewhere in Germany. He rather obviously left various passages out as he read aloud, my mother glancing at me from time to time and frowning and shaking her head, but it slowly became evident from what he was saying that soap, the big blocks the size of half-bricks, could be connected in some way with human bodies; and the next time I smelt the fatty smell of it, and felt the flecks of foreign objects and the bits of grit embedded in its nasty yellow substance, I was certain. Something very bad indeed had happened to our soap, and therefore something just as bad could be expected to happen to those of us who washed ourselves with it.

I stopped using the soap after that, and no amount of pleading or threatening would make me start again. When my father started to get annoyed with me, my mother suggested quietly that it was his fault, for thoughtlessly reading things out from the papers that a child shouldn't hear. My father, rather more loudly, insisted that my mother had something to do with it – and her mother, and Garden Cottages, and perhaps the Catholic faith in which she had been brought up and had never entirely been able to throw off. The path the row followed was familiar and well-worn, and, as rows will, it very satisfactorily deflected my parents' attention from me, as they quickly forgot what, precisely, they were arguing about in the first place.

'Impossible,' my mother said, getting up and walking out of the room. 'You're completely impossible.'

Even to this day I dislike using soap. Especially the pale yellow kind.

ON THE EVENING OF Thursday 16 May Lord Wavell, the large, awkward, kindly soldier who now served as the penultimate Viceroy of India, sat down at a microphone in Sir Edwin Lutyens' incomparable government buildings in New Delhi and in a low, rumbling voice delivered a broadcast about the country's future.

> I speak to the people of India at the most critical hour of India's history. You will have studied the government's statement, most of you, and may perhaps already have formed an opinion on it. If you think that it shows a path to reach the summit at which you have been aiming for so long – the independence of India – I am sure you will be eager to take it. We should much have preferred that the Indian leaders should have themselves reached agreement on the course to be followed. We have done our best to persuade them, but it has not been found possible.

The demand in India for independence had always been there, to some extent and among some people. It became a concrete demand in 1917, when Mohandas Gandhi was elected leader of the Congress Party; and after the growing anger of the interwar years, when the British came to accept that it was inevitable that they would leave India but no one could agree how, when, or on what terms, the issue came to a head on 3 September 1939 when the then Viceroy, Lord Linlithgow, blandly announced that India, like Britain, was at war with Germany. He had not consulted a single Indian politician before doing so.

The Indian Army served the British cause loyally throughout the war, and played a significant part in the Allied victory. But it was always clear that the price for their efforts was Indian independence; and when a Labour Government came to power in 1945 the moment was at hand.

The trouble was, India's main political groupings were deeply at odds. The Congress Party, headed by Gandhi and with Jawaharlal Nehru (who had supported Britain during the war) as one of its most significant leaders, wanted the newly independent state to take in the whole of British India. The All-India Muslim League, headed by Mahomed Ali Jinnah, ascetic, tall and almost skeletal, wanted a separate independent state for India's Muslims, which would be known from the initials of its main provinces as Pakistan. Jinnah's grandfather had in fact been a Hindu, and for many years Jinnah himself had co-operated closely with Gandhi. Then they quarrelled; and from that quarrel arose the future partition of British India.

Hindus outnumbered Muslims in India by about three to one at this stage: there were approximately 250 million Hindus, and more than 80 million Muslims. Violence between them was always close. Linlithgow, the Viceroy who brought India into the war, was treated with implacable hostility by the Congress Party; but the Muslim League under Jinnah was prepared to give continuing British rule its backing, as long as it was settled that the British would agree to give separate independence to Pakistan. The British were deeply uncomfortable about this idea, and never formally agreed to it; but the Muslim League, knowing its negotiating strength, behaved as though the British wholeheartedly intended to create the nation of Pakistan.

Directly the war was over, the new Labour Government was determined on moral as well as practical grounds to give India its independence as quickly as possible. But it wanted to create a single state, not two; and by strong and effective diplomacy a team headed by one of the Government's strongest figures, Sir

Stafford Cripps, managed to create a constitutional structure which would give each of India's provinces a satisfactory amount of self-control, whether they were predominantly Hindu or Muslim. But India would be kept together as a single independent nation by having a Constituent Assembly in charge of foreign affairs and defence at the top of the structure. It was a clever plan, which gave almost everything to almost everybody, and Jinnah took the extraordinary step of accepting it and agreeing to set aside the aspiration for an independent Pakistan and accept the British proposal.

Then Nehru overplayed his hand. The plan was acceptable to the Muslims only because the Constituent Assembly was necessarily lacking in serious power. Nehru, with Gandhi's backing, demanded that it should be much stronger – which in turn would mean that Congress would have a far greater say in the future government of India. Jinnah, who had been heavily criticized for his early compromise, took fright and backed away from an agreement. Soon he was demanding a fully independent Pakistan again.

Maybe the Constituent Assembly idea would never have worked anyway: these elaborate constitutions which are constructed like road bridges to get over some major problem on the ground below often collapse when they come face to face with reality. But it would have protected Britain from the accusation over the decades that for its own divide-and-rule purposes it wanted to leave two separate states behind it, not just one. The horrors of partition, with its millions of casualties, might have been avoided if only India had been kept together.

Poor old Lord Wavell, sitting nervously at the microphone and clearing his throat before making his big announcement, certainly wanted a single independent India. He belonged to a generation which could scarcely imagine India independent at all, let alone divided into two newfangled states. By the time he made his broadcast it was perfectly clear to most senior politicians in Britain and in India itself that the British mission's plans for a Constituent Assembly didn't stand a chance. Still, his broadcast was well enough received by Gandhi himself:

> There are some who said the English were incapable of doing the right thing. I do not agree with them. The mission and the Viceroy are as God-fearing as we ourselves claim to be. Whatever the wrong done to India by British rule, if the statement of the mission is genuine, as I believe it is, it is to discharge an obligation which they have declared the British owe to India – that is, to get off India's back.

But the British proposal came to nothing. Soon, London sent out its final Viceroy, Lord Louis Mountbatten, to negotiate the hand-over of power to two states, one headed by Nehru and the other by Jinnah. When he arrived a few months later, on 22 March 1947, Mountbatten, glamorous, dashing, good-looking, intelligent, received everyone's attention and, despite their suspicions, the leading Hindu and Muslim politicians were charmed by him. As for slow, anxious old Lord Wavell, who had carried on trying to keep India together when it would have been easier not to bother, no one took much notice of him as he left; with the sole exception of Jawaharlal Nehru, who paid a fine tribute to him, even though it would have been easier and more popular to have stayed silent.

The British were nothing like as generous. The next day's *Times* reported Mountbatten's arrival in a story several columns long, even though newsprint was so scarce at the time that plenty of other news had to be sacrificed for it. An inch or so up from the bottom of the same page is an item of eleven words, date-lined Bombay:

> Lord Wavell and his party left Karachi this afternoon for Britain.

That, we could say, was the moment at which, after three centuries, traditional British India came to an end.

Life in Britain itself was grey, and seemed likely to get greyer still. On 16 May Herbert Morrison, one of the leading members of the Labour Government, had a gloomy announcement to make when he met the press in Washington. After long negotiations with the US Government he had been obliged to agree to give up an extra 200,000 tons of American grain which he had hoped to be able to send to Britain, so that they could be diverted to India and the British sector in Germany. Morrison had hoped that since the 1945 harvest had been reasonably good the Americans would send other grain of their own to help out in India and Germany.

But although the negotiations were friendly enough, Morrison was faced with the basic and perfectly understandable question: why should Americans have to go short in order to help Britain meet its own requirements? Because the British people are already facing unprecedented shortages, Morrison replied; to which the American negotiating team merely shrugged their shoulders.

At a press conference afterwards, someone asked Morrison if there would now have to be bread rationing in Britain; something that had never quite happened, even during the war. Morrison, usually imperturbable and inclined to fiddle with his pipe when faced with difficult questions, was uncharacteristically flustered.

'I'm not sure,' he answered. 'I don't want to do it if I can help it ... It doesn't smell good to me. But the British Government will have to decide how to carry on as at present and squeeze through till September – it will be an awfully tight squeeze, a sheer gamble – or compel more economies on the British people.'

Directly they read that, most British people will have guessed that things would shortly be a lot worse. It was usually a safe bet during the 1940s.

The only good news that day was slight indeed: the Board

of Trade announced that there would be a modest increase in cigarette supplies in June, and Government departments had released all but thirty-three of the 493 hotels they had requisitioned around the coast as part of Britain's wartime defences. The orders came through for the last American servicemen to leave Britain. From now on the only Americans in uniform serving in Britain would be graves registration men, and soldiers on leave from more difficult places in continental Europe.

Someone paid £2,520 for Rubens' painting *The Holy Family with St Anne*, which showed that there was still some money around. The Oxford Union voted by 176 to 39 not to accept women as debating members. And the grand, statuesque, extremely formal and distinctly elderly Queen Mary, accompanied by Princess Alice and the Earl of Athlone, visited the Stage Door Canteen in Piccadilly, one of London's favourite dance venues. 'They watched hundreds of servicemen and women dancing the "hokey-cokey" and other modern dances,' said *The Times* rather disdainfully.

Wednesday 12 February 1947

Sun rises, 7.22 a.m.; sets, 5.08 p.m.
Lighting-up time: 5.38 p.m.
Maximum temperature: 30°F; minimum: 29°F.
Sunshine: nil.
Strong easterly winds. Cloudy. Occasional light
  snowfalls during afternoon and early
  evening. Frost day and night.

THERE IS A LUMP, not unlike a blister, on the little finger of my left hand: just as painful, but oddly hot and cold, and with a nasty reddish colour to it. I can't help touching it, exploring the pain it produces, testing its strength and its power to hurt me. It is fascinating: and anyway there isn't much else to think about. I show my finger to my old, balding brown bear, which is stuffed with strips of wood which keep escaping from a hole somewhere near his left ankle. The bear, who has no name, seems sympathetic. He should be: he was a gift from Colonel Cody to my mother in 1907, and has suffered quite a lot himself over the years. He must have been one of the first teddy bears in existence, named after the aggressive American president Theodore Roosevelt, who led a shooting-party in the American wilds to hunt bears. My bear's dark button eyes look into mine, and he seems to understand me; even though part of me realizes perfectly well that he is just an inanimate object.

The chilblain on my finger is more painful than ever, as a result of my constant investigation of its qualities; and it has now become a subject of contention between my father and mother.

'All I said was I couldn't believe you would put that child in a place where he could get chilblains all over his hands.'

My mother's voice replies, quiet, submissive, yet uncowed. My father talks over her, loud and excited.

'But you know how bloody cold it is. You've allowed him to be covered with chilblains when it's colder than at any time within living memory.'

Any time since 1867, my mother counters. A new sub-argument branches off: are eighty years (her mathematics are always swift) really beyond living memory? And anyway the BBC has been saying it's only the coldest since 1940: minus sixteen degrees Fahrenheit. There follows a range of further emotions: anger, mockery, hurt, resignation, silence. Nothing will now be properly harmonious between them for some hours.

Even at the age of two and a half, it is obvious to me that things are worse than ever between my parents. Everything reinforces this impression: the volume of sound, the looks on their faces, the way every argument ends with an angry breaking-off, the slamming of a door, the refusal to speak. A year or so later I will try pleading with them or distracting them in some way to get them reconciled; but for now I have no idea how to go about it, or even, perhaps, what it is that I should go about. So I just lie on my bed and press the chilblain on my finger as a kind of distraction.

'How did he get it, anyway?'

'I suppose his little glove must have come off yesterday.'

'It's freezing enough inside here, let alone outside.'

'I can't ever remember it being this cold.'

A silence; suddenly they're dangerously close to agreeing with one another.

I know it has been horribly, bone-cuttingly cold for a very long time now, inside the flat as well as outside it, but how we combat it I cannot say. Nor can I remember anything about the place, except its grandiose name – 'Madras', Bedwardine Road, Upper Norwood – and the fence around its garden. I seem to think we were on the ground floor, though this would argue that my father had more money to spend on rent than he can possibly have earned from his current job. The house was a rangy, red-brick neo-gothic pile, put up in the 1860s for some newly-retired middle-ranking Indian civil servant just in time for what would remain one of the coldest winters for eighty years.

But I do remember the ferocious, cruel, insinuating cold of 1947; so bad that, despite the shame, I prefer one night to wet the bed rather than get out on to the brown lino and use the little pot under the bed; until the warmth turns to bitter chill and I am colder than ever, as well as humiliated and apologetic.

It is curious and somehow mildly frustrating that neither my mother nor my father is ever angry with me, even when I ruin the sheets and stain the mattress. They do not use me directly in their wars; they do not appeal to my judgement or my preferences to try to bolster their own case against each other. Neither of them comes to me quietly and tries to poison me against the other. On the contrary, they seem to me to like each other more when they are separate than they do when they are together.

'Daddy will be so proud of you when I tell him.'

'Look at the lovely little hat Mummy has knitted for you. Come on, try it on.'

All their efforts are directed towards persuading me that they are ordinarily loving parents; yet they seem to make no effort whatever to be what they pretend.

Outside the window, the snow is a good three feet deep. A month ago, I loved it; now, like everyone else in the country, I have come to loathe it. But it isn't snow anyway; it is a hard, dark, reddish-brown layer that covers everything and gets more and more leathery as each freezing day passes, darkened from its original white by the dirty, acidulous air of London. From time to time another layer of white covers the disgusting carapace, but within a couple of days that too has lost its cleanliness and merged into the general cruel dirt. I have fallen over so many times and hurt myself that I fear the ice as much as any brittle-boned seventy-year-old. I hate going out, and cry if I am forced to: big, gulping sobs which make my parents look at each other doubtfully, and which remain with me in lesser and lesser eruptions and snivels for minutes afterwards. A line of silver ropes down from my nose, but no one does anything about it. These things have become too commonplace for anyone to care about.

As usual, my mother comes and goes, and since I hear her talking from time to time about Epsom I suppose she is still living part of her life there. Not at present, though: the trains and buses are all affected by the endless freeze, and she is stuck in Upper Norwood. She doesn't like any part of Norwood, Upper, Middle, Lower, West, South. One day I will come to realize why: Norwood is Simpson territory. It's not just that they live there; it's because they built various parts of it. The Simpsons were once one of the big families of the area, and it was their construction firm which carved it out of the surrounding woodland and turned it into row upon row of grey- and red-brick housing, each with its little arched doorway and its little grace-notes of oak-leaves and acorns to show that culture has reached an area as starved of the finer things of life as this.

Still, parts of it were once quite grand, and many of the richest London businessmen bought vast, ugly mansions here, designed in styles from fourteenth-century France to seventeenth-century Italy, in order to breathe its pure air in preference to that of North London. Norwood features occasionally in novels and short stories about London during the last quarter of the nineteenth-century, and Conan Doyle set part of a Sherlock Holmes story there. But the Simpsons didn't build these houses; they were too canny for that. They realized that the big profits lay in the long rows of middle-middle- to lower-middle-class housing, where the owners didn't complain or produce their own architects, and didn't have fancy ideas about the kind of houses they wanted.

By now the Simpsons are no longer grand; two World Wars and two serious slumps have made sure of that. But they still act as though they are, and my mother, whose best claim to fame is that her grandmother abandoned her husband and ran off with an American showman, is not the kind of person they think a Simpson should marry. Certainly not a handsome, amusing, promising Simpson like Roy.

His promise is taking some time to come to fruition, all the same. My father has left the Croydon factory behind – he didn't want to go back to it, of course, but anyway the demand for bullets, shells and bombs has dropped markedly and the place has closed down. Like hundreds of thousands of demobbed soldiers, my father cannot find a job. There are copies of the *Star*, the *Evening News* and the *Standard* everywhere in the flat, with his characteristically bold arrows and circles in the 'positions offered' columns; but at present the best he has been able to find is selling disgustingly made furniture in a shop owned by a monster of meanness and depravity called Drage – 'Do you know what that swine Drage asked me to do today?' – and then, as a sideline, selling football pools, something whose basic principle I can never quite grasp.

Now, though, the great freeze has closed Drage down (it will soon put him out of business for ever, something my father will both exult in and regret), and the icy pavements and power-cuts make it difficult to go from door to door persuading people they could earn the top prize of £75,000 by next Saturday night if they get the right combination of draws. For me, all these years later, the figure of £75,000 still has the ring of immeasurable wealth about it; whereas £100,000, though certainly a decent whack of money, now seems quite moderate.

And so my father, like so many others in Britain at the moment, is at a loose end: nowhere to go, nothing to do.

'Why don't we go and take Johnny to see my mother?'

Joyce is not enthusiastic. 'Besides, she doesn't like me.'

'Oh, you know how she is: she doesn't like anyone.'

'Exactly.'

'Oh, come on, Joyce.'

'No, darling. You go alone. She wants to see you. She won't want to see me.'

'But you know what'll happen – she'll pick a fight with me.'

'Better with you than me. After all, you are her son.'

After that the voices rise and fall for a while in mild irritation, self-defence, and eventual half-agreement. Finally a kind of result is reached. My father starts to wrap me up himself: something which, after the chilblain, he feels my mother cannot quite be trusted to do. I am going with him alone.

I remember little about the journey. For another year or so, most of my memories seem to be indoor ones. But I do remember walking along Marlow Road, watching the little house get closer and closer, with the ugly brown snow-banks piled up along the pavement. A slight sprinkling of snow overnight had covered them a little, and the frost which had followed had bonded the new to the old. The soot from the chimneys – people were burning anything they could lay their hands on, including even books – had already begun to settle on the new layer of snow.

I suppose I should nowadays find my grandmother's house rather charming: a decent-sized little suburban cottage, square and semi-detached, typical of the kind of place my great-great-grandfather George Simpson and his son Alfred have built all round here: streets and streets of them, all neat, all small, all eminently adapted to the dwellers' station in life. My grand-mother received her house a few years earlier, when her poverty became acute and her father's fierce attitude towards her relented a little. She has done nothing to the house since then. The ugly dark brown paint, applied by some of A. F. Simpson's workers several years before the war, is now peeling from the doorjambs and window sashes. A few scraggly bushes rise up cautiously out of the snow, as though they are peering at us, keeping watch to protect the house. A silver birch of some depressingly weeping variety grows in the middle of the next-door garden, giving my grandmother's house a little extra protection.

'Let's hope she's up,' my father says.

I can't quite understand this: we've been up for hours. But my grandmother, having had a difficult life, finds it hard in her early sixties to get out of bed on bad mornings: especially with the cold and snow.

He raps on the downstairs front window, where she has her bedroom. The heavy dark velour curtains are firmly closed.

'Eva! E! It's Roy. I've brought Johnny.'

There are noises from inside: reluctant, resentful noises. After a cold while, the chain rattles on the front door and an assembly of coats and scarves appears for an instant before vanishing.

'Oh God,' the bundle moans as the door closes.

We sit in the kitchen. It is very old-fashioned, with a scullery, a big square open sink with a single cold tap, and a copper for doing the washing. The only concession to modernity is the little lavatory off the scullery: A. F. Simpson & Co. always goes in for indoor plumbing; only the working-class have outdoor lavatories, and these are not intended to be working-class houses. In the kitchen itself is a big table with a heavy turkey table-cloth like a carpet, three leather armchairs which must have been new in 1920, and a variety of attractive but very old-fashioned landscapes on the wall: 1870s, like the house, I should say. There is also a triptych of paintings showing some fox-terriers approaching and eating their master's dinner, then running away. A huge domed radio like a cathedral dominates one wall. Through this, every major world event of the past ten years or more has passed, from the Abdication crisis to victory over the Japanese.

Nearby, under a cluttered mantelpiece, is a large gas fire. At present, with the gas pressure very low at best, and cut altogether at worst, it is fairly useless for heating the room. The fire is controlled by a meter, which takes pennies (for twenty minutes of gas) and shillings (for an entire morning, afternoon or evening session). My father has fixed the meter so that my grandmother can use the same penny and the same shilling each time, extracting them when they run out. He has some scheme, too, for dealing with the gasman when he comes round to clear the meter. Between them, my father and his sister, my aunt Daphne, pay for the gas fire. There was simply an open range here before that, and my grandmother's idea of lighting a fire was to pile up some paper, firewood and coal together haphazardly, pour a bowlful of petrol over it all, and throw a lighted match at it from the other side of the room.

My grandmother is an Edwardian and a bohemian: a genuine one. When she finally comes into the room, more or less dressed, though her grey hair is standing up wildly and there is a cigarette in the corner of her mouth, she looks pretty strange, even to me: I am used, through my mother and my half-sister Pat, who is starting to be a beauty, to women who dress well and look after themselves. Yet even I can see that Eva Simpson must once have been very beautiful: that upright carriage on a woman who is taller than average, those fine grey eyes, that clear skin, those full lips despite their sketchy smear of lipstick, all tell their story.

My view of my grandmother is heavily influenced by old black-and-white films: *Sunset Boulevard*, for instance. She even looks a little like Gloria Swanson. My grandmother could well have been an actress, with her looks and her clear diction; it was probably only the strait-laced low church principles of her family that stopped her going on the stage. Eva was always the wild, unhappy beauty of the family, and in the late 1890s they were lucky that she didn't break out and shame them all. In order to stop her, they broke her spirit.

'Hello, Johnny darling.'

She bends down and gives me a perfunctory, tobacco-flavoured kiss. I am nervous of her, because she is capable of flaring up into a savage passion over nothing; yet at the same time I can see that she treats me on a basis of equality with herself and everyone else. She never speaks to me in baby-talk, and she will ask my opinion and listen to it as carefully as if I were twenty instead of two.

'That really is most interesting,' she will say when I confide in her, and she seems always to mean it.

My grandmother is highly principled, and utterly fearless; there was a time when she would spend part of every day standing at the bottom of a steep hill in Norwood, attacking any carters and horse-riders who whipped their horses up the sharp gradient. Attacking them physically, that is, with a cane or an umbrella; and if the police were called, they would be far too scared of her scathing tongue to stop her.

Now she turns the hallowed radio on loudly, being slightly deaf. *Workers' Playtime*, a lightly patronizing programme of cheerful music for the lower classes in their factories, is on. My father has to shout over the music to make himself heard. They talk, of course, about the cold.

'And you know the power will go off again at two o'clock.'

'Oh God,' she groans, running her hand across her forehead and looking more like Gloria Swanson than ever. 'Is there nothing that can be done? Why doesn't the Government . . .?'

My father doesn't want her to start talking about the betrayal of Mr Churchill. He is still something of a radical, though he has long given up his support for Anarchism, and has now, like so many one-time firebrands, started to take the long road to the right. He voted Labour in 1945, but he has already come to dislike the Atlee government, which hasn't helped him get a decent job and keeps cutting his food ration. All the same, he doesn't want his mother to tell him how bad everything is.

'Let's have a cup of tea.'

Conditions are fairly bad in the food cupboard, and he has to clean it out before he can find the tiny amount of sugar she has left, and sort out the tea from other things.

'Dried milk all right?'

She nods. Dried milk is all she can afford on the tiny allowance her father, now ninety, still gives her.

So she sits in the big leather armchair, a Juno wrapped in shawls, one ancient blue furry slipper swinging from her toe, appreciating her cup of tea. I suddenly feel very sorry for her loneliness, and go and take her hand. She responds with immediate affection, as though she had expected I might do something of the kind. But she doesn't want me to stay.

'Go and sit down, darling, and let Auntie E drink her tea. Nice boy, that. Intelligent. He looks a little like—'

Apparently I remind her of some long-lost Simpson relative. She and my father may not have political views in common, but they are fellow-worshippers of Simpson blood. It will out, apparently: and it has outed in me.

There is still enough of the glamorous Edwardian in her to resist with passion the idea that I might call her 'Granny'. She is touchy about her age, and has gone through all her books, which are many, erasing the years she or others have written in them. Just as she tries to keep the world at bay by getting up at eleven each day, or later, so she tries to rub out time by getting rid of the evidence for it.

'This awful weather,' she starts again.

My father looks at her warily, as if he thinks she is going to tell him that Mr Churchill would never have allowed it to get this cold. Or perhaps, more sombrely, he is worried that the hunger, the darkness and the gloom will push her to suicide. Many years later he told me he had always expected she would kill herself one day, and was surprised that she hadn't.

Why all this anguish and unhappiness? It is quite plain, really. Eva Simpson was a child of a different era, a different world. Her parents had been solid, charming, educated mid-Victorians, fine-looking, confident, well-to-do – and utterly conventional. Their view of things was completely settled, and not even the two great wars against Germany which destroyed every last fragment of their world managed to penetrate my great-grandfather's quiet study, with the bound volumes of Dickens and Thackeray in its shelves, and the gentle vanished landscapes of East Anglia on the walls. I imagine that Alfred Simpson, generous though he was to the poor and the deserving, would have sung the familiar words from Mrs Alexander's hymn of 1848, written just a year or so before he was born, with much approval:

> The rich man in his castle,
> The poor man at his gate,
> God made them, high or lowly,
> And ordered their estate.

Alfred Simpson was a gentle if firm paterfamilias, who reread all the novels of Dickens every year, and finished them for the last time a few days before his death in 1949 at the age of ninety-one. Four years earlier I had been taken as a baby to see him: an imposing figure sitting in his garden wearing a panama hat and an alpaca jacket. He reached out his old, slender, blue-veined hand, which had in its time shaken the hand of a man who had voted for Pitt the Younger's war measures against Napoleon in the House of Commons, and took my pudgy little fist. My fingers opened out, as a baby's will, and I seized hold of his delicate old forefinger.

'Who can say, when they look at the beauty of a child's hand, that it has not been made by a loving God?' he asked; and though any atheist could knock forensic holes in that, it remains for me a fine and gentle sentiment, behind which may indeed lie some greater truth.

Alfred Simpson would much rather have been a teacher than the head of a building firm. He voluntarily made a patriotic gift to the Government of all the horses owned by the business for pulling carts, long before there was any question of their being requisitioned. A. F. Simpson and Co. might otherwise have grown to the dimensions of the other big nineteenth-century building firms, like Costain and McAlpine; Alfred's foreman was the Wates who started a large firm of his own. According to family legend, Wates vanished for good from the office one Friday night with the petty cash.

The company dwindled as a result of my great-grandfather's generosity in handing over his horses, and (my family always maintained) the dishonesty of his employees. More probably it went down the drain because it wasn't run properly. By the time my great-grandfather died, the business had declined to a little jobbing builder's with a single small workshop at the end of a side-road.

Alfred and Annie Simpson had five children: Eva, Harold, May, Elsie and Vera. Eva, tall, beautiful and wilful, was the only rebel among them. Born in December 1884, she had the superb profile that the American illustrator Charles Dana Gibson made fashionable throughout the Anglo-Saxon world as 'the Gibson Girl'. She learned to think for herself, insisting on going to the Congregational church where the members elected their minister and where God sometimes faded to a benevolent spirit, rather than an angry Creator. She wore corsetless, flowing gowns which showed her fine figure to its most natural advantage. She campaigned for women's rights, and was arrested and threatened with gaol; though when she smiled at the magistrate from the dock he let her off with a fine. In the tight, conventional little world of Norwood, she was remarkable and very shocking. And she was deeply in love.

Rex Bailey was a year older than Eva, and a distant cousin: a tall, fair-haired, cricket-playing man with plenty of ambition and intelligence, but no money. The Baileys were not on the Simpsons' level at all, and they did not mix with them socially. Rex, through ability and hard work, had hopes of becoming a solicitor; and the moment Eva met him she knew this was the man she would love for ever.

Her parents, predictably, were furious. They already knew who Eva was going to marry: not Rex Bailey, but the eldest son of the other big family in the Norwood area, Herbert Fidler, whose father was a publisher. It was a natural alliance, so obviously advantageous in all respects that Eva's blindness to its benefits angered her parents as much as it baffled them. Alfred Simpson spoke to Rex Bailey's father, and Rex Bailey sorrowfully packed his bags. After one last meeting with Eva, he left for a new life in Australia. For the next three decades, every Christmas Eve, her birthday, she would receive some little token from him, which she kept with great care and secrecy. Sometimes there would be a letter with the gift, telling her that, no matter how settled he was in his new life, and no matter how pleasant his growing family might be, he would never stop loving her or wishing that she had come away with him, as he had begged her to do.

But Eva Simpson, though she could brandish a banner for women's rights, knock a policeman's helmet off, and throw stones at the windows of Number 10, Downing Street, couldn't ignore the wishes of her parents. She duly married Herbert Fidler instead.

Herbert's father, John, was a publisher, and held a senior position with Cassell. Earlier in life he had travelled the country for them, and once, when he was on a trip to Dundee, he had been involved in the Tay Bridge disaster. His railway carriage balanced frighteningly on the broken bridge all night long, and John Fidler and the other passengers dared not move in case it too crashed down into the river below. It was always said in the family that his hair went white during the hours he waited to be rescued.

John was a lifelong Liberal, and stood several times for Parliament; though with such little success that even in the great Liberal landslide of 1906 he failed to win a seat. But he was certainly a man of some moral courage. He was strongly against the Boer War, and a little sliver of yellowing newspaper in my father's documents records the fact that he was arrested for his part in a demonstration in Whitehall. Since he was determinedly non-violent it seems that he was released without charge the following morning; though he spent the night in a police cell.

Herbert was born a few months after Eva, in June 1885, the youngest of three brothers; stocky, ugly, adventurous, tough, wayward and heavily spoiled by John Fidler's wife Julia. He played rugby for his school and his county, and was encouraged by his adoring mother to regard himself and his own interests and desires as the only thing that mattered in life. And from the moment he first saw Eva, at the age of fourteen, he decided that she was what he wanted.

Bertie pursued her in every conceivable way, determined to overcome the distaste she invariably showed for him. Once, in racing for the opponents' line with only a full-back in front of him, he stumbled and cut his kneecap badly on a rusty scythe which one of the groundsmen had accidentally left there. A doctor in the crowd sewed up the cut carelessly, leaving bits of grass and earth in the wound, and Bertie was forced to have his knee re-opened and cleaned an hour or so later. Then he walked three miles to the Simpsons' house to pick up Eva for a prearranged date. Characteristically, she changed her mind when he got there and refused to go out with him.

But the Simpsons and the Fidlers were determined that Eva and Bertie should marry; it would be the best match socially for both families. Slowly, Eva's strong, upright father and her compliant mother wore down her opposition. The marriage between Bertie and Eva took place with great pomp at the local Unitarian church – as advanced social and political thinkers, both the Simpsons and the Fidlers had given up the Church of England many years before – and it was the biggest social occasion of 1908 in Norwood. They were both twenty-three.

In the 1970s an elderly Simpson cousin described it to me. Her parents had slipped down the social scale (her father drank and couldn't keep a job) and so none of them was invited to the wedding. Nevertheless, she wanted to see something of it, and took a horse-drawn bus past the church at precisely the moment when she thought the bride and groom would emerge.

'You have never seen anyone look so miserable as poor Eva,' the cousin said. 'She could have been at a funeral.'

Still, the couple had a splendid and highly enjoyable honeymoon at Villefranche-sur-Mer, on the French Riviera, and spent some time in Paris on the way back. Bertie had already begun his career as a dress-designer, and wanted to see whether he could achieve anything in the capital of fashion. With his usual cockiness, he decided he could; and although Eva was scornful of his presumption she was quietly excited at the prospect. It seems to have been her beauty, rather than his designs, which attracted the buyers; but he held a show in Paris every spring for the next five years afterwards, and each time, with Eva as his model, it was a success.

Herbert and Eva lived a bohemian life in London, spending a good deal of time at the theatre and the music-hall. To please her, he became involved with the growing suffragette movement, and Herbert once joined a group of men who chained themselves to the railings outside the Houses of Parliament; he, too, was released from court without charge. They were on the fringes of various artistic groups; the Georgian poet John Drinkwater was a relative, and lived nearby; they would occasionally go to the parties he gave, for other poets like the quiet, reclusive Edward Thomas, the up-and-coming Walter de la Mare, Robert Frost. Their house in Norwood was impeccably furnished with the best of Arts and Crafts furniture. She kept a few last remnants of all this for the rest of her life: in her house in Marlow Road were a superb dining-table and chairs, and a mirror of beaten copper with a depiction of a Viking ship above the glass; these were all that was left after everything else had been sold off.

Bertie, although he was an accomplished artist and a good chess-player, did not fit into this kind of society as well as Eva. He remained an active sportsman, and as early as his twenties he showed ominous signs of becoming a heavy drinker. His loveless marriage with Eva cannot have helped. Yet it wasn't loveless on his side, just on hers. Bertie adored her for the rest of his life; I remember him forty years later, by now an almost absurdly fat old man, getting his best suit cleaned and brushing his bowler hat with great care before taking her out to lunch.

'Wish me luck!' he said roguishly as he pulled the front door to behind him.

But Eva had no time for him, before or later; though she was delighted with the elegant tea-dresses and evening gowns he designed for her in his showrooms in Margaret Street, off Upper Regent Street. One particular dress, in apricot silk with stitching *à la japonaise*, became well-known, and brought him in a good deal of money.

For some years after their marriage, Eva and Herbert remained childless. There was a good deal of quiet comment in the family about it, and the younger males nudged each other and recalled that Bertie was a dress-designer. In fact the couple had taken a deliberate decision not to have children until later. Both of them understood the value that Eva's looks represented to the business, and pregnancy would interfere badly with it. My grandmother, with her habitual disconcerting frankness, explained to my father that you could easily buy condoms in Paris; they were, she said, made from sheep's bladders. My father later passed all this on to me. It was clear that Bertie was an enthusiastic husband, but Eva was never at all interested in the physical act of love and did what she could to put him off.

By the end of 1913, though, they decided that they should give in to the family's expectations and have a child. Eva was approaching twenty-nine, and her career as a model was all but over. The following St Swithin's Day, 15 July, Roy was born in what was then the smart but raffish London suburb of Brixton: the kind of place where actors and artists lived. He was a wilful but affectionate and intelligent little boy, whose childhood was immediately blighted by the First World War. It broke out nineteen days after he was born.

The war changed everything for families like the Fidlers and the Simpsons. John Fidler, the pro-Boer, was instinctively against it, but felt obliged to keep loyally quiet about his doubts. In the Fidler household, though, there was none of the curious sense of relief which the start of the war brought to so many British people: the sense that the German Kaiser's antagonism to Britain had finally shown itself openly, and could now be dealt with. There was fury that German troops should have invaded the territory of a neutral country, Belgium, in order to attack France, and even instinctive pacifists like John Fidler felt strongly that Germany was very much in the wrong.

The Fidlers had a daughter, Florence, and two other sons: Stanley, the youngest, who did everything he could to keep out of the forces, less from principle than because he was seriously frightened of being hurt; and Jack, the eldest child, who had been commissioned in a rather smart regiment, the Royal Horse Artillery, in 1907, but was discharged as unfit after he became almost totally deaf. Eccentric to a degree, he had been part of the detachment which fired the twenty-one-gun salute in Green Park for Edward VII's birthday in 1909; and although he had gone the rounds beforehand ensuring that all his men had put wax-balls in their ears to protect against the noise, he forgot to put his own in.

Uncle Jack was seriously odd. He was once sued by an opera-singer with whom he had fallen deeply in love. Each night he would sit in the same box at Covent Garden with a bottle of champagne to drink and a large bunch of red roses to throw on to the stage at the end of the performance; until the unfortunate moment when, in his excitement, he threw the champagne-bottle at her instead of the roses, and her legs were cut by flying glass.

Bertie was a much more circumspect character, like his

brother Stanley. Yet unlike him he realized that it would be social disaster for a young man not join up. Somehow, perhaps because of his reasonable grasp of French, he managed to wangle himself a job in a particularly secret department in the War Office, and did some kind of undercover work in France and Belgium. The family used to say he was mentioned in dispatches for his courage. He himself told me, in a single burst of confidence when I was twelve years old, that he had made five journeys to the Continent by submarine during the war, and that each time he had to change from the uniform of the Royal Navy into civilian clothes while the submarine was under the North Sea.

Perhaps it was all true. He never spoke to my father about his wartime service, which was unusual for him: he was characteristically boastful and open about everything else, and particularly about his prowess as a rugby player and his cartooning ability. In fact I have only been able to trace one of his cartoons, published in the early 1920s: a rather unfunny drawing in *Punch*, which shows two ragged boys, one of whom is eating an apple.

'Can I 'ave the core?' the smaller boy asks.

'There ain't goin' to be no core,' the larger one answers.

Both Eva and my father, from bitter experience, were disinclined to believe anything Bertie said. But the point about his war service, whatever it might have been, was that he scarcely ever spoke about it; so maybe it was true after all. There certainly were agents who kept in contact with the relatively powerless resistance movements in Belgium and German-occupied Northern France. Could Bertie, who spoke French, whose bonhomie was famous and whose self-confidence never faltered, have been one of them?

The Ministry of Defence in London is unwilling to provide any details, even at this late stage, about secret service personnel, and there seems to be no record of his service anywhere else. Apart from what he told me himself, the only evidence I have for his wartime activities comes from a montage of sepia photographs of members of the family in uniform which someone must have put together in the latter stages of the war, and which I still have somewhere. My grandfather, looking rather smug in a white roll-neck sweater and a Royal Navy jacket, stares out arrogantly at the camera. Someone else (not my grandfather himself, who had unmistakably beautiful flowery handwriting) has inscribed firmly and confidently underneath 'Bertie – Secret Messenger'.

'OH, MY GOD,' my grandmother groans, rubbing her fine long hands in front of the feeble gas fire. 'It really is detestably cold. Will it ever be warm again?'

There is always something of the tragedienne about her, though her acting is for herself, not for an audience.

'Of course it will.' My father is inclined to be irritable with her today. 'You think there'll still be snow on the ground when it's summer?'

'Who can say, nowadays?'

She goes off into a little reverie, whistling tunelessly and almost soundlessly to herself.

'The first really freezing winter I remember was in 1915, when you were just a baby.'

I am immediately interested: stories about my father or any of my relatives as children have a particular fascination.

'That was when poor Harold—'

I don't really suppose all this happened as neatly and tidily as I remember it, because life so rarely does. But my father, in later years, always insisted that my grandmother had only just mentioned his name when there was a knock on the door.

'Oh God – supposing that's Harold now.'

She motions to my father to go and see, and he looks through the curtains of her bedroom, beside the front door. There is an angry rumble from the doorstep.

'I know you're there, Eva – I can see you peering out at me. For God's sake, let me in. It's Harold. I'm freezing cold out here, you know, and I've nowhere else to go, and no money. Let me in. You can't just leave me outside like this.'

I am terrified by the voice, and perhaps more by the concept: the cold, the hunger, the evident misery, the sense of anger and betrayal.

My father tiptoes back into the kitchen, but the voice follows him.

'Let me in. Go on. Please.'

'You mustn't, whatever you do.'

My grandmother seems almost as frightened as I feel, and my father does too. I realize afterwards that it isn't quite fear, though Harold could occasionally be violent, but embarrassment and an almost paralytic uncertainty about how to treat him. If I were older, I hope I would ask them what was so wrong about letting the man on the doorstep come into the relative warmth of the house when it was so cold outside; but I can't form the words, and probably can't even form the concepts behind them. I start to cry.

'Bloody kid – shut up!' my father whispers.

He is so rarely angry with me that I'm shocked even more. I sob more loudly.

'Oh Roy, how could you?'

There is another muffled shout from the doorstep, and I begin to wonder if something even more dreadful will happen: an attack on the door, an angry eruption into the house.

More sobbing.

But I don't suppose poor Uncle Harold could possibly have heard me. After a minute or so and some quieter muttering, the presence on the doorstep shuffles off. My father hurries to look through the curtains as he leaves, and I creep up behind him. I have the faintest image, no doubt much enhanced by imagination and by a later, dreadfully awkward meeting with him face to face, of a thin, tall, bent figure in black, shambling through the ugly snow.

It is hard to associate this figure with the tall, good-looking young man Harold Simpson had once been: the captain of his school, a good cricketer and rugby player, a first-rate public speaker. At the time the family imagined all sorts of glories and honours for him: he would go to Cambridge, enter politics, and rise inevitably to become Prime Minister by, perhaps, the late 1950s. In August 1914, to their pride and alarm, Harold insisted on volunteering for the East Surrey Regiment straight out of school, at the age of nineteen.

Once, in the kitchen of her little house in South Norwood, Eva told me how, with Roy as a baby at her breast, she and her sisters had sung the song of the day to Harold as he prepared to go, with their parents looking uncertainly on. Her eyes glistened with tears as she sang.

> Oh, we don't want to lose you,
> But we think you ought to go.
> For your King and your Country
> Both need you so.
> We shall love you, and kiss you,
> And with all our might and main,
> We will greet you, love you, kiss you
> When you come back again.

On 4 August 1914 Harold went down with the rest of a sizeable crowd to the town hall in South Norwood, which had been turned into a temporary recruiting station, signed the necessary papers, and was given his shilling. It was, he told his sisters later, the last time that any non-commissioned officer was polite to him, until he received a commission a few months later. He spent most of 1915 being trained, along with the rest of 'Kitchener's Army', and went to France with his regiment the following spring.

When they left, they went from Waterloo station. The area in front of the barriers was jammed with soldiers saying goodbye to their families. Harold's parents had stayed at home, but Eva had brought Roy, who was nearly two, and the other sisters had come with her. The Simpsons were not a demonstrative family, and in the surrounding noise they kissed Harold quietly, and held him, and pressed little gifts into his hand: a penknife, a pair of fingerless mittens, a small box of sugared almonds. His parents had already given him a silver Longines wristwatch, which he was wearing. He resisted the temptation to glance at it now.

No one cried. Harold grinned awkwardly at his sisters, and got into the carriage while his friends looked out enviously at the four attractive young women who stood on the platform, smiling. They were still smiling as the train slowly started moving out of the platform, taking him and his old life and his old hopes and his entire world with it.

> Brother Bertie went away
> To do his bit the other day,
> With a smile on his lips,
> And his lieutenant's pips
> Upon his shoulder bright and gay.
> As the train pulled out he said,
> 'Remember me to all the birds!'
> Then he wagged his paw,
> And went away to war,
> Calling out these pathetic words:
> 'Goodbye-ee! Don't cry-ee!
> There's a silver lining in the sky-ee!
> Don't cry, old thing! Cheerio! Chin-chin!
> Napoo! Toodle-oo! Goodbye-ee!'

Harold and his men and hundreds of thousands of volunteers like them were earmarked to take place in the Great Push of July 1916, which was expected to punch a major hole through the German line, thus at a stroke relieving pressure on the French at Verdun and rolling back the Germans. Their reserves would be drawn in, and they would be defeated as well. Then another Big Push would finish them off. The initial operation would probably last ten days, some of the senior officers thought. This year the war really would be over by Christmas.

A couple of weeks before the Big Push was due to start, on 1 July, the East Surreys, part of 18th Division, marched up through the town of Albert, and saw, as hundreds of thousands of soldiers had seen and were to see, the big gilded statue of the Virgin and Child on the town's basilica, knocked out of position by a shell early in the war. It was hanging over at a precarious angle, as though the Virgin was offering her Child to the men who were about to sacrifice their lives. The war would end, the soldiers used to say, when the statue finally fell. Extraordinarily, that was exactly what happened.

The countryside reminded many East Surreys of the countryside south of London: rolling downs, rich soil, fine woodlands. The front line they took over was in fact three lines of trenches, up to 200 yards apart. These men were in peak condition, physically and mentally, and Harold's letter the day before the battle – no one said these things might be the soldiers' last words to their families, but everyone knew it – was enthusiastic and slightly bantering; my grandmother showed it to me once. It was written in some haste, in pencil, in Harold's firm, characterful handwriting. He clearly believed, as everyone on the British side did, that they were about to take part in the culminating battle of the war.

This was the first time he and his men had seen shell-bursts and shooting at such close quarters; many of the 1914 volunteers had seen action the previous year, but Harold and his men were new to the front line. Everyone knew the dangers; as they marched up to the front line they passed the vast pits which the labour battalions were digging. The dead would soon be placed here. Yet human beings are capable of infinite self-delusion, and the great majority of Harold's men will have felt certain that they themselves would survive. It's how we're made.

They shuffled up through the narrow, winding trenches,

noting here and there that parts of dead horses and mules, and even occasionally dead German soldiers, had been used to shore up the trench-walls. The East Surreys took over positions that were intended for less than half their numbers. One by one, at different places along the trench, selected soldiers were allowed to get up on to the firestep and look through the officers' periscopes at the strange sight of the enemy trenches 100 yards away. Harold had his own periscope, bought at the Army and Navy Stores in Victoria Street on his last leave in May. Through it, he must have gazed in surprise and horror at the complete devastation of the area opposite: worse, if anything, than the destruction on their side of the line.

Yet there was no real sign of life: once in a while a German sniper would fire at the British trenches if he saw a target; but here along the line of the Somme things had been quiet. Everyone on both sides knew that something big was about to happen: it was quite impossible to hide the preparations for an attack as big as this. A kind of peace settled over the two front lines, and the rumble of artillery was a long way away. For now.

Seven days before the battle, the British began shelling the German lines: a devastating, hideously destructive, all-encompassing noise that was louder than anyone had ever heard before. It was intended to cut the German wire, blast the dugouts, and destroy every vestige of human life in the enemy's trenches. The British assumed this was happening: it was hard to conceive that anyone could live under the appalling onslaught of the guns. The East Surreys scarcely had to worry about shelling or counter-attacks from the German side. Yet the barrage looked and sounded worse than it really was. The guns were ordered to cover an area of German territory that was too deep, and the destruction was not as bad as the British believed.

Harold's men eventually managed to get their heads down by about ten-thirty on the night of 30 June. Everything was ready for the big attack the following morning. Harold and the other officers made certain the men were as comfortable as possible, though only the most stolid among them, or the most tired, were able to sleep. Then the officers too lay down and tried to rest. The greatest battle in history was just a few hours away.

At 6.15 the men were roused by their NCOs, who moved along the line, nudging them into full wakefulness. The shattering noise of the great guns, so continuous that it was usually impossible to recognize it as a series of individual explosions, grew even louder. In the last few minutes before the start of the battle the British artillery intensified their firing rate twofold. Exactly at 7.20 the ground shook with the shock-wave as a gigantic mine went off under the German lines at Hawthorn Redoubt in the northern sector. Eight minutes later, almost simultaneously, two other enormous explosions happened under other parts of the German line. The time by Harold's Longines watch was 7.28: two minutes to go.

He and the other officers were certain that no human beings could possibly survive the destructive power of the artillery on this scale. The East Surreys were expecting to walk across no man's land virtually unopposed; and after the unthinkable hammering of the past seven days, it seemed entirely likely.

At 7.30 o'clock precisely, the guns stopped. The silence was so sudden, so marked, that it seemed like noise of a different kind. Many men along the line noticed that in the minute which followed, larks rose up and began singing in the sky above the trenches. Then, seconds later, the whistles blew for the attack and men rose up in waves, hundreds of thousands of them, along a line many miles long, an inundation of dark brownish-khaki like a massive flood.

But then the machine-guns opposite opened up, raking the advancing wave and dropping hundreds, thousands of them as they queued up to get through the barbed wire, often left entirely uncut by the shelling. Not far from the East Surreys, the 740 men of the 1st Newfoundland Regiment had to mass at a single opening point; 684 of them were injured or dead within two or three appalling minutes. The 10th West Yorkshires losses were even greater: 710 killed or wounded.

The Germans had suffered terribly from the artillery barrage, but they hadn't been destroyed. Their trenches were dug far deeper and had been rendered much more permanent than those of the British, because Germany was fighting a defensive war while the British and French were on the offensive. The 7.30 attack had been too well signalled, and the minute which elapsed between the silence of the great guns and the launching of the infantry attack had given the dazed German defenders just enough time to run to the surface and man their machine-guns.

One or two of the wiser commanders had anticipated something of the sort. The 17th Highland Light Infantry (known as 'the Glasgow Commercials') were ordered up out of their trenches at 7.23 and waited only forty yards from the German front line before attacking exactly at 7.30. Nothing like this battle had ever been fought before, and every tactic was experimental. The British Army paid hugely for the experience it gained.

Lieutenant Harold Simpson clambered out of the trench with the rest of his men at 7.30. At this point the only danger was from British shells dropping short: surprisingly large numbers of them were defective in one way or another. As they reached the German wire the East Surreys saw for themselves the lack of destruction the shells had caused, and cursed the people who had made them. Still, there were enough gaps for a majority of the men to get through quickly.

The East Surreys threw themselves on to the German front line. Harold, athletic and fit, was one of the first to jump over the lip of the nearby trench, and he was in it and ready just as the first Germans came out of their deep dugouts. The

Feldwebel who led them up fired at Harold just as Harold fired at him, but his bullet went wide while Harold's was true to its aim. The *Feldwebel* was badly injured in the neck, and the soldiers bunched up behind him shouted that they surrendered. Harold left three of his men to disarm them and take them back to the British lines, while he ran on with the others along the line of the trench.

At first they had things almost entirely their own way, and in the first twenty minutes they had killed five Germans and captured thirty-six others. From everything they could see, the Big Push was succeeding. After a while they halted, and the East Surreys gathered together to work out their own strength and losses. Along the German line as a whole 104 of them had been killed, including several lieutenants, all the captains, one major and the adjutant who, unusually, had come with them. Harold was one of the few junior officers who had survived.

The colonel of the East Surreys, who had also insisted on joining in the attack, looked at the assembled men and told Harold that he should take over as Captain. It was a moment the Simpson family was to be immensely proud of; for decades afterwards, they would always say, 'Harold was promoted on the field of battle.'

The inevitable German counter-attack came about half an hour later: a great angry wave of men in field-grey uniforms rising out of the ground and charging them with bayonets. Seventy or eighty were killed in the new no man's land; at least twenty got into the trench, and a dreadful hand-to-hand battle began, in which the weapons were trenching tools and knives, and you felt the rank breath of your enemy in the face as you tried to stab him and avoid his blows.

These were the battles the men feared the most; and they ended with men's eyes being put out and their brains splattered all over the already slippery duckboards at the bottom of the trench. 'I'm afeard there are few die well, that die in a battle,' says the private soldier Michael Williams in *Henry V*; and as ever Shakespeare was right.

Harold and his men defended their trench against three more attacks; and when the Germans finally faltered it was Harold who shouted the order to 'jump the bags' and attack the second German line. It took them very little time and effort; here at least the Germans were beaten. Harold wandered around the deep network of shelters amazed by their solidity and their air of permanence. Some of the dug-outs were fifty feet deep, with pictures on the walls and pleasant, looted furniture. One had a wine cellar, and Harold had to appoint two of his most reliable men to guard it.

They began the battle for the third line of trenches. Here, the Germans' morale seemed weaker, and a couple of bayonet charges captured it at the cost of only ten East Surreys. By now Harold was some way ahead of the rest of the regiment on either side of him, and he sent a messenger back to the colonel to report his progress.

Maybe the messenger was killed or injured; maybe he merely got lost in the vast complexity of the two front lines and the continuing battle. The colonel did not hear that Harold had captured the German third line; and when he called in artillery support to soften up the third line he did not make any exceptions. Harold and his group of twenty men had only been in the third line for a few minutes when the first British shells started to land on it. Most of them were killed.

When the rest of the East Surreys took the line as a whole, they found Harold lying on his side at the bottom of the trench, and thought he was dead too. He had a gaping wound in the side of the head and was unconscious. Then someone heard him sigh, and called for a stretcher party. It took the best part of an hour for the two stretcher-bearers to get him over the old no man's land, which was still being hit occasionally by shells, to a field hospital behind the lines. There, one of the surgeons recognized him, and put more effort than he might at saving the life of someone so badly hurt.

Harold lay in the over-heated recovery tent for two weeks after his rudimentary operation. Sometimes he was feverish, and thought himself back in London or at school; at other times he was entirely rational, and able to think about his life. It was clear to him that the only worthwhile existence was back here in France with his fellow-officers and his men. Once the quartermaster stopped off on a mission to a supply dump behind the lines, and told him that the men missed him. Harold took the decision to get fit as quickly as possible and return.

The family were immensely proud of him when he finally came back on home leave. He couldn't walk for some months, and they squabbled about which of them would push his wheelchair around. When he became a little better he took a succession of local girls up to town, to the theatre and to supper at the Café Royal. Harold was a hero, and received a hero's welcome; yet Eva said he always looked uncomfortable and out of place, and seemed incapable of sustaining a proper conversation.

He had taken to smoking a pipe in the trenches, and although his parents disliked tobacco they did not feel they should stop him smoking, even in the house. But the use of the pipe became a defence for him: he would break off for minutes on end, tamping down the tobacco and making several efforts to light it. Afterwards, his sisters realized he had never once spoken to them about conditions in the trenches, and had only referred to the fighting on the Somme in the sketchiest of ways.

He read the newspapers with a particular voracity each morning, but would soon throw them aside in anger when it was clear they could tell him nothing about what was really going on at the front. There was still no official indication that on 1 July, the first day on the Somme, the British Army had suffered the worst losses in its entire history: 60,000 men killed or injured.

As the battle slowly began to peter out, Harold's mood became darker. He no longer invited girls to go with him to the theatre, and they were less enthusiastic about accepting anyway; it might be fun to be seen with a genuine hero, but the long silences and the gruff, sometimes hurtful rejoinders across the dinner-table weren't fun at all. The girls would look round them at the other couples, the men in khaki or regimental evening-dress, holding the girls' hands and looking meaningfully into their eyes, and reflect that being with Harold was nothing like as nice as that.

By the spring of 1917 Harold was able to take proper exercise, and told his parents he was going to report for a fitness examination. Once again, they felt they couldn't protest. Alfred Simpson had sacrificed the future of his company to the national interest; now, it seemed, he would have to sacrifice his only son as well. As he left the house that morning, Annie brushed his greatcoat with its captain's pips and started hesitantly to say something.

'Don't, mother. Don't be stupid.'

Harold stormed out, slamming the door behind him. He had never spoken to either of his parents like that before.

He was back in France by the beginning of June 1917, but it wasn't the same. For a start, he had been transferred to another regiment: the Royal West Surreys. He didn't know any of the officers there, and they didn't know him. He was morose and silent, and seemed to most of the men like a relic from some distant age. The life-expectancy of a British subaltern on the Western Front was two weeks; a man who had served here twelve months earlier seemed to them like the Ancient of Days.

Harold shared a damp, inadequate dugout with another captain, who had been a commercial traveller from Preston before the war. They did not become friends. They had one record, my grandmother told me, and played it endlessly.

> At seventeen, he falls in love quite madly
> > With eyes of tender blue.
> At twenty-four, he gets it rather badly,
> > With eyes of a different hue.
> At thirty-five, you'll find him flirting sadly
> > With two or three or more.
> When he fancies he is past love,
> > It is then he meets his last love,
> And he loves her as he's never loved before.

Not many of the officers Harold was serving with survived to twenty-four, let alone thirty-five. He himself was twenty-two.

He had once been the gentlest of men – it was the one quality which people felt might hold him back, particularly if he went into politics – but after his injury his character changed completely. In some trivial argument, possibly about the record, Harold's temper flared up, and he called the other man a bounder and a cad. The colonel reprimanded Harold sharply.

Already there was talk of the next Big Push, and on 7 June 1917 it came: the Third Battle of Ypres, which would later be known as Passchendaele. Now the tactics were different: the British had perfected the notion of the creeping barrage, which dropped a rain of shells on the German positions just a short way in front of the advancing British troops. There was to be no deadly pause before they climbed out of their trenches, no terrible butcher's bill as they lined up to get through their own wire.

What went wrong now was the weather. Many of the early objectives were achieved, but the men were quickly bogged down in completely inadequate positions and found it hard to resist the ferocity of the German counter-attacks. Like the Battle of the Somme, Passchendaele petered out in the autumn. Virtually no territory had been gained. There were growing mutiny in the French and Russian ranks, though not among the British; but the officers were dubious whether they could keep their men going indefinitely.

During the 1920s it became habitual to regard the First World War as not only a grotesque waste of human life, which it was, but also as a prime example of the stupidity of the generals, and particularly the British generals. It is only now, almost a century later, that the opinion of military historians has shifted. The generals, it seems, were quick in learning the lessons of the terrible conditions of the Western Front: the supremacy of the defence, with its machine-guns and barbed wire, and the appalling difficulties of dislodging the German troops from their strong positions. Yet in the summer and autumn of 1918 victory came, precisely along the lines the British and French had always planned.

A general like Sir Herbert Plumer, a distinctly unmilitary figure with a drooping moustache, a slouch and a pot belly, was immensely careful with the lives of his soldiers, and found the usual British obsession with mindless discipline irritating. Once, before a major offensive, a meeting of senior staff officers was called to discuss the habitual failure of Canadian soldiers to salute their officers. After forty minutes, Plumer couldn't keep quiet any longer.

'Well, gentlemen, I don't think there's much wrong with the saluting of the Canadians. Nearly every Canadian *I* salute returns it.'

And he brought the meeting to an end.

None of this mattered much to Harold. On the second day of the battle he had been hit on the forehead by a piece of shrapnel, and had again been fortunate to survive. He was unconscious for several days, and woke to find himself in another field hospital. He was blind. The doctors assured him he would soon regain his sight, and by the end of the first week he did.

But it wasn't the joyful experience he had expected. His face was a mess; his eyes stared out balefully at the world from the damage around them. At first he tried to persuade the medical board to allow him to go back to front-line duties, but they told him the concussion he had suffered to the brain meant that he would never be able to fight again. Harold broke down in tears in front of them, and they hurried him back to convalescence.

His parents and sisters tried to hide their shock when he arrived home; no one had warned them about his disfigurement. They found it impossible to persuade him to leave the house, and perhaps they were a little grateful that he didn't; people were used to the sight of injured men, but there was something quite disturbing about Harold: a savagery, a despair, which made you want to avert your eyes immediately.

And so Harold's sisters and former girlfriends no longer wanted to hold him, love him and kiss him when he came back to them. Within a year the war was over, and everyone wanted to move on, to think about the new post-war world. Harold was a reminder to everyone of how bad things had been. One of his former girlfriends, Chrissie, stayed with him and married him; but she was the one whom Harold's parents had liked the least, and she was a feckless girl, unable to find work in the new, freer conditions after the war.

Harold himself suffered terrible headaches, which made his temper ferocious. He couldn't abide anyone's company, not even Chrissie's, when he was in the grip of one. Employers who were at first prepared to overlook Harold's dreadful appearance soon felt they had to get rid of him. Medicine seemed to provide no relief; only drinking helped. Harold drank every penny his parents gave him, and he took to dropping in on his sisters to ask for money. When they refused, and even sometimes when they didn't, Harold would roar insults at them; his facility with words, his beautiful speaking voice, now served to alienate even the last few who remained loyal to him.

After years of sticking by him, even Chrissie faded away, and by the end of the Second World War Harold lived somewhere alone: he would never tell anyone where. I myself met him only once, at the end of the 1940s, obeying as best I could my father's instruction not to look at his face.

'The boy won't look at me,' Harold snorted.

'Of course he won't; why should he?' asked Eva, as sharp-tongued as he was.

Some years later, perhaps in the late fifties, a policeman came to call on Eva. He told her that Harold had died in the night, lying on a bench at Waterloo station which had apparently been his only home for some time. The policeman had brought his effects round to her: an old, charred pipe, a wallet containing a little shag tobacco, a box of Swan Vestas matches, three-quarters empty, an envelope containing a curt letter from Eva, with her address on it, and all the money he had in his pockets: twopence-ha'penny.

'I could see he was a gentleman, though, mum,' said the policeman, and he handed her a separate brown envelope. Inside she found a silver Longines wristwatch. Somehow, it had stayed with him through everything: safe from the stretcher-bearers and the hospital staff, safe from the pawnbrokers when his fortunes collapsed, safe even from the other vagrants who lived rough, as he did, at Waterloo station. It meant something to him: his last reserve of self-respect, perhaps, which was worth more even at the hungriest and worst times than the hot meal and the bed for the night which the watch would have bought him.

I've still got Harold's wristwatch, and I occasionally wear it on big occasions: a beautiful object, engraved on the back with an impressive, aristocratic crest which the Simpsons certainly weren't entitled to.

Unlike Harold, the watch is unmarked in spite of everything it went through. Did he ever think, as he lay on his bench at the end of his life, dirty and weak, of the strong, confident young Harold Simpson who had worn it and said goodbye to his sisters at the same station more than forty years before?

Harold gave everything for King and Country: his decency, his mental balance, his self-respect. If he had only given his life, it would have been a great deal easier for everyone.

And particularly himself.

ON WEDNESDAY, 12 FEBRUARY there was nowhere throughout the day or night in Britain where the outside temperature was above freezing. A system of fuel control was in force throughout the entire country, and an emergency Whitehall committee described the national situation as 'dangerously critical'. Only six days' supply of coal remained. The domestic use of electricity was forbidden for five hours under Defence Regulations – which, as a way of preventing virtually anything the Government did not like, were a hangover from the war years. All street lighting was switched off, except at road junctions where there was heavy pedestrian traffic after dark, and streets where essential road-works were being carried out. The only objects of any kind which could be illuminated by electricity were traffic signs and bollards.

People found themselves turning back to the old ways, as they had rarely if ever been obliged to do even when the Blitz was at its height. At railway stations, in offices and houses, old-fashioned oil lamps provided the most reliable light, while in the north of Scotland, Northumbria and Yorkshire, horse-drawn carts proved better than trucks and cars at getting food supplies through to villages and outlying houses which had been cut off. Many of those railway services which had not been cut off by the snow and ice were cancelled to allow coal trains through. 'The production and movement of coal,' said a Government announcement, read out over the BBC that day, 'have absolute priority.'

Dog-racing, the printing and publication of magazines, and

the BBC's own television service and its Third Programme on radio were all prohibited during the crisis, in order to conserve power. The last of these measures, in particular, brought a howl of well-expressed rage from the country's intellectuals. The Third Programme provided, someone wrote to *The Times*, 'a dash of spice in the philistine hot-pot. To sacrifice it makes cold comfort colder still.' One of London's leading breweries, Fuller's, warned that the capital's supply of bottled beer would be exhausted within ten days. People were no longer as willing to pull together as they had been during the war. A senior official in Manchester said the way people there had disregarded the call for voluntary cuts was 'disgraceful'. In Luton, loud-speaker cars toured the streets calling on people to 'play the game'.

Yet slowly, as February wore on, the emergency measures had their effect, and the weather became a little less grim. By Tuesday 18 February the crisis ceased to be the lead story in the newspapers, and accounts of the King and Queen and Princesses Elizabeth and Margaret sailing off to the warmth of the South African winter took its place. No one, in those pre-tabloid days, suggested they were fleeing the winter; though several writers reminded their readers that the trip had been arranged months earlier, long before there was any suggestion that the weather in Britain might prove to be particularly bad.

The following Tuesday, 18 February, was the seventeenth successive day without sunshine anywhere in the country, the longest sunless period since 1880. There were more snowfalls over the next weekend, but by Wednesday 26 February the extreme crisis was over. Nevertheless everyone realized that the rationing of fuel was now certain.

Even during the worst of the freeze, criminals remained active. On this day, Wednesday 12 February, a leather suitcase containing £500 worth of US war bonds was stolen at King's Cross station, while a gang broke into the home of Mr Leonard Chandler in St John's Wood and got away with furs worth

£1,600: a considerable amount of money. A prisoner called Eric Davis, who had been serving five years' penal servitude for burglary, escaped from Wandsworth prison.

At the same time a one-man crime wave was finally brought to an end when Fred Westbrook, a deserter from the South Wales Borderers, was found guilty of manslaughter at the Old Bailey and given a heavy gaol sentence. He had killed Aloysius Abbott, an aircraftman from Jamaica, in New Cavendish Street, London W1, and fired at two policemen before he was caught. He pleaded guilty, and asked for forty-four other offences, mostly of breaking and entering, to be taken into consideration. Westbrook was only twenty-seven, but he already had fourteen previous convictions. Once, when he was stopped by two policemen on Putney Bridge in south-west London, he had jumped down on to the foreshore of the River Thames, twenty feet below, and got away.

A sinister little pamphlet called 'Pre-frontal Leucotomy in 1000 Cases' was published that day by the Stationery Office at a price of sixpence. Based on the theory that '[s]omething must be done in some mental illnesses to break the connexion between the patient's thoughts and his emotions', it examined the results in a wide variety of patients. When successful, it said, cutting the physical links between one part of the brain and the rest had enabled a third of the people whose cases were recorded to resume their everyday activities 'without that emotional tension and preoccupation with hallucinations and phantasies which has hitherto handicapped them'. Another third had shown signs of improvement, though not to the point where they could be discharged from hospital. And the rest? No details were available, except that 3 per cent of them had died. It showed, said one medical writer, that the operation was well worth while in carefully selected cases. Today, pre-frontal leucotomy would be regarded by many surgeons and psychiatrists as a quite unnecessary form of torture.

Several newspapers carried articles about Mrs Agnes Linklater of Beostar, Bressay, in the Shetland Islands, who was celebrating her 101st birthday. She had never, it was reported, seen a tram or a train, or been in a cinema or theatre.

The travel agents, even in the grey, limited days of 1947, were offering ways to escape the cold of Britain. The more expensive newspapers carried advertisements inviting people to follow the example of the Royal Family:

FLY TO SOUTH AFRICA

In Our Luxurious 32-seater Bristol Wayfarer Aircraft
(Cocktail bar. Smoking allowed.
Light refreshments served in the air.)

Aircraft is manned by a crew of six including Air Hostess.
NO NIGHT FLYING.
The journey is undertaken in easy stages.

Safety And Comfort Are Our Only Considerations.
Bookings can now be accepted for March and onward.

Skytravel Ltd, Liverpool Airport, Liverpool 19.
Tel. GARston 4031 (10 lines)
Telegrams, 'Skytrav', Liverpool.

The cost was £250: four months' wages for a shop assistant, but even after that terrible winter had finally relented, thoroughly worth it.

Friday 2 April 1948

Sun rises, 6.35 a.m.; sets, 7.34 p.m.
Lighting-up time: 8.04 p.m.
Maximum temperature: 53°F; minimum: 41°F.
Rainfall: 0.15 inches.
Sunshine: 2.6 hours.
Strong westerly wind, decreasing slowly. Bright
*   intervals, with occasional local showers.*
*   Fine in early morning and late evening.*
*   Ground frost in exposed areas.*

'AND NOW, LADIES AND GENTLEMEN, to demonstrate to you how delicious and wholesome the residue is, I'm going to get my little boy to come up and drink it.'

He speaks as we as ever, and he is frank, self-deprecating and charming. Even I can see that. I'm proud that so many people should listen to my father with respect and attention. It's just that, of all the many things I hate about the Ideal Home Exhibition, the thing I hate most is drinking the Residue.

It is worse than being petted by people I have never met, worse than being patronized by the commissionaires at the gate as I come in each morning ('Hello, look who's here! What are you demonstrating, then, young fellow-me-lad? Baby food?'), even worse than having to carry a note to other stands in order to get free samples for my father and his colleagues: 'Please give Bearer two cups of coffee in the accompanying mugs, one black and the other with milk and two sugars . . .' I do not like being a Bearer. It makes me feel as though I am some kind of pack animal. Or a bear, perhaps, with something strapped to its hairy back.

'I don't want to be a Bearer.'

'Well, you are one if you're going to bring Auntie Norah and me a cup of coffee. Look, dear old Johnny-boy, it's just the word everybody uses. No one will take any notice.'

My father, it seems to me, has no sense of the ridiculous, and no understanding of the embarrassment all this will cause me. Also no very great grip on the way things usually turn out.

'Oh, so you're a Bearer, are you? Well, Bearer, here you are – two coffees, and make sure you don't spill them. Bearer, indeed; whatever next? I don't know.'

That was half an hour ago. Now it is time for me to take the terrifying walk up from the back of the stand, through the women and the occasional man sitting in folding chairs on either side of a narrow gangway, and climb on to the stage to drink the Residue. And that is much, much worse even than being a Bearer.

'Isn't he sweet?' twitter the older women.

The first time I did this, my face was fiery red, my tongue seemed far too large, and I found it difficult to get the Residue down at all. My father was cross, but I felt we were both lucky I hadn't gagged on it. Over the days the exhibition has been going on, though, I have gradually and reluctantly got used to the humiliation of being put through my paces like a performing bear. Like a Bearer. I may actually have come to like the attention, just a little, but I find this hard to acknowledge. And now, after all these years, when I have addressed entire stadium-loads of people, and appeared hundreds of times on live television in front of hundreds of millions, I still feel like an awkward child making his way through the audience, with the ordeal of acting and speaking just ahead of me.

Of course my father finds it hard to understand my reluctance to perform, because he patently enjoys it so much. No one is as persuasive and amusing as my father when he is in front of an audience; I understand this entirely, because I have myself been his audience so often, and can see (at least, I think I can) that he gives just as good a performance when we are alone and he is telling me a story as he does when he is trying to persuade an audience of grey-faced, grey-haired people that they should buy one of his Easiwork pressure-cookers.

Even at my age, I can see that Easiwork has not made my father's work easy. This pressure-cooker is a big thing made of gunmetal, with curious high arching clamps and an outsized whistle on the top of it. My father thinks it looks like some sort of explosive device, a naval mine perhaps, and he and his friends have endless running jokes about people coming to the stand and complaining that they knew someone whose arm or leg has been blown off by a pressure-cooker. As a serious-minded child, I am inclined to believe these stories, and I always feel uneasy when the Easiwork cooker is on the boil, the steam begins to issue out of it and the whistle sounds. Suppose my leg is blown off, like the others?

My father's big competition in the pressure-cooker line, the Prestige Commodore, is on show at a stand not far from ours. The Prestige Commodore looks a lot less explosive and a lot more normal than the Easiwork version: essentially it is just a saucepan with a pressure-gauge. Prestige and the people who make it and demonstrate it are our deadly enemies, and I cannot understand it when my father goes across and has an uproariously jolly time with the people on the Prestige stand. I have a profound sense of hostility to them and of loyalty to Easiwork, and I sometimes go and stare balefully at their horrible smooth product, so much more stylish and saleable than our own, just to put them off. The Easiwork pressure-cooker, by comparison, is the underdog, ugly and awkward, and I have adopted it as I might have adopted some ugly, stupid kid in my class; except that at this stage I don't go to school.

Decades later, when I was reporting from Afghanistan before the fall of Kabul in November 2001, I wandered past some shops in the town of Charikar, where I had based myself. Looking idly inside one of them, I saw a pressure-cooker on a shelf at the back. It had been made in Iran, but it was a perfect imitation of the old Easiwork model which my father had once demonstrated: right down to the whistle and the small containers for Brussels sprouts and cabbage, which made the Residue what it was. I bought it on the spot, of course, as an act of filial piety. But remembering all those tales from more than fifty years before, I have never attempted to use it. It stands on a shelf in my office, and if anyone asks me what it is, I echo my father's joke from our days at Olympia: 'The design is based on a naval mine, only it comes with rather more explosive power.'

I have never seen so many seething crowds or so many fascinating objects as there are on display at Olympia. When my father is trying to sell pressure-cookers I like to wander round, squeezing through the gaps in people's legs and lodging myself in places outside the current of people where I can hang around and watch what is going on. It never seems to occur to anyone, not even the protective 'aunties' who are working with my father, that it might not be safe for me to be on my own like this. There are as many abductions and murders of children in 1948, proportionately, as there will be sixty years later, but we are less aware of them in these immediate post-war years, and much less convinced that they represent a serious threat: perhaps because the newspapers do not dwell on the terrible details.

And so I stroll around, avoiding attention, and gazing at the extraordinary things on display: machines that can eviscerate oranges or turn carrots into liquid; entire sitting-rooms of furniture on which I can sit as long as I don't stay too long; whole gardens with little fountains and real goldfish swimming in the ponds, genuine flowers growing in the flowerbeds (though not wallflowers, disappointingly) and lawns made of real grass which have to be clipped every morning with a set of shears, the cuttings being swept away just as my father sweeps away the bits after he has cut my hair. In 2003 I bought a house in London with a garden like this; it has a sixteenth-century brick wall and a little pond, and lights to show up the place at night-time, and although I bought the whole thing, house and all, partly for the brick wall, another reason was that the garden reminded me of the ones I used to wander round at the Ideal Home Exhibition.

There are several stands which purport to show the Kitchen

of the Future; and a women's magazine has one which tells you How to Make the Best of Things: shiny stoves with large gas or electricity rings, kettles (but not electric ones), outsized blenders, refrigerators big enough to climb into, a primitive washing-machine. It isn't the kitchen of the future at all, of course; only a few years later kitchens had far outdistanced these, which were really just the Kitchens of the Present.

Another stand, run by a women's magazine, concentrates on making the best of things. It tells you, for instance, how to make cauliflower soup for eight people.

> One large cauliflower
> One teaspoon margarine
> One medium onion
> Two tablespoons semolina
> Two quarts reconstituted milk
> One heaped teaspoon nutmeg
> Evaporated milk
> Salt, pepper.

The result – try it, if you want the authentic taste of the late 40s – is quite nasty. You are left, not with the taste of cauliflower, not even with the Residue, but with the ersatz flavour of artificial ingredients.

As I wander through the thicket of legs and shopping bags and walking-sticks, carrying a cup of coffee in each hand, I feel perfectly safe. Everyone assumes, if they notice me at all, that I must be with someone else, so no one takes any notice of me. Then I hear a pleasant, well-modulated voice somewhere above my head.

'Hello – it's Johnny, isn't it?'

A particularly tall woman is looking down at me: attractive, dark-eyed, with brilliant red lipstick. I am on a level with her nylons, but recognize her even so. Her name is Penny. Penny Dane.

I nod warily.

'So what are you doing in the furniture section? Taking a look around?'

I nod again.

'Well, I'm sure you aren't lost, but even so you might want to bring your cups of coffee back to Easiwork with me.'

A long, warm, white hand descends on my shoulder. Rather pleasant.

'I can't bear the Ideal Home; do you like it?'

I have never really stopped to consider what I think about it; it's just there, a fact of existence like autumn or unemployment. But now I feel called upon to commit myself.

'No, I don't like it either.'

Even this early in life, I want to be agreeable if possible, and I realize suddenly that it is perfectly true that I don't like it. In fact, I like it as little as I like the Residue.

'Too many people, I always say, with too little money and too few coupons.'

She says the word properly, not like Sir Stafford Cripps.

'Listen, it's almost time for my demonstration. It only takes three minutes – won't you watch me?'

Penny, tall, stately and rather cold, is an actress who often comes to visit the Easiwork stand. She works for a household gadget company nearby, where she pretends to be a beautiful automaton. It's hard for me to think, as I write this, that Penny Dane must now be in her eighties, if indeed she is still alive: in my memory she is eternally young, as though she really is an automaton who cannot age.

She puts down a new and streamlined make of steam iron.

'Unobtainable at present, ladies, for love or coupons!'

She turns stiffly, as though requiring oil.

'But soon the hour will come!'

She points mechanically at an electric clock. Then she picks up a shiny electric kettle, and pours out some imaginary water in order to make an imaginary cup of tea. Her movements are exquisitely timed and charmingly elegant, as she raises the empty cup to her lips, with just a faint hint of metallic awkwardness to convince you that she is indeed nothing more than a beautiful machine.

And then, as I watch, an unruly boy of around ten moves through to the front of the crowd. His shirt-tail is hanging out of his shorts and his thick grey socks have fallen loosely over his ankles. He has bruises and scabs on his shins. Slowly, deliberately, he rolls up a small piece of paper, chews it to make it malleable, and flicks it with his middle finger at the back of Penny's gorgeous swanlike neck.

The result, from his point of view and even from mine, is superbly satisfying. The elegant, beautiful robot slams the cup down, and leaps across the stage at the boy, shouting, 'You bloody little swine! I'll get you!' There is nothing mechanical or stiff about her movements now.

And of course she does get him, right in front of the stand where two slightly older women are demonstrating a primitive electric carving-knife with which, if you have the necessary strength and enough time at your disposal, you can slice a joint as long as the meat isn't too tough. Gripping his shoulder, Penny gives the boy a tremendous slap round the side of the head, which makes his ear go scarlet instantly. Then she stalks back to the ironing-board and the kettle, but not to work. She raises her handsome eyes and stares challengingly at the audience.

'I can't do anything more here, so I don't know what you're all staring at.'

And she picks up her elegant jacket and storms off home, forgetting me entirely.

So now I am left to make my way over to the Easiwork stand, still holding the coffees. The audience are already in their seats, and the time has almost arrived for the next pressure-cooker demonstration. My father is starting to fret. No time to drink the coffees, and anyway they're cold. I hang my head, and he clucks his teeth.

'Oh well, never mind. I suppose I shouldn't have asked you to go.'

'Yes, please ask me,' I say humbly. 'I don't mind going, and next time I'll be back quicker.'

'So you tell me.'

Placating my father always takes a long time, I find, and requires long minutes of obedience and meekness before he will consent to be mollified. This time, though, there is a deadline.

'Ah well, never mind, old chap, we'd better get on with the demonstration. They're all waiting.'

He runs his fingers through his hair, straightens his tie, and walks down to the dais.

The demonstration takes ten minutes ('Can't give them more than that, their little brains can't take it'). He puts the ready-cut pieces of carrot and cabbage and Brussels sprouts into their respective containers and fills the pressure cooker with them, as though they are the explosive charge. He talks the audience through the entire process with jokes and great charm, and at the end of it the steam inside the bomb-like object builds up and the whistle on top of the pressure-cooker blows loudly.

'Good Lord!' says my father, with heavily feigned surprise, 'can it really be ready so quickly?' And then, to forestall any hint of scepticism in the audience, 'Well, actually I know it is, but I always say that, just for effect.'

The great strength of my father's credibility is that he convinces himself while he is talking that everything he says is absolutely correct. When he sells his pressure-cookers to his audience, therefore, he is also selling them to himself. Just as he used to know perfectly well that the football pool he was selling was less generous than others, so now he knows perfectly well at some level of consciousness that his pressure-cookers are heavier, smaller in capacity and perhaps even a little more dangerous than others. Yet at the critical moment, when the potential buyer wavers and falls under the spell of the hypnotic, confident patter, I am certain that my father genuinely believes the cooker he is selling is the best there is.

In the same way I have seen a famous journalist telling an interesting and delightful story about a place which I happened to know she had never been to and an incident which she could not have witnessed. Yet you couldn't call what she said a lie. If you had had a Bible handy, she would have sworn on it that every word she said was true; and she would have been absolutely certain, for the brief time she was under the influence of her own convincing rhetoric, that everything had happened precisely as she said.

'You know, ladies and gentlemen, this machine is so reliable and fast that I have no need of looking at my watch. And of course the vegetables will be ready for eating the moment I take them out of the cooker.'

He starts to take them out, steaming hot, and the air around the stand is filled with the throat-catching savour of cabbage. He samples each container – to make sure, he tells his friends afterwards, that the vegetables really are done. 'Sometimes the bloody things are still raw, so I can't dish them out.'

Not this time. I know, because he invites people from the audience to come up and sample them.

'You see? Full of freshness and their own natural goodness. Of course, I'd like to put a nice juicy piece of steak in there as well, but I used up my ration days ago, and the butcher would want to know why I need twelve pounds of steak a week.'

More laughter. Then the moment I have come to loathe.

'But there's one thing more, ladies and gentlemen. After we've taken out all the vegetables, there is still something left. And to show you how good that is, I'm going to ask . . .'

But I am already on my way up to the front, squeezing between the large ladies on either side of the gangway. It is time for his little boy to try the Residue.

'His name's Johnny.'

A little maternal sigh rises from the audience.

'Here you are, Johnny.'

I am standing on the stage, looking up at him as he smiles out at the audience, oozing charm. He hands me a small, thick glass of a lightish, translucent, greeny-yellow liquid.

'Be careful,' he mutters. 'Don't for God's sake drop it.'

The Residue is warm to the touch, and smells pretty strong; sometimes I wonder if it isn't urine, freshly drawn, and think I might gag on it when I smell it. But instead the characteristic pungency of leaf vegetables enfolds me. All I have to do now is drain the glass and hand it back to my father with, if possible, a smile.

And suppose I don't like it? I asked him once. What would happen then?

'You will like it,' my father said earnestly, anxious that this idea shouldn't get a foothold in my mind. 'It's delicious. And really good for you.'

This cannot, I know, be true: I am already aware that some inalienable law always seems to separate goodness from niceness, and to place a barrier between them. The stuff about its being delicious and good for me is just part of my father's sales patter, only this time I am the one who is buying. Yet somehow I always agree, simply to keep the peace between us.

And now here I am, standing in front of an audience of maybe twenty adults, with a glass of Residue and my father's reputation as a salesman in my hand. And like my great-grandmother Madame Cody in her red tights, I am prepared to sacrifice my own comfort and safety for the sake of the act.

I drink it down under the lights.

'So what do you think, Johnny?'

What I really think, of course, is that I'm sick to death of drinking the Residue, day after day, and I want to go off and play somewhere. But that wouldn't be professional. I put on a smile and nod.

'Good?'

I nod again.

'Well, there you are, ladies and gentlemen. You can't say fairer than that.'

Polite applause ripples around them, and at least one person seems to be interested in buying an Easiwork cooker. One purchaser per demonstration will provide us with just enough commission to keep going, he tells me. It's one of those things I would rather not know about, because it worries me to know how little money we have, but I suppose it helps to ensure that I do my side of the job.

Afterwards, before I can tell him about Penny, he hisses irritably in my ear, 'You're supposed to *say* how good it is when you drink it. You mustn't just stand there, grinning like a monkey.'

I feel I've let him down, and have to apologize again. But because he has actually sold two cookers during this demonstration, not just one, he's in a good frame of mind. He makes me tell the story of Penny and the kid three times in all, with all the required gestures. But he tries to hush me when I say 'You bloody little swine' too loudly.

Unfortunately the phrase stays in my head. The following Christmas, when the well-to-do family of a Sunday school friend of mine invites me to a pantomime – *The Babes in the Wood*, I think – I watch in horror as the hero and heroine are captured. Carried away with the excitement of the spectacle, I jump up in the box and say, 'The swine! The bloody swine!' just like Penny.

My friend's mother covers her child's ears with her hands, and then whispers something about me to him. He barely speaks to me after the performance is over. My father feels he has to write the family a letter of apology, and there are no more invitations from them. But my father finds it very funny, and tells his friends about it; and over the next few weeks I have to act this out again and again, too.

Working for Easiwork is a definite step up the scale for my father. He has finished with selling football pools and Mr

Drage's badly made furniture, and after an interlude during which he went from door to door with gadgets made by a firm called Kleenezee he has found something a little more suitable. People are desperate for a life which is a little more easy – or easi, or ezee for that matter; but selling things to them isn't easy at all, and nowhere near as profitable as the advertisements for sales staff imply.

SOMETHING ELSE HAD come into his life as well: a new dynamic, which would change his life in many ways and encourage this upward social movement away from the old shabbiness to something altogether more prosperous. What united many of the people he now found himself among was their religion: they were Christian Scientists, and he would soon become one himself.

Nowadays, as I write this, the tide in Britain has long receded from organized religion of all kinds, and Christian Science, with its emphasis on mental healing and the power of thought, has been left farther up the beach than most. It has even declined in the United States, where the oddest and most counter-intuitive forms of religion seem to prosper. So it is hard to remember that Christian Science once seemed like a genuine threat to the more established religions, and that in Britain it was a faith which the wealthy and titled were particularly drawn to.

Today the grand churches, modelled on Byzantine and Roman and Gothic styles, have often been sold and turned into concert halls, or blocks of flats; but then the Sunday services and the Wednesday testimony meetings, where people stood up and related examples of how Christian Science had healed them, were packed. It was a religion which seemed to be going somewhere.

From the start, my father liked everything about it: the presence of so many wealthy, well-born people, the American-ness of much of its readings and ritual, and especially the idea that you could be responsible for your own body and your own health, mental as well as physical.

My father had grown up detesting the old things, the old attitudes. He was young and impatient and anxious for change: he hated the established politicians with their wing-collars and their umbrellas and their strangulated old voices, who had done nothing for the country except feed its self-satisfaction. He was a natural extremist, who craved colour and excitement. He took part in several anti-Fascist marches in the East End of London, attacking the uniformed followers of Sir Oswald Mosley with young Communist groups. But he was attracted more by Anarchism, which was of course far less structured than the Marxists. At the age of twenty-two he volunteered to fight for the Anarchist brigade in Spain, only to change his mind ingloriously as the train started to leave Victoria station with the Anarchists all on board. My father jumped back on to the platform.

Once, encouraged by too much rough red wine, I told this story over dinner when I was reporting on a gathering of international Anarchists in Venice in the 1980s. At first there was silence and a certain anger; then an elderly Italian down the table raised his voice.

'The true Anarchist never follows the herd.'

I and my father were applauded to the rafters.

Even when he was an Anarchist he adored the Prince of Wales, and was deeply angry when the Establishment forced him to abdicate as King. He never could stand the Conservatives, and had trouble finding himself a lodging-place among the political parties.

Now, during the 1940s, he is a Liberal, partly because he dislikes the atmosphere of state control and official snooping which the Labour Party has introduced, and partly because the Liberals are now decidedly odd and seem as close to extinction as a rare species of animal. He loves the notion of belonging to a small coterie, almost a secret society, and is liable to produce a copy of the *Manchester Guardian* at public gatherings, rather as a spy might make some self-conscious and rather unnatural signal at a prearranged rendezvous, in the hope of making contact with other Liberals.

In the same way he took to Christian Science instantly when he came across it among the out-of-work actors and actresses at the Ideal Home Exhibition. I didn't spot the moment of his conversion, because adults towered over me like giant trees in a rainforest and I found their conversation largely incomprehensible. Yet it was clear even to me that he found their company attractive, because he did his hair with particular attention, and spoke more roundedly and deeply than normal. He didn't seem to be especially attracted to any individual: it was the group he liked, jokey, nice-looking, self-deprecating and relaxed. The Christian Science came, I should guess, as something secondary. Liking the company of the group, he eventually decided he liked the ideas that bound them together.

My mother, not being interested in these ideas in any way, assumed that he was interested in the actresses because they were attractive and available. In fact, they were all very well-behaved. Although I wouldn't necessarily know what I was observing, I am sure I would certainly have spotted the signs if my father had fallen in love with one of his new friends. No: it was their attitude to life which he was suddenly in love with.

And it was certainly the case that the Christian Scientists he met at the Ideal Home Exhibition were a cheerful, happy, jokey lot, relaxed and unstuffy. His own friends and family seemed gloomy and limited by comparison. It was the first time he had encountered any religious people that he approved of; he had loathed his Anglo-Catholic school as much as he hated the Dickensian ministers of his family's Congregational church, who seemed to believe that money and worldly success rightfully belonged to the upper-middle-class people who turned up to hear them preach every Sunday, while outsiders who were poor and unsuccessful deserved their poverty.

My father loved the idea that you could heal yourself of illness – and of poverty, for that matter – through prayer and thinking the right thoughts. He hadn't had a particularly good time with conventional medicine. His doctor was an old drunk called O'Callaghan, who tried to inoculate me as a baby but allowed his hand to slip. He cut my arm open with the needle; I still have the scar. The medical officer at my father's factory was another drunk who habitually misdiagnosed the problems of the patients who came to see him, and was responsible for at least one death. When my father joined the Army, the dentist who examined him, being paid by results, insisted on taking out any tooth that was less than perfect. As a result, my father lost four of his front teeth, and had to wear dentures from the age of thirty. Turning his back on this kind of medicine was scarcely difficult. Anyway, my father loved the idea that you could circumvent the claptrap of the educated, the wealthy, and the pampered who were after your money, and heal yourself through your own unaided efforts. Even before he met the Christian Scientists, he had found and bought a book called *Your Mind Can Heal You*, and for a time it was his favourite reading.

'According to this,' he would tell my mother, 'if you simply concentrate hard enough on harmonious thoughts, even cancers have been known to shrink.'

'Wonderful, darling. And what about the rent money? That's shrinking quicker than anything.'

But *Your Mind Can Heal You* had something to say about that too. Thinking harmonious thoughts could make you rich; the author adduced his own life as evidence of it.

Christian Science was a good deal more sophisticated, and my father soon decided that the author's harmonious thoughts had included ripping off Mary Baker Eddy's own work, *Science and Health*, pretty extensively. My father certainly did find both prosperity and health, though in the end he became terminally short of money and died of a heart attack at the age of sixty-five. But by that stage he had drifted away from it, bored with its strict rules. He was much too independent-minded to abide by someone else's system for ever.

I don't suppose anyone nowadays would seriously deny that the way you think affects your life, your health and your happiness. The *Irish Times*, that literate and enjoyable newspaper, once began an editorial on the strange and colourful ways of a highly questionable Irish politician with the words, 'The things that happen to people are like the people they happen to.' That encapsulates a great deal of my father's philosophy of life, and it seems pretty much unanswerable to me; though maybe this is because I grew up with such ideas.

So we didn't go to doctors any more; and since for me doctors meant drunken old O'Callaghan, I was perfectly happy. Instead, we prayed, and we read *Science and Health*, and if necessary we called a Christian Science practitioner, who would pray for us. And things went remarkably well. Perhaps they would have anyway; after all, people throve before medicine became a real science. But my father seemed more at ease, a little less anxious about money and jobs, and I liked going to the Christian Science Sunday School. We sang hymns and had the Bible and Mary Baker Eddy read to us, and since (according to some American scholar) Mrs Eddy used a greater variety of words in her writings than any other writer in the entire corpus of literature in English language except Shakespeare, I found myself absorbing a remarkably wide vocabulary.

The dominant figure in my father's new group of friends was a handsome, motherly lady called Mollie. I realize now, when I look back on my childhood self, that I tended to identify Mollie – *Auntie* Mollie, inevitably, since I now lived a life surrounded by women who were close to us but not related – with Christian Science and Mary Baker Eddy herself. Christian Science was very much bound up with the female principle, and the church was to be full of able, intelligent, slightly dominant women. Auntie Mollie was all those things.

I was a bit scared of her; and even now, when she has been dead for decades, the thought of telling her to her face that I've left the church, and my first wife, and lived long years in adultery, is alarming. Not that Auntie Mollie was ever cross with me, or harsh in any way: on the contrary, she was jolly and generous and gave excellent parties (without alcohol, of course). But she was monumentally *good*, and I found that intimidating.

My mother hated the church, the ideas, and most of all the women. I suppose she still thought, at this stage, that she and my father might have a future together, even though she would now spend a week or so with us and then go back to Epsom to be with Pat and Michael for the next few months. With the enthusiasm of the new convert, my father was always telling her how wonderful Christian Science was, and how she would like his new friends.

'Yes, dear, I'm sure I would. Now shall I start to get a meal ready for Johnny?'

'Oh, I can do that later. I just thought you might like to meet some of them.'

'Not really, Roy. You know I don't like meeting people very much. And they sound a bit too noisy for me.'

A pause, while my father defends them against the charge of noisiness.

'And anyway I simply don't believe in all that business about healing yourself. What would you do if Johnny went down with something bad?'

'I'd get on the phone to a practitioner.'

'And they'd all start praying, I suppose. So what would you do when the praying didn't work? Would you be prepared to watch him get seriously ill?' She meant die, of course.

My father was never short of answers, and he soon talked my mother into silence. But it wasn't the silence of agreement; she never, as far as I know, went into a Christian Science church, or looked at a page of *Science and Health*, or met Auntie Mollie and the others. But I didn't die as a result of Christian

Science treatment. On the contrary, I grew tall and thin and active, and immensely healthy.

And was I happy? I had no reason to think I wasn't. I was more self-contained than many children, I suppose, and therefore required less entertainment than I would if my circumstances had been different. I would have liked more harmony in the home, but so do most children whose parents are unsuited to each other. I wasn't frightened of violence, I wasn't hungry, I wasn't miserable. The worst I could say was that I felt sad about the way my parents were. And I was as worried about money as my father, without having the least understanding of how to get more of it, or of the consequences of not having enough. Would we be thrown out into the streets? Would we die of hunger? It wasn't clear to me, and that in itself was disturbing.

Still, a couple of weeks after the incident of the Residue at the Ideal Home Exhibition, my father got a new and better job, representing a company which produced a number of well-known magazines; this was the result, he announced to us both, of positive thinking. My mother also had a job, something to do with wool, and Yorkshire, and a strange carpet-making instrument that looked like a large pair of scissors. You could make your own carpets and mats with this, though even my mother with all her patience and dexterity had an impossible time trying to make the wretched gadget work. But from now on there would be no one at all to look after me. I would have to go to a day-nursery.

For me, this was simply hellish. I detested the lumpish woman who ran it, I loathed the food, and most of all I loathed being separated from my home and my parents. My father would take me in the morning to the bus stop at the top of Crystal Palace Hill, and as we were going along I would promise him that today I would be good and wouldn't cry; and then he would hand me over to the conductor and give him the money – a penny – and make sure he knew exactly where to put me off, and as the bus started off down the hill I would break out into shattering sobs that racked my chest and made my throat sore for a long time afterwards.

The lumpish woman, or maybe one of her acolytes, would be at the bus stop to meet me, and I would be taken across the road and indoors. I hated it all so much that I succeeded eventually in putting it completely out of my memory. I can remember images and experiences from other aspects of my life at this time with the greatest ease; yet virtually the whole of the day-nursery experience has gone from me as completely as if I had wiped the recording. It is only by a process of deduction that I can even work out where the day-nursery was; even though I could take you by the hand to every one of the places where we lived, and show you the precise spot where someone said something to me, and exactly what they said.

Yet all I can remember of the day-nursery is crying, getting on the bus, and being met by the woman. Whatever else happened there has vanished, at least from my conscious mind. But I assume that unpleasant things must have gone on; for instance, someone at the day-nursery force-fed me tomatoes, and ever since, I have never been able to eat a raw tomato without retching.

My father, once he had solved a problem, was always reluctant to open it up for discussion again; but he could see how miserable the day-nursery made me, and he soon began to realize that this wasn't going to be the answer he'd thought it would be. Perhaps I told him how I was treated, though I somehow doubt it: a strange system of *omertà* seems to grip young children and prevent them from telling their parents what is really going on at school and elsewhere, and I may have been too scared or too inarticulate to explain what was happening to me. And of course it is perfectly possible that nothing really bad did happen, though the evidence of the tomatoes is suggestive. For long years afterwards, certainly until I was in my teens, the very words 'day-nursery' were enough to make me shudder.

'TAKE A LOOK AT THIS, old chap,' says Uncle Hedley in his husky smoker's voice, and pulls a pen conspiratorially out of his inside pocket.

Uncle Hedley is a natural ally of mine: tall, bent, balding, getting on a bit, distinctly unglamorous, and with a tendency to be gloomy among all these bright, charming, optimistic Easiwork people at the Ideal Home Exhibition. He is Auntie Norah's husband: a non-Scientist, as the others would say, and inclined to slink round the back of the stand for a cigarette. The Christian Scientists don't smoke or drink, and my father has already given up doing both. Everyone is very nice to Uncle Hedley, but he remains a bit of an outsider. Not to me, though. He treats me like a friend instead of a child, and I appreciate that.

He holds out an interesting silvery object: a writing instrument, clearly, but neither a pencil nor a fountain-pen.

'Try it out on this bit of paper.'

I scribble with it, not being able to write yet. It seems to have a pleasant flow, and leaves a confident blue furrow behind it.

'It's called a Biro. I just bought one while I was demonstrating down at my stand. Can't get one for you as well, I'm afraid – much too expensive. But this is the future all right. One day they'll be a lot cheaper than they are now.'

In the spring of 1948 a Biro ballpoint pen, just released on to the market, costs £1 14s. 10d.: to get an idea of the equivalent nowadays you'd probably have to multiply by about forty.

Even the refills are expensive, though the price is coming down fast. In the press that morning a leading retailer announced it was reducing the price from 5s. 8d. to 2s.

This whole business of newness is important and emblematic. All over the Exhibition, and all over London, and soon all over the country, people are starting to experience an unfamiliar sensation: the feeling that, even in these dreary, shortage-ridden times, our post-war world might just possibly be capable of turning out goods which are better than pre-war ones. It's only the very beginning, but the feeling that we are inhabiting the ruins of a destroyed civilization is starting to fade.

If I were only aware of it, these indications, as tentative and vulnerable as the spring flowers which are showing their heads in the unseasonably warm weather outside Olympia, are all around me at the Ideal Home Exhibition. In the women's clothes, for instance. Many of the women on the stands and in the crowds that are pushing their way along the passageways between them are showing distinct signs of a change in fashion. Their dresses are a little more flowing, a little less regimented, the shape gentler and more rounded, the waists narrower, the skirts longer, and there is often the faint *susurrus* of petticoats. Real colours, and not just Government-controlled Utility shades, are starting to come back.

A little over a year before, at 10.30 on the morning of 12 February 1947 at 30 Avenue Montaigne in Paris, a new fashion house had been launched: La Maison Christian Dior. The 'Corolle' line which Dior showed off was completely different from anything the other fashion houses had come up with in Paris that year: a slender bodice tapering down to a tiny waist, from which the skirt burst out in all its fullness. There were no sharp angles, no awkward shoulders; breasts and hips were padded out, skirts were longer. Everything was rounded and full and very feminine. No more clothes like uniforms, with buttons and pockets and epaulettes and short skirts.

Women weren't warriors and workers any longer, they could be mistresses and mothers again.

Christian Dior himself had no intention of starting a revolution against austerity. He didn't even think his New Look was particularly new; indeed, he didn't use the expression at first himself. He felt he was looking back to the beginning of the twentieth century: the time when, as it happened, my grandfather and grandmother used to hold their annual fashion show in Paris. Dior later wrote:

> I thank heaven I lived in Paris in the last years of the Belle Époque. They marked me for life. My mind retains a picture of a time full of happiness, exuberance, and peace, in which everything was directed towards the art of living. The general, carefree atmosphere derived from the illusion that the existence and capital of the rich as well as the thrifty lives of the poor were immune from any sudden reverse.

There had been no British newspaper reporters at 30 Avenue Montaigne that morning in February 1947: no one thought French fashion could possibly be news at a time of austerity. So it took a little time for the New Look to cross the Channel. Yet when the few fashion magazines left after the war began to tell their readers what had happened, there was indeed a small revolution, a rebellion against the dreariness which had gripped everybody for so long. To the British, depressed and tired and disappointed (with intentional irony, people had resuscitated the dreary old slogan 'Don't you know there's a War on?', which had been used from 1939 to 1945 to justify every shortage, every curtailment of liberty), the thought of a return to old-fashioned opulence and beauty was irresistible.

And there were other green shoots to be seen, if you were willing to be optimistic. Eros was back in his place at the centre of Piccadilly Circus, his bow and arrow pointing accurately down Shaftesbury Avenue (nowadays, re-sited, he points in the wrong direction). In 1947 Princess Elizabeth married Lt Philip Mountbatten: inexplicably, the gloomy month of November was chosen for the wedding, and the bride was restricted to 100 coupons for her outfit, but the occasion glittered in the rain and cold, and most people seemed to feel better as a result. According to *Vogue*, the Dorchester Hotel commissioned a design from the artist Graham Sutherland for the new carpet in its luxurious drawing-room. Even the popular songs of the day had a feeling of change and movement about them: 'Open the Door, Richard' and 'Don't Fence Me In'.

Some people were predictably scandalized, especially by the New Look. The President of the Board of Trade, the gloomy, severe Sir Stafford Cripps, who dominated the entire period of the Labour Government, instructed the British fashion industry to keep skirts short and resist the new fashions from France. Obediently, a leading functionary of the unsuitably named British Guild of Creative Designers announced, 'We cannot give way to Paris's irresponsible introduction of the longer skirt . . . [T]here will be few long skirts in Britain next season.'

Bessie Braddock, a redoubtable old warrior for working-class politics, who was built along the general lines of a Sherman tank, called the longer skirt 'the ridiculous whim of idle people'. British women hadn't, she said, agitated for skirts to be longer. 'Their strong feeling is that skirts should be left as they are.' Mrs Mabel Ridealgh, another tough Labour MP with a dress sense to match Bessie Braddock's, agreed.

> This so-called 'New Look' is an utterly ridiculous, stupidly exaggerated waste of material and manpower, foisted on the average woman to the detriment of other, more normal clothing. The average housewife won't buy it.

Later, Mrs Ridealgh announced that one particular store had told her it had to alter 75 per cent of its clothes, because women felt silly in longer skirts and wouldn't buy them. When she was pressed about this, it turned out that the store in question was the Co-op in Mansfield.

It all went to show how little the serious, unfrivolous, well-intentioned, puritanical Mrs Ridealghs, Stafford Crippses and Bessie Braddocks understood the real, underlying mood of the British people. Yet it is possible to sympathize with them. The war had been a time of remarkable liberation for many women, and the feminists in the Labour Party were worried that alongside the soft, feminine clothes from Paris the British would re-import all the old ideas about women: that they were essentially decorative, kept at home for the diversion of the men, who did all the work. For a few months after the unveiling of the New Look, plenty of other politicians and leader-writers agreed that Christian Dior's fashions should be resisted. Even the opinion polls showed that a majority of people were against longer skirts and feminine padding.

But that was because they didn't really know what it was all about. Directly women, and men too, had a chance to see the New Look for themselves, everything changed. In October 1947 Christian Dior brought his clothes and his models over from France and settled in the Savoy Hotel. The newspapers were suddenly full of it all, especially after the seventeen-year-old Princess Margaret started wearing longer skirts. On 3 March 1948 she appeared in public in a pink coat with three velvet rings at the hem; on 13 March, ten days later, she wore the same coat at another public function – and now it had been lengthened by another velvet ring. The day Uncle Hedley showed me the Biro, an advertisement for a perfumier appeared in the newspapers:

> TODAY IN BOND STREET
> The new hour-glass waist and . . .
> Atkinson's eau de cologne.

Another advertisement, for Fenwick's department store, was more specific:

A ballerina suit, with softly-rounded shoulders,
page-boy nipped-in jacket, gaily swinging skirt to give
the new fashion look. Exciting colours and gay mixes.
18 coupons. £5 12s. 6d.

When the Easter Parade took place in Hyde Park at the end of March, the New Look was everywhere. The phrase itself was being adapted for everything from cars to politics: everything seemed to be in danger of having a New Look.

Even literature. In 1948 George Orwell, already seriously ill with the TB which killed him less than two years later, published both of the books for which he is most remembered: *Animal Farm* was one. For the other, he switched the last two figures of the year around and called it *1984*. It drew its descriptions of urban dreariness and mind control from the things Orwell saw around him, as well as from his awareness of Russia under Stalin. When the year 1984 finally arrived, it was notable how little like the book the circumstances of life had actually turned out to be; the problem proved to be rampant capitalism, not Marxist-Leninist absolutism. Even so, Orwell's grasp of the threat to decent, rational human life from political extremism gave *1984* its power and its lasting relevance.

My father, perhaps because of his dabbling with anarchism and his interest in Spain, read *1984* not long after it came out, and a year or so later talked about it to me at great length. He was as much of an individualist as Orwell himself, and in after-years I saw something of him in Winston Smith, the book's hero.

What I recalled most strongly from my father's account of it was the danger that governments could reach back into the past and change it out of all recognition, rewriting the documents and destroying the truth. I picked up a little of my father's own fear of this; it underpinned my interest in history at school, and in later years it played some part in my decision to be a journalist. It seemed to me that I would, like Winston Smith, at least be in a position to know something about the past for myself, and not be forced to rely on the lies people might tell about it later.

American literature certainly had a New Look about it: in 1948 Norman Mailer published *The Naked and the Dead*, which had a ferocity and an honesty which no contemporary British novel could match, and for much the same reason that American writing about the First World War had mostly been less effective than British: in the Second World War the Americans suffered more. What was new in British literature was the extraordinary phenomenon of the verse play. Christopher Fry's dull and essentially undramatic works were received with excitement on both sides of the Atlantic – perhaps because no one wanted to be thought a philistine for not liking them. They turned out to be a step backwards, not a step into the future.

T. S. Eliot also threw his considerable intellectual weight behind the verse play, in particular with *The Cocktail Party*. To those who admire Eliot, *The Cocktail Party* can nowadays be a bit of an embarrassment; awkward, heavily humorous, and somehow *wrong*. But at the time people were still deeply impressed and intimidated by Eliot: perhaps it was all the Italian and German and French he put into his poetry. The humorist James Thurber, writing in the *New Yorker*, was sceptical about it all.

> Ever since the distinguished Mr T. S. Eliot's widely discussed play came to town I have been cornered at parties by women, and men, who seem intent on making me say what I think *The Cocktail Party* means, so that they can cry 'Great God, how naïve'.

1948 was Eliot's year. He published one of his best books on literature and society, *Notes Towards a Definition of Culture*, and he received the Nobel Prize for literature and the Order of Merit. Usually these are awarded long after a writer has ceased to produce anything of merit, though not quite in Eliot's case.

Personally, I prefer to think of him going to work at Faber

& Faber on the number 19 bus, as he did throughout 1948, reading his manuscripts and thinking up unlikely rhymes. It may have been about this time, too, that he hailed a taxi in the Gloucester Road, near his flat.

'Hullo,' said the driver, 'it's Mr T. S. Eliot, isn't it?'

Eliot, rather flattered, agreed that it was. The driver was encouraged, and started talking about other intellectuals he had met.

'You know, I picked up that Bertrand Russell the other day, and I said to him, "Go on, Mr Russell, you're the greatest philosopher in the world – what's it all about, then?" And do you know, he couldn't tell me?'

Eliot's widow, Valerie, vouched for the story in a letter to the *Independent* newspaper in the 1980s. Eliot himself told it often. He was jollier than was generally imagined, and not necessarily as fearsomely highbrow. He once stumped an entire literary gathering by quoting a long passage of prose from memory, and asking the audience to identify it. No one could; and then he told them it was the climax of 'The Valley of Fear', a Sherlock Holmes story.

Far more characteristic of ordinary taste than Orwell or Eliot was the novelist Angela Thirkell. My father disliked her books, after having read just a few pages of one of them. She wasn't in any way anti-intellectual – on the contrary, her grandfather was the painter Burne-Jones, and her father had been professor of poetry at Oxford – but she sounded like the voice of resentful upper-middle-class Britain, though without the savagery and spite of Evelyn Waugh (whose own best days as a writer were now pretty much over).

'We have seen the end of civilization,' says a character in one of her books, *Love Among the Ruins*, which came out in 1948. 'It began to crash in 1789 and this is its last gasp. It's a sickening thought, but there it is. All our scrattlings and scutterings, our trying to save a bit here and a bit there, are useless. We are out of date.'

It wasn't entirely true in 1948, and eventually both the aristocracy and the upper-middle class in Britain managed to reinvent themselves on a smaller and less dominant scale; but Angela Thirkell spoke for the tens of thousands of people who felt the Labour Government was determined to root them out, once and for all. 'I'm all for levelling,' you would hear people say again and again, 'but it ought to be levelling up, not levelling down.' In other words, they hoped that the social change would be on their terms, and that their standards and their sophistication would predominate. You only have to turn on a television set nowadays – as I write this I have just watched a large, toothy blonde on a Channel 4 programme describe with some precision how she makes sure her lovers are up for the job – to see how wrong they turned out to be.

TELEVISION WAS A British invention, and adapting it for broadcasting into people's houses was a British achievement. The first moving image was transmitted by John Logie Baird on 2 October 1925, using, mysteriously, a ventriloquist's dummy called Bill. The BBC then hired him and started its broadcasting service in 1927. Although Baird died poor, with his achievement insufficiently recognized, Britain – that is, the BBC – began broadcasting the world's first regular television service on 2 November 1936. It was closed down for the full extent of the war, and longer, and only reopened in 1946, in time to broadcast the Victory Parade from London. The signal for this was faint and blurry, and the farthest it reached (and that only by a fluke of meteorology) was Somerset. But now the BBC was able to broadcast live to most of Britain from Westminster Abbey, as Princess Elizabeth married Philip Mountbatten, and from the White City during the Olympic Games of 1948. When, a decade later, the BBC took over the White City to build its own television centre, Corporation folklore maintained that the management had spotted it as a useful site while the athletics events were going on.

Yet in its early days no one took television seriously as a means of mass entertainment until the early 1950s. It was starved of cash, and (apart from a few visionaries) the best people stayed with radio, where the big audiences were. Not surprisingly: the programmes were arid and boring. This was anti-television.

11 am–12 noon:	Demonstration film
3 pm–4 pm:	Designed for Women
8 pm:	Amateur boxing
8.30 pm:	Picture Page
9.15 pm:	Boxing cont.
9.45 pm:	Newsreel
10 pm–10.15 pm:	News (sound only)

The news was broadcast without the benefit of vision because the BBC felt that the look on the face of the newsreader as he (it was always a he, of course) read the words might somehow distort the meaning or add an element of bias.

Those who worked for television were united in a largely unsustained belief that one day it would be the main source of information and entertainment in Britain. According to another piece of BBC folklore, the head of BBC Television, an amusing, slightly raffish Anglo-Irishman called Maurice Gorham, decided to make a personal appeal to the Director-General himself, to demonstrate to him how cheap and unimaginative much of the entertainment on television was, and how an injection of real money was required so that the BBC could start making proper programmes. Gorham assumed, probably rightly, that the Director-General, a bluff, kindly man called Sir William Haley, who came from a working-class background yet had risen to be editor of *The Times* and then head of the BBC, didn't watch much television.

So he arranged a viewing at Lime Grove, where the main television service had its headquarters: a rambling, ugly yet numinous set of brick buildings down a suburban side-street in Shepherd's Bush. Among the poor-quality items Gorham showed him was an embarrassing music-hall evening; by this time the music-hall was close to collapse. It proved to be a serious tactical error on Gorham's part. One of the songs which the music-hall artists sang was 'Lily of Laguna', and Sir William loved it. He was still whistling it as he got into his chauffeur-driven car outside in Lime Grove. 'Thanks so much – haven't enjoyed an evening so much in years,' he said as he was driven off, still whistling.

Maurice Gorham watched the large black car as it receded down the road, and reflected, accurately, that the great days of television programming would probably be some years away yet.

We tend to think of television as the most characteristic and effective form of mass communication in our new century, at the very forefront of technological achievement. Yet on Friday 2 April 1948 it was celebrating its twenty-first birthday, with a grand anniversary dinner at the Waldorf Hotel in London which was hosted by the Television Society (not yet 'Royal' at this stage). The Society's chairman, who boasted the Dickensian name O. S. Puckle, warned his audience of broadcasters, administrators and other luminaries that although Britain was still ahead of the rest of the world in television, the margin was starting to narrow. The Americans were our leading competitor, he said. Maurice Gorham's recent successor as Director of BBC Television, Norman Collins, was reassuring. The present system of transmission, which used a 405-line picture, would last for many years to come. (It did.) There were frequent demands for a 1,000-line picture, to make the broadcasting of colour television a possibility, but there was no question of its happening for a while. In 2005, as I write this, it still hasn't happened.

Not long after the dinner took place, Norman Collins travelled round the United States, observing the already depressing quality of American broadcasting and gathering the evidence for a BBC position paper which would oppose the introduction of commercial television. This decline, Collins's paper said, could happen in Britain if we weren't very careful. His paper convinced the Lord President of the Council, Herbert Morrison, who was in overall charge of the BBC and a strong defender of public service broadcasting.

In the meantime the BBC decided to upgrade the post of Head of Television to a Controllership – the BBC equivalent in all sorts of ways of a Cardinal's hat. Norman Collins had campaigned for this, and naturally expected to get it; only, in the appalling way the BBC often has, Sir William Haley gave it to someone altogether different. Collins's nose was put out of joint, and he resigned. He set up a company dedicated to breaking the BBC's monopoly. When Herbert Morrison was shifted to the Foreign Office after Ernest Bevin's death, the BBC lost its greatest defender.

By the time the Conservatives won the election of October 1951, the BBC's monopoly was no longer secure; and Norman Collins, still angry, was campaigning hard to break it. The new Conservative Government, which disliked the BBC on ideological grounds, was only too happy to do so – and Norman Collins played a distinguished part in creating the Independent Television Authority. One day, that would lead, not only to a new spirit in television, and to thousands of superb and lively new programmes, but also to having a busty model called Jordan describing on camera – with appropriate hand-gestures – why her boyfriends were never bored in bed. Among other things, of course.

FRIDAY 2 APRIL 1948 marked a critical moment in the Soviet campaign against the division of Berlin. Stalin wanted to force the Americans, the British and the French out of Berlin, and the fact that the city was set deep in Soviet-controlled territory gave him his opportunity. Claiming that the Western allies were sabotaging the work of the Four-Power committees, the Russians set up strict traffic controls on the roads leading to Berlin. The aim was to cut off supplies of food to those Berliners who lived in the Western-administered sectors. The Americans, British and French all issued statements insisting that they would remain in Berlin, and when the Russians tried to break the agreement which allowed trains from West Germany to pass freely through East German territory to Berlin, the three Western allies put military escorts on the trains with instructions that no Russians or East Germans would be allowed to board them.

On this day the first train from Berlin tested the Soviet will. It had an RAF officer, Wing-Commander Galloway, on board. At the last station before the West German border a dozen Russian soldiers and thirty or more East German policemen were waiting to board the train. They wanted to inspect the travel documents of everyone on it, and maintained they had the right to arrest anyone whose documents were not in order. Galloway was the model of tact. His orders were, he said, that no one could board the train, but he would have no objection if the Russians wanted the passengers to hold up their documents at the windows to show them. That wasn't what the Russians wanted.

The train was moved into a siding, and the passengers, nervous but determined not to be browbeaten, set up tables beside it and started to have a picnic. Wing-Commander Galloway was worried the Russians would swoop down and arrest them all, but eventually, after hours of patient negotiation, it was clear that the only safe way of breaking the stalemate was to let the train proceed. The passengers cheered, and the train crossed the border to safety. The Russians wouldn't be so lenient again.

Soon the only link between West Germany and West Berlin would be by air; and with all other means of transport cut, the Western powers would be obliged to keep Berlin supplied by a massive airlift. For the moment, though, this seemed unlikely. The correspondent of *The Times* was supercilious about the idea:

> Talk of an 'air bridge' to Berlin is picturesque, but it would be foolish to suppose that, if the worst came to the worst, the allied community and forces here could be maintained by this means alone.

Within a short time the air bridge was the only way of supplying Berlin, and it worked.

In other parts of Eastern Europe the Soviet grip was also getting stronger.

Prague, Friday 2 April

Today's issue of the semi-official Communist newspaper *Rude Pravo* announces that the workers' militia, which paraded with new arms while the Communists were seizing power in Czechoslovakia last month, is to be 'legalized' as a permanent auxiliary police force.

Six unnamed persons, presumably Slovaks, have been

arrested on a charge of having helped the Slovak Democrat and member of Parliament Dr Michail Zibrin to escape from the country.

The Communist authorities announced that four classes of people would not be allowed to play any part in the political life of the country:
1. Those who had collaborated with the German Occupation of Czechoslovakia.
2. Those who had spoken against the people's democratic order, or organized groups of listeners to foreign broadcasts against the Republic.
3. Saboteurs in factories, black marketers.
4. Corrupt officials.

The United Nations issued an urgent call for a truce between the Arabs and Jews in Palestine, with the withdrawal of Britain, as the mandated authority, now less than six weeks away. Sir Alexander Cadogan told the UN Security Council that Britain was not prepared to continue its impossible and increasingly dangerous task of holding the ring in Palestine beyond 15 May, even to help maintain a truce.

That afternoon at the village of Hulda, between Tel Aviv and Latrun, a large group of Arabs ambushed a convoy taking supplies to the beleaguered Jews of Jerusalem. Five vehicles were captured or destroyed, and the rest turned back. Five Arabs and two Jews were killed in the fighting, though later the bodies of fifteen other Jews were found nearby. It looked as though they had been taken prisoner and murdered. Fifty lorry-loads of food were needed each week to keep the Jewish population in Jerusalem supplied; this week nothing like that number had arrived.

Pandit Nehru, prime minister of the newly independent Republic of India, announced that the British national anthem would be played when a military tattoo ended in New Delhi that evening. As long as India remained in the Commonwealth, he said, 'God Save the King' would be played on all formal and military occasions, and the Indian national anthem afterwards.

In Britain the duties of doctors under the new National Health Service were set out. The NHS was due to start on 5 July 1948. Local councils would have lists of available doctors, and people would have to go and find the name of someone they wanted to be their GP. They would have to take him or her a medical card or a signed application form, and would be given a card in return. Doctors would not be allowed to have more than 4,000 patients on their books. They would receive a fixed annual fee of £300, and would also receive a capitation payment per patient, together with payments for temporary residents.

An advertisement in that day's newspapers shows two rugged forty-year-old men sitting and talking, while a young and pretty woman wearing the New Look walks past them, carrying a machine like a typewriter.

> 'Doing a spot of reorganizing, eh?
>
> 'Well, the Chief seemed to think we were going into a bit of a decline. Even hinted darkly that things are not what they were.'
>
> 'So you've moved down into old Hemingway's office and he's gone up to the second floor?'
>
> 'And Grimes has moved into Burkitt's room, and Miss Oxley's gone down to the basement with her *vade mecum.*'
>
> '*Vade mecum?*'
>
> 'The thing which Miss Oxley is now never without. It's a SUMLOCK Adding-Calculator, dear boy, to assist her with her costing problems.'
>
> 'Costing? But I thought she was the girl who sent out the invoices?'

'That was in the pre-SUMLOCK era. Miss Oxley
now labours deftly under the sobriquet of The "Cal-
culating Queen".'

The advertisement was for London Computator [sic] Ltd,
1 Albemarle Street, W1. Things really were starting to change,
in all sorts of ways.

Tuesday 1 November 1949

Sun rises, 6.53 a.m.; sets, 4.34 p.m.
Lighting-up time: 5.04 p.m.
Maximum temperature: 50°F; minimum: 33°F.
Rainfall: nil.
Sunshine: 2.4 hours.
Light to moderate easterly winds, mostly fair.
*   Local fog morning and night in industrial*
*   areas and near large towns. Rather cold for*
*   most of the day.*

I AM AN OUTLAW. Not the kind I will shortly start reading about in Richmal Crompton's William books, a naughty middle-class kid who wanders round the countryside committing small-time acts of mild aggression, but genuinely outside the law, liable if not to arrest then certainly to being caught and questioned and forced to go to school. It is a constant worry to me. Sometimes I dream about it, and wake up terrified.

Later, of course, I would come across children who have made my own experiences seem so mild that it is shameful even to suggest that there might be any similarity: children from Rwanda, from Sarajevo, from Belfast, from the lower depths of the American slums. All the same, at the age of five I feel myself to be watched and hunted, and I know that I have to keep under cover, out of sight.

The day nursery is finished for me; maybe I brought myself eventually to tell my father enough about it for him to realize that I couldn't go back. Anyway, I am too old for that now. There is a school nearby, but Anerley Primary is pretty rough and my father refuses to send me there because he knows what his family would say if they knew he did. Although I have no understanding of this ludicrous snobbery, I am very anxious not to go there. The Anerley kids scare me. In particular there is a gang of brothers and cousins, dark and almost shaven-headed and supposedly lice-ridden, who go to the school; or who are at least based there loosely from time to time, when they aren't ranging round the area stealing things from shops and beating up kids smaller than themselves. Like me.

One afternoon my father and mother sit down with me at home, make me a cup of weak, sweet tea, and explain the position. My mother is living with us again, and life seems quite attractive. From time to time there are noisy rows and tears, and terrible scenes about money, which are worse still. But just to have my parents together seems right and proper, even if they don't get on.

'Joyce and I had another screaming set-out,' I would hear my father tell his mother occasionally, but it seemed to me that he was the one who created the set-out; for the most part my mother would listen quietly, refuse to join in, and finally walk out of the room.

Now, though, they are in agreement about whatever it is they are going to tell me. I am nervous: this is something about my future, I can see. Something important.

My father starts to explain it all. Because I am five now, the law says I have to go to school. What's more, he's found a very nice school to send me to – nothing like the day nursery, he adds quickly, before I can say anything. It's got a purple uniform, my mother says, as though that is something which will particularly attract me.

'And it's called the Crispin School. It's in Penge, just a bus ride away.'

I see there is something else, though: a but is coming.

'The problem is, dear old boy, I can't afford to send you there for the time being. You know – things are rather difficult at the moment.'

There's another pause, and I wait for another but. It takes a little time to arrive, but when it does I understand more. I can't go to this nice new school, where the kids are the opposite of rough and the teachers are all charming, for another year. But I won't have to go to Anerley Primary in the meantime. Instead, I will have to stay at home secretly whenever my mother and father are away, and not let anyone know I'm around. Because if the police get to hear about it, my parents will be in trouble and I'll be put straight into Anerley Primary.

Actually, I'm sure I would have had a perfectly good time at Anerley Primary, regardless of the dark-haired tribe of kids there who frightened me (their name, I now remember, was Connor, and it struck fear into a lot of hearts). But that is the effect of hindsight. At the time, my father wasn't only worried about what his family would say, he probably didn't even have the money or the coupons to buy me a uniform for Anerley, cheap though it was. What my mother thinks, I don't know. She keeps quiet, her dark brown eyes watching me closely.

'So I'll have to play indoors.'

'Exactly.'

That is about as much of it as I can properly take in.

'And you really won't be able to go out at all in the daytime, or else they could catch you.'

If I were a little older, I might go further into the implications; but I don't. What of course my father means is that I will be a kind of prisoner sentenced to a year's house arrest in a form of solitary confinement.

'Won't I ever be allowed out?'

Yes, it seems I will, but just not at times when other kids are at school.

'You mustn't tell anyone about this. It's our secret.'

I don't really have any friends anyway; kids who live the strange wandering life I do rarely get the chance of making any. And there's the odd business about our social status: my father doesn't like me to play with the local kids, who are common. I don't mind not playing with them in the slightest: in fact, I'd rather be on my own than be forced to spend time with children I don't like. Loneliness won't be a problem.

'What about going to see Auntie Eva?'

Auntie Eva is my grandmother; more depressive than ever, apparently, and therefore unable to look after me at the moment. As for Daphne, my father's sister, she has a full-time job.

'The main thing is, you mustn't tell anyone. No one at all.'

'Roy, are you sure it's right to do this to him?'

'Of course I'm sure. Johnny won't mind, will you?'

I shake my head: I can't think of anything to say, anyway.

'Because if you did tell anyone, Mummy and I would get into an awful lot of trouble.'

I don't tell anyone; indeed, this is the first time in fifty-five years that I have broken my vow of silence. At first it was from fear, then from habit, and soon it ceased to have any relevance or any interest to anyone and I pretty much forgot about it. Except of course that you never really do forget about such things; you just put them away in some small, broken-down cupboard at the back of your brain, and only come upon them by chance, years afterwards, when you're searching for something else.

Soon my mother will be gone again, and my father will leave early in the morning and come back tired but jolly in the evening. It's a hard life for him, and he has as little social life as I do, which matters to him. During the day, I stay at home with a couple of sandwiches and a glass of milk which I have to drink when the little hand is on one and the big hand almost comes up to join it.

By this stage I can read: not particularly well or accurately, and certainly not out loud to an audience, but with increasing speed and confidence. Every Saturday we go and get more books from the local library, books about talking mice and rabbits and pigs, and I pile them up for the coming week, as many as they will let me take out. The limit is six.

'He's a good little reader, isn't he? I'm surprised he's got enough time to do all this reading. Doesn't he ever want to get out and play with his friends?'

'Ah, well,' says my father, casting round for an answer, 'you see, the fact is – well, he likes to have a lot of books to choose from.'

He grips my hand hard, in case I say something awkward. I don't. I believe that all of us – my father, my mother and I – will be arrested and gaoled if anyone finds out I'm not at school.

I select the books I want to read by sitting down on the floor in front of the shelves and looking for attractive titles and names. I like names, in particular: Alison Uttley sounds good to me, though I can't decide whether it's a man or a woman. So does Hugh Lofting – something high and noble about him. But a glance at the words on the page shows these books aren't quite for me yet. I still need something a bit easier, with fewer and shorter words than either Hugh or Alison use.

But I have long since lost interest in books which patronize me by breaking up the words into hyphenated syllables. That was why I stopped reading *Chick's Own*, a comic which my father used to buy for me. *Chick's Own* was relentlessly patronizing.

> Oh dear!' says Dil-ly the Duck. 'I am ver-y sorr-y that you have fall-en down the well. But you do look ver-y funn-y down there!'

Against my better judgement, I was persuaded by my father to write a letter to *Chick's Own* as part of some competition it was holding. I could tell this was a waste of time. The prize (a day at the *Chick's Own* office, which might, I felt, have presented all sorts of existential problems for an outlaw like myself – having to say which school I went to, and so on) didn't seem to be worth the effort. And of course I didn't win it anyway. I simply received a letter from the Editor's office. It was typewritten and the notepaper was decorated with chicks, ducks, and out-of-scale piglets. Infuriatingly, even the text was in baby-speak. It, too, is in the bag with my father's documents.

The Editor's Office,
Chick's Own,
Fetter Lane,
London E.C.4.

Dear Johnny,

Wil-fred and Dil-ly and all their friends here at the Chick's
Own off-ice were ver-y glad to hear from you. We are pleased
you like our news-pap-er. Thank you for your ent-ry to our
com-pet-i-tion. I am ver-y sorr-y that you did not win it, but
please keep on read-ing about our joll-y ad-ven-tures.

    Much love from all of us.

There is a scrawl at the bottom which could be anything.

'I knew I wouldn't win,' I say passionately, when I have
opened the letter and puzzled out its contents. But I am
absolutely charmed to have received a letter addressed specifi-
cally to me, of course, and will keep both it and the envelope
for the rest of my life. Fortunately it doesn't occur to me that
this will only be the first of a long series of rejection notes.

Comics and magazines will soon be one of the mainstays of
my world: both the ones my father disapproves of, like the
Dandy and the *Beano*, where patently rough kids do fierce
things to one another and are rude to grown-ups, or footballers
win against incredible odds, or unfeasibly large characters like
Desperate Dan knock people through brick walls and eat pies
with entire cows, horns and all, cooked lightly into them. There
are strange conventions: Lord Snooty, for instance, wears a
shiny top hat, an Eton collar and a monocle at all times, yet his
pals seemed like ordinary kids. We all seem to accept the notion
of an aristocrat, who, in spite of all the strange forces of class
resentment and snobbery which were evident at the time, is
presented as an attractive character.

My father particularly disapproves of Desperate Dan. This
is because when Dan sits down to eat his cow pie, with his hat

on and his gigantic napkin tucked into his neck, he puts his hairy fists down on the table on either side of the plate, with his knife and fork sticking up in the air. This is a Bad Influence. Yet my father doesn't need to worry: I'm not tempted to hold my knife and fork like that. Anyway, I'm more interested in the physics of punching someone so hard that they go right through a brick wall; would the hole in the bricks really be human-shaped?

There were comics during my childhood which were less objectionable from the point of view of class and manners: *Lion*, and *Magnet*, for example, which were still firmly in imperial mode: insouciant white men in topees, carrying revolvers, held sway over uncountable numbers of Africans wearing skins and headdresses. Usually the Africans were nice, but a bit stupid – comically so. The Chinese were usually the villains; they were dressed as mandarins, with round hats and long gowns, and sometimes they had very long nails.

And then there were the comics which my father thoroughly approved of: the *Eagle*, which was bright and colourful and famously had Dan Dare, Pilot of the Future, fighting off the Treens on the front page. I liked Dan Dare – something about the clean-cut jaw, I suppose, and his strange uniform, like a ticket inspector in blue overalls, and his superiority to the rest of his crew, especially the rather obtuse Digby. For some reason, though, my favourite feature was Luck of the Legion, on one of the inside pages: not, clearly, one of the leading features. Perhaps I preferred something which seemed to be halfway real to out-and-out fantasy like space travel, which I assumed would never happen in my lifetime. I much preferred reality. I suppose I was a rather literal-minded little boy.

Luck was British, of course – what else? But he was fighting for the French Foreign Legion alongside all sorts of ludicrous French characters with long moustachios in what I now understand was the North African desert: great expanses of yellow on the pages, with lines of camels and white forts in the distance, and the water-bottle as much in evidence as the rifle. This caught my imagination, and enhanced the interest of a hymn which we later sang at the Crispin School, and which seemed to suggest that there was something particularly godless about the desert sands.

The back page of the *Eagle* was devoted to the doings of a Biblical character, usually St Paul, which meant that middle-class parents felt happier buying the comic for their children. I quite liked this too, because of the characters in their flowing robes and the fact that quite a lot of action seemed to be involved with the Mediterranean; I suppose I also took a ghoulish interest in the martyrdom of various unfortunates, from St Stephen to St Peter. You couldn't easily see death portrayed anywhere else. Even at the cinema people would fall down dead out of camera shot, or die behind a curtain. In the *Eagle* they were strung up on crosses, sometimes upside down, or shot full of arrows. The *Eagle* was to me then what Old Master painting was, a decade later.

The middle pages of the *Eagle* were taken up with showing how things worked: atomic power stations, oil refineries, the *Queen Mary*. This wasn't really to my taste at all; and as I grew older it became clearer and clearer to me that I had no interest whatever in science or engineering: very much my loss, I know, but you might as well find these things out early on.

The other magazine my father approved of was the *Children's Newspaper*, 'conducted', it said pompously on the mast-head, 'by Arthur Mee', which made it sound like an orchestra, or perhaps a bus. I had the impression that Arthur, with his weird name (there was a book in the junior library about three koala bears called Riddle, Mee and Ree, which made it hard for me to take him at all seriously), was a rather oleaginous character, inclined to grovel before royalty and England's famous past. Of course I was a royalist and a patriot at the time, like everyone else, but even at the age of five I felt that Arthur Mee was overdoing it a bit.

And the fact is that although I remember the format of the *Children's Newspaper* very well, and the feel and look of its pages – it was a bit smaller than a modern tabloid – and although I read it faithfully every week, as best I could, I cannot now remember a single story from it: not a good story for a newspaper, even a children's one. Worse, I can't remember any single column or feature in it, nor even the kind of story it used to report on: things to do with kids, I suppose, though it would be a tremendous solecism to call the readership of the *Children's Newspaper* 'kids'. They were children, and that represented a huge and unbridgeable social difference. The *Children's Newspaper* exuded a middle-class confidence and security, as though everything were going to continue being exactly how it had been for decades: even though you only had to look around you to realize that it wasn't. But I suppose you knew, if your child read it, that he or she would turn out well and wouldn't hold their knife and fork upright on either side of the dinner-plate. Or terrorize the neighbourhood, like the Connor family.

MY PARENTS AND I weren't really middle-class, and yet we weren't quite not. My mother's family was so deracinated that it took its tone solely from Colonel Cody, the showman and friend of royalty. My father was pretty deracinated too, though the Simpson and Fidler families were archetypically, achingly middle-class; none more so. As a result we lived our lives in a kind of social weightlessness, like Dan Dare in his airlock, neither one thing or the other. Dickens and Thackeray would have called us 'shabby-genteel', I suppose, though we were much shabbier than we were genteel. But my father, having been degraded as thoroughly as it was possible to be, thrown out of the middle class with the door slammed in his face and the badges of rank ripped from his uniform, was determined to get us back in there. If that meant that this week I couldn't read the *Dandy* because it offended his social susceptibilities, so be it. We – he and I, at any rate, because he had his serious doubts about my mother – were upwardly mobile. We were on our way back to claim our own, and we would do it soon. But for the moment, at any rate, we were shabby-genteel, like characters in an early nineteenth-century comic novel.

We had moved quite recently, shifting a quarter of a step further up the scale. Now we had two big rooms at the top of a large, angular, ugly late Victorian house, not built by A. F. Simpson & Co., in a street more or less parallel to Crystal Palace Hill. We were to stay at 41 Lullington Road – the house has long since been demolished, and a much uglier row of

1960s houses has been built in its place – and a few of the most important events in my entire life would take place there.

One of the rooms was a kitchen, with a big table, a gas stove and a skylight. The other seemed to me to be vast, but I suppose it wasn't. It was big enough for my parents' large double bed, and for my own bed, which was folded up every morning. There was another skylight in the ceiling, through which I could look out at the clouds and imagine myself in a ship; and there was a cupboard under the eaves which ran almost the full length of the room but was only about three feet high. This cupboard was, I think, the best thing about our flat for me. It was dark, and therefore more than a little frightening at first, but all my toys were kept in there and for strange womb-like reasons I used to prefer sitting in it with a candle or a torch to being out in the main room.

We shared a bathroom with everyone else in the house. It was down on the first floor, and really was enormous. There was a gigantic and very old geyser which heated the water, and was inclined to explode. More than once my father shouted to me to get out of the room because of the smell of gas, and lighting it was a dangerous business: he would throw a lighted match into the middle of the room first, to clear out the gas, and would then very gingerly hold another lighted match as close as he dared to the window in the geyser. The gas would then catch light, and the entire geyser would explode. Little bits of hard black stuff would fall from it on to the floor and into the bathwater, and my father would swear long and effectively: his education at sea had been quite impressive in that way.

We weren't allowed to have baths very often: maybe once a week. I didn't mind: it was so cold in winter, getting out of the bath in a room whose temperature was about the same as that of the open air, that I much preferred it when my father, perhaps nervous about the geyser, would say he didn't think I was dirty enough to need a bath for the time being. 'For the time being' meant another week. There was a picture hanging over the bath, by the children's artist Mabel Lucie Attwell, showing a distastefully cute little girl with her knickers showing – knickers always do seem to show in pictures like this – and a poem to go with it. For some reason I took against it with the greatest intensity. Sitting on the loo, which was beside the bath, or in the bath itself, I would read the poem over and over again and so committed it, unfortunately, to memory. Like some irritating pop-up message on a computer, I can't delete it from my mind; and it still comes back to me at the stupidest moments:

> Please remember, don't forget,
>   Never leave the bathroom wet.
> Nor leave the soap still in the water –
>   That's a thing we never ought'er.
> Nor leave the towels about the floor,
>   Nor keep the bath an hour or more
> When other folks are wanting one.
>   Please don't forget, it isn't *done*.

My father hated the picture and the poem as much as I did, but when I asked him to take it down he said he couldn't; it belonged to the landlord.

The landlord was a Mr C. Swift. I had forgotten him entirely until I found one of my father's surviving documents: an old rent-book. The name brought a face and a figure with it: short, stocky, red-faced, and not at all unpleasant; generous to my father, and quite nice to me, I remember. Even in the 1960s, when it became fashionable for anyone under the age of twenty-five to regard landlords with loathing for their well-known habit of grinding the faces of the poor, I was less hostile to them than others, remembering Mr Swift.

This particular rent-book starts on 1 January 1951 (we arrived in Lullington Road at some point early in 1949), and it ends on 25 June 1953, when we moved to an altogether better and larger flat near the Crystal Palace; a big upward step for us. The rent of our two rooms was £1 12s. 6d., and week by week the rent-book shows that my father paid it promptly. There is nothing in the arrears column for the entire duration of the rent-book: quite an achievement for him, I suspect. On 13 August 1951, four days after my seventh birthday, the rent went up by sixpence to £1 13s. 0d. A sixpence was a little cupro-nickel coin small enough to be hidden in a Christmas pudding for luck, and in real terms it is worth something like a pound today: not a huge amount, but enough to make the difference (as Mr Micawber points out in *David Copperfield*) between comfort and ruin.

My father loved Dickens, identified strongly with Copper-field, found Micawber, with his fecklessness and iron-bound optimism, unbearably similar to his own father, and always wanted to write a sequel to *David Copperfield* about the Micawbers in Australia, where they emigrated at the end of the book. Like so many of his ideas, it was a good one; and also like so many of them, he did nothing about it.

Flicking through the rent-book, I find some 'Notices to Tenants' on the inside back cover. These have a suitably Dickensian tone:

> By the 2nd Geo. II. C. 19, secs. 3, 4,5, it is enacted
> 'That any Tenant or assistance removing Goods to prevent Distress, shall pay the Landlord double the value of the Goods, if under the value of £50.'
> Complaint may be made to two Justices, who are empowered to enforce payment, or commit the offender or offenders to the House of Correction for six months.

The second regnal year of King George II was 1728. It seems extraordinary that I should have been brought up in a flat regulated by a law 220 years old, which, if broken, would have meant that my father might have been sent to a House of Correction. The obligations of the landlord are also set out, on the back page of the rent-book, and there is advice about where my father should apply if the landlord fails to meet them; but it shows how antiquated some things were in Britain, even at the halfway point of the twentieth century.

My father himself hated that kind of thing.

'Disgusting old bastards,' he would have said; the bastards in question being the people who ran the country, the politicians and judges and bishops and generals and doctors. And the police. My father, who never entirely lost his anarchistic streak, disliked the police intensely. Once, years later in rural Suffolk, when he was in his country gentleman phase, a policeman stopped us for speeding. My father was distinctly aggressive to him, and in the end he let us off with a caution; but as we drove off my father yelled the most appalling imprecations out of the window, something about hoping his guts fell out and his balls shrivelled up. The policeman pretended not to hear. I was quite shocked, but my father went on for several minutes about how stupid and vicious the police were; I suppose it was the last faint vestiges of the young man who had once thrown bricks at the Fascists in the East End, and at the policeman who tried to protect them.

My father never lost a certain outlaw quality himself. I notice that on the cover of 'The St. Paul's Rent Book', where Mr Clive Swift originally wrote 'Mr R. Simpson, 41 Lullington Road', the address has been erased and rewritten; and it looks as though it has been done by my father, for some obscure purpose of his own. Throughout his documents you often come across a sense of something rewritten, changed, improved in some slightly nefarious way. Sometimes it represented a way of earning, or saving, money. Sometimes it was to disguise his age, or to cover up for something else he didn't like; he once burned his passport because he didn't like the picture ('It fell into a log-fire by accident,' he told the Passport Office: an uncharacteristically lame excuse, and they were reluctant to give him another one until he said he'd write to his MP to complain about them). My father was a dodger: a charming, intelligent, very funny dodger. I loved and admired him immensely, but I think that even then I understood I would always have to keep an eye on him.

One aspect of this dodger status was his ability to come up with an answer to absolutely everything; he prided himself on it. He was remarkably, inventively plausible, and could coax you into doing or even feeling almost anything he chose. An example: I was absurdly fixated on the cheapest and most primitive of toys – an empty matchbox which I somehow managed to persuade myself was a tube-train, with a door that opened laterally; a stick from the park which was a gun or a sword, depending on the century of my game; and, most loved of all, a little red plastic monkey with a curling tail. I remember the shop in Upper Norwood where we bought it. Plastic toys were pretty rare at that time, so this was neither cheap nor primitive; but it was small, basic, and intensely lovable.

I adored the monkey's face, with its wise, protuberant eyes and its paws that seemed to beg for affection and interest. When its tail snapped off, I was desolate; but my father, realizing we wouldn't be able to find another toy like this, explained to me that monkeys often lost their tails. Their mothers bit them off, he said, perhaps as a sideways hit at my own poor mother. I hadn't appreciated that you had to be careful of your mother in this distinctly castrating context, and was grateful I didn't have a tail myself. But I accepted that such a thing could have happened to my monkey, and continued to love it, broken though it was.

Slowly, though, as I read more books about the jungle and saw more pictures of monkeys, I came to realize that there was no monkey species on earth which was bright cherry red. This worried me a good deal, like religious doubts afflicting a Victorian clergyman: was the object I adored really quite as it should be? One evening I put this to my father as he read his *Manchester Guardian* by the feeble heat of the one-bar electric fire, and my mother made us a dish with cauliflower and white sauce and one small rasher of bacon. One memory, I have noticed, can often trail a series of others behind it, and now as I think about the monkey I can smell the cauliflower cooking on the stove.

My father considered the question. He too liked honesty and realism, and the monkey's redness was certainly pretty hard to believe.

'All right,' he said at last, 'I'll get hold of some brown paint and we'll cover him up.'

When my father committed himself to doing something like this, he always did it. It was an act of faith with him, and he might spend hours which could have been dedicated to something more profitable simply in order to keep his promise. The very next day he bought, or borrowed, a tin of paint the precise colour of excrement, the shade people still used on wood panelling in the 1940s, just as they had in the 1880s; the shade, indeed, that A. F. Simpson & Co. had painted the inside of my grandmother's house. He dipped the monkey into it, coated it pretty heavily, allowed it to dry, then gave it back to me that evening.

I was delighted. The monkey looked really genuine to me, assuming you could accept that its mother had bitten off its tail when it was a baby. The paint made it impossible to see the monkey's charming little eyes, but I knew they were in there somewhere still, and I remembered very clearly how wisely they twinkled.

It was a couple of weeks later before the paint started chipping off. I was appalled, and showed my father at once. He managed not to be irritated; in fact this kind of thing never did irritate him. He saw it as an intellectual challenge.

'Look, dear old boy, all animals that live in the jungle get terrible sores from time to time. And guess what colour the sores are.'

I thought about it, then slowly understood.

'Red?'

'Absolutely. The red bits are just sores on the poor old monkey.'

I bought it: for a while, at any rate. Then one of the legs snapped off while I was playing with it. I knew my father's invention would produce something else that was plausible: he would tell me that plenty of monkeys lost their legs to passing jaguars or crocodiles, but somehow I had come to the end of the pretending. I got my matchbox that doubled as a tube train, put a piece of cotton wool into it, and laid the poor old three-legged, tailless, sore-covered monkey to rest in it. It lay around for a bit, then, like all the other toys of childhood, it simply vanished.

There must have been other tenants at 41 Lullington Road, but I can remember only one: Mrs Ivy Rayner, who lived on the ground floor and was a kind of trustee, working on behalf of Mr Swift the landlord. It would be impossible to forget Mrs Rayner anyway. All his life my father collected people like her – eccentric, odd, sometimes rather embarrassing, and always with some particular way of speaking, some tic, some accent, which my father, whose ear was as quick and accurate as an African parrot's, could imitate.

Maybe this sounds spiteful and a bit treacherous, but he wasn't like that at all. He would go to endless trouble to help people, and would spend far too much of his time with them, listening to their problems and giving them advice. But the price he charged for his care and interest was to make fun of them afterwards: not generally, in any way, and certainly not so they would realize it, but just to his real intimates. And because he was fundamentally good-hearted, as well as because they provided him with an endless supply of anecdotes, he never abandoned them. As he remounted the social ladder which his Micawber-like parents had so spectacularly descended, and went from Lullington Road tenant to the ownership of a big house in Norwood, then another in Putney, then a vast country house on the Suffolk coast, he stayed in close touch with all the people who, like Mrs Rayner, he'd met along the way. They might not quite fit into his new existence, but that didn't matter to him. He never learned to become a snob, and drew great enjoyment from their company.

Mrs Rayner was definitely odd: a dark-skinned, dark-haired woman in her late forties with a sallow skin and black rings under her eyes, skeletally thin, who nevertheless habitually wore short-sleeved blouses from which her thin, bony white arms appeared like some strange sea-creature's. She walked around like Groucho Marx, taking long strides and keeping her centre of gravity remarkably low. And she was the mistress of some startlingly awkward phrases. When we first moved into Lullington Road her husband was in an oxygen tent in their bedroom at the back of the house, dying of some terrible lung disease. He was a nice old boy, slightly embarrassed by his wife's constant bossiness and importuning. Directly we arrived in the house, Mrs Rayner insisted that I had to go and see him. At five, I was reluctant and awkward about the idea.

'No, you go in there and say 'ello. You can get right into the oxygen tent with 'im. 'E won't mind.'

Every inaspirate was said with special emphasis, as though she wanted you to notice that she wasn't using her aitches as a matter of policy, and every vowel sound was somehow extended and drawn out: ''Eeeee won't mind.'

I hung back, nervous about entering the presence of sickness.

'Ooh, go on, 'e won't bite you. Get under the curtain.'

She pushed me in with her bony hands, lifting the clear plastic curtain and propelling me on to the old man's bed. He was dreadfully sallow, and found even the slightest movement difficult; yet when he rolled up his eyes to show that she treated him in the same way as he treated me, I liked him immediately. Breathing, even in the oxygen tent, was very hard for him, and being there meant little more than listening to the sound of it, raucous and painful, and smiling at him from time to time. Yet the strange thing was, I came to like it. The tent was a place of peace and quiet, and the old man quickly realized I didn't mind if he carried on reading the paper: the *News Chronicle*, my father's own favourite. I listened and watched and enjoyed looking at the outside world through the distorting prism of the yellowish plastic of the tent. It felt like being in *Through the Looking-Glass*, a book I had recently started reading and could scarcely understand yet.

Poor Mr Rayner didn't last long. Soon after we moved in my father came down one morning and found Ivy in floods of tears.

'I gave 'im 'is pot and told 'im to go, and I went to make 'im a cup of tea. Then I put my 'ead round the door, and said, "'Ave you been?" And 'e'd gone.'

My father was very sympathetic, and quite a comfort to her, but for the rest of his life that was one of his staple stories.

Ivy Rayner had a magnificent collection of malapropisms, which she used to produce with a certain defiance, as though she knew they were wrong but dared you to laugh at them: the Conservatory Party, the Natural Health Service, the BBC Live (instead of 'Light') Programme. Years after we had left Lullington Road she came to see us at our big house in Upper Norwood, just as I arrived home from school.

'It's all so bloody expensive, Ivy,' my father said. 'Now he's started playing rugby, he has to have all new equipment. The latest thing he needs is a scrum-cap, to protect his ears.'

''Eee don't need no scrum-cap. I'll knit 'im one, and that'll keep his ears safe.'

It was nice of her, and she would certainly have done it; but even my father, who disliked the snobbery of my new prep school, and certainly didn't enjoy having to buy me all these extras, could see that a knitted scrum-cap might not entirely fit the bill. Especially since Mrs Rayner only ever seemed to use bright pink wool for knitting.

NOW THAT MY FATHER is going out to work every day and I have to stay behind, Mrs Rayner keeps an eye on me. It's clear she doesn't really like children or know what to do with them, but twice a day, morning and afternoon, she brings me a cup of weak tea with a couple of biscuits, rather as though she might bring food to a potentially dangerous animal in a cage. My father (or my mother, on the few occasions she isn't either travelling or in Epsom) prepares me a sandwich, an apple and a glass of milk for my lunch. I can hear Mrs Rayner downstairs, her broom knocking aggressively against the wainscot, *House-wives' Choice* or *Workers' Playtime* loudly on the radio, and that keeps me from feeling abandoned. And when she goes out in the afternoon I know it won't be too long before my father comes home.

So I lie on my parents' bed under the skylight, sometimes reading and sometimes staring up at the clouds. I have come to relish my loneliness. I talk to myself and to my two teddy-bears, who sit side by side on chairs, facing me, and listen attentively to what I have to say. They are the crew of my ship, the soldiers I command, the other inhabitants of my desert island. Some-times I tell them stories from the books I'm reading: *Alice, Peter Pan, Tom Puss Tales*, Grimm's fairy tales, a Peter Parley's Annual from 1885 which my grandmother lent me, a floppy green-leather-covered Lamb's *Tales from Shakespeare* (my father reads to me from this, night after night, especially *Cymbeline*, which for some reason is my favourite, until his head droops and he slowly falls asleep), *One-Man Wallopem, The Wind in the Willows*.

Because I have nothing else to do, I read massively. The following year, when I am finally released from prison and allowed to go to school, my English teacher estimates I am at least three years ahead of the rest of my class in reading; and, listening to the things the other kids read, it seems to me that my teacher is being conservative; or, as Mrs Rayner would say, conservatory. So, far from setting me back by making me stay at home, my father is actually helping my education enormously; though I don't imagine a school inspector or a magistrate would see it that way. I do not have the slightest discrimination, and read everything I can find: good stuff, stupid stuff, grossly old-fashioned stuff, incomprehensible stuff. My father, who dreams of being a writer himself, keeps a big collection of a magazine called *Argosy* on the shelf behind his bed: monthly anthologies of short stories and poetry. *Argosy* is seriously middle-brow, but quite good all the same. I can scarcely understand a word in it, of course, but that doesn't stop me trying.

At this stage my father is still a salesman for an agency which sells magazines, and he has to tramp around the newsagents and bookshops of London trying to get them to stock things like *John O'London's*, *John Bull*, *Illustrated*, and *Picture Post*. There are always a few display copies of them around, and I spend a day at a time browsing through each one. This gives me a strange idea of the world at large. I must have been one of the few five-year-olds in Britain, for instance, who knows what the battlefields of South-East Asia and Korea look like; yet I have no understanding whatever of it all, and remember asking my father nervously whether the Koreans – I pronounce it 'Korans', as though we are fighting an army of holy Islamic writing – might be coming to get us.

Because I mostly read for myself, and rarely hear how things should be pronounced, I make worse mistakes than Mrs Rayner. For instance, one of my comics contains a character called the Falcon, who rights wrongs and descends on people from the roofs of buildings; I am convinced for several years to come that it is pronounced Flacon, and it takes quite an effort to change my mind about it.

My favourite book, or at least the one I spend most of my time reading, is a guide to world cinema, big and green and printed on shiny coated paper that has a tendency to stick to itself when I drop my tea on to it. I probably spend more time with that book than with anything else, puzzling out the titles of the films and trying to work out from the single frame which illustrates each one what it is all about. I managed to lose the book when I took it to school with me the following year, but when my father started taking me to the cinema in earnest after my sixth birthday we saw several of the films I had read about. It was always tremendously exciting to me to spot the moving-picture version of the still frames I had stared at so often: *M*, *Broken Blossoms*, *The Birth of a Nation*, *King, of the Khyber Rifles*. I knew them as another child might have known football stars or the characters of the latest cartoon: Harold Lloyd, Mae West, W. C. Fields. My father approved immensely, especially where Fields was concerned. He was one of my father's great heroes.

> *Greenhorn:* Ah, poker – is that a game of chance?
> *Fields (shuffling the cards with immense skill):* Not the
>   way I play it, no.

Fields reminded him powerfully of his own father, especially in the 1935 version of *David Copperfield*, where Fields played Mr Micawber. The combination was irresistible: the portly, heavy-boozing, instinctively dishonest persona teamed up with the grandiloquent no-hoper who always believed that better times were just around the corner. Fields as Micawber even looked like my grandfather. My grandfather's favourite expression was 'When my ship comes in'; as for Micawber,

> I have known him come home to supper with a flood of
> tears, and a declaration that nothing was now left but a jail;

and go to bed making a calculation of the expense of putting bow-windows to his house, 'in case anything turned up,' which was his favourite expression. (David Copperfield, chapter 11.)

My grandmother, on the other hand, was distinctly like Mrs Micawber, with her superior background and her inability to cope with the ordinary tasks of daily life.

Experentia does it – as papa used to say.

In all of this, my father felt he played the part of David Copperfield himself – disregarded by his parents, forced to make his own way in the world from an early stage, wiser than those around him yet too young, too weak and too poor to stand up for himself properly. I suppose most of us feel like that occasionally: David Copperfield was Dickens's own rather self-pitying portrait of himself, and his real-life parents were even more like my father's than the Micawbers were.

Most of us can recognize something of ourselves in the book; even I – and I certainly wasn't neglected or badly treated, as Copperfield and Dickens and my father all were. Both my father and mother acted in what they thought was the best way for me, and ignored their own interests; that, in a way, was their small-scale tragedy. But even for me there were points of similarity with David Copperfield. I had to learn to look after myself at an early age, and I was an observant little boy, older than my years in some ways and not in others; so that there are parts of *David Copperfield* which very definitely strike home.

'Somebody's sharp.'
'Who is?' asked the gentleman, laughing.
I looked up quickly, being curious to know.
'Only Brooks of Sheffield,' said Mr Murdstone.
I was relieved to find that it was only Brooks of Sheffield; for, at first, I really thought it was I.

AT SOME POINT during my year as a prisoner, my grand-mother's depression lifted a little, and she announced that she would be able to look after me occasionally. It was far from being a complete solution to the problem, even now, because she was unwilling to come to Lullington Road and my father didn't have the time to take me to her house in the morning and pick me up at night. The only answer seemed to be for me to make the journey on my own. But because my grandmother still couldn't wake up before eleven, and schoolchildren would be in class by then, we had to work out a compromise between us. I would wait at home until the new programme for young children on the radio at lunchtime had finished, and directly it ended I would take a bus down the hill and travel the two miles to my grandmother's house.

I was rather annoyed by the programme at first, because it was entitled 'For Children Under Five'. I had ceased to be Under Five in August, and it felt as though the radio people were taunting me by providing a programme which was delib-erately not quite intended for me. Then I realized that no one would know or care if I listened to a programme that I wasn't eligible for any longer; not even my father, who was inclined to say, 'That's good, old chap,' if I talked to him about it when his mind was on something else. And anyway I rather liked the songs they sang, and the stories they told.

'The time is five-and-twenty to two,' the announcer would say, and there was something about this old-fashioned formu-lation which pleased me. My father had a very strong sense of history; some years later, when he was better off, he became a professional genealogist, and (with the help of his business partner, Brian Brooks, who played a major part in our upward mobility) started to make his interests work for him. Everywhere we went, he would point out the old buildings and tell me what had happened in a particular spot. He also began interesting me in logical problems.

'Is that a new rail or an old one?' he once asked, when the train we were on passed a siding where the rails were red with rust.

'An old one,' I said immediately; it seemed pretty obvious.

'Well, if you think about it, it's the old rails which are shiny, because the trains have been running along them for ages. The rusty ones are quite likely to be new, aren't they, because they haven't been used much?'

I suppose there might be a flaw or two in the logic, but this engaged my interest vividly: not everything, I began to understand, was as obvious as it seemed.

The programme for children under five had a nice historical touch too, with stories and poems about knights and princes and beautiful maidens, and London Bridge falling down, and Dick Whittington turning back at the key moment and becoming Lord Mayor of London.

Later the programme metamorphosed into *Listen with Mother*, and it became social suicide at school to admit that you had ever, even when you were extremely young, listened to it. Especially in my case, since I no longer had a mother with whom I could listen to it. But I liked the frank, friendly voices of Daphne Oxenford and the others, and I especially liked being asked 'Are you sitting comfortably? Then I'll begin.' I would flop down on a cushion in the middle of the room and prepare myself for the experience.

Sometimes – these are things I have never confessed before – I would also march round the room singing the programme's more familiar songs:

> Horniman and Sir,
> Off we go together.
> Horniman and Sir,
> We don't mind the weather.
> Splashing in the puddles,
> Walking in the rain,
> [– something I don't remember, then –]
> Here we go again.

Horniman and Sir, I assumed, were names for the left and right feet respectively. What an extraordinarily interesting world this was, I thought, where even your feet can have names.

And then there was

> Hob shoe hob,
> Hob shoe hob,
> Here a nail and there a nail,
> And that's well shod.

Or something like that, anyway. It's been superglued into my memory in this fashion for more than half a century.

When the music ended, and it was time for me to go, I would put my coat on, go downstairs, tell Mrs Rayner I was leaving, evade any possibility of a kiss from her, and dodge out through the front door and down the steep steps to the streets. My entire life would one day be decided on those steps, but I scarcely stopped to notice them.

I had tuppence in my pockets, two large, friendly brown coins with someone's head on them. Queen Victoria's, maybe, an old lady wrapped up in a veil (though you occasionally came across earlier coins which showed her as a young woman, with the rather intriguing hint of a bosom), a succession of old men, Edward VII and George V, and a younger one who brushed his hair back from the front with a parting on the side, much like my father: that was George VI.

I would examine these things with great interest and intensity, turning them over and looking at the date and the figure of Britannia with a helmet which, when the coin was a bit worn, looked like a beaky nose. Underneath was the date: 1897, 1908, 1936. The past, when I was a child, seemed a great deal closer than it does now that we have been through such huge technological and economic changes. People had been sitting in buses, paying their fares with big brown pennies, for at least 100 years; and I understood that I myself was a part of this pattern.

Later, when I went to school, my father would ask me if I would mind walking home, because tuppence a day was a bit expensive for him; but for the moment, since I was only five, I could take the bus in both directions.

'Penny, please,' I would squeak to the conductor.

He would take a child's penny ticket, a little piece of thin card with a big red 'C' on it, from among all the other variously coloured tickets in his wooden holder, select the stage which was printed down its edges, and which marked the point at which I got on, and press down on a little lever which cut a round hole in the side of the ticket. Conductresses (though never the conductors) were called 'Clippies'.

Later, when I was in the company of other kids, I started collecting these tickets; and of course the best ones to have were unclipped, and had higher values and brighter colours: sixpence, sevenpence, eightpence. Later still, when my friends and I were more sophisticated, we would specialize in collecting tickets which had attractive or interesting numbers: AA 22222, for instance, or WC 12345. Once, not all that long ago, I stood in a bookshop listening to a man explaining to the assistant why he was taking books off the shelf and holding them out with the edges pointing downwards.

'I collect old bus tickets,' he said, 'and you often find someone's left one in as a bookmark. They fall out this way.'

My bus would stop in the main road, and I would have a quarter of a mile to walk to my grandmother's house, down the commonplace suburban streets my great-grandfather's firm had built, with names like Wheatcroft Road, Samos Road and Stembridge Road; and I made up little stories to myself about how they came by names like these. I remember one or two still, but they were too silly to repeat. The streets were almost empty of vehicles, since people who lived in areas like this rarely had cars; just bicycles. The houses were demarcated from each other and from the road by privet hedges. If Norwood had to select a characteristic plant, like American states do, it would have to be the privet, thick, impenetrable, and deeply petty bourgeois.

By now it would be two-thirty, and my grandmother would certainly be up, though not necessarily dressed.

'Hello, dear one,' she would say as she opened the door, puffing on her inevitable cigarette: Craven 'A's, which I used to go regularly to Mr Luck's corner shop close by to pick up for her.

'Twenty Craven 'A's, darling, and tell Mr Luck I'll make sure to pay him at the end of the week.'

'Yes, well, tell your granny I'm not made of money, and she's had two packets from me already, and a quarter-pound of tea which she promised me the coupons for. She'll have to pay me on Friday, and that's flat.'

Mr Luck's has long since vanished, and there is no shop within a quarter of a mile of 111 Marlow Road today: but the road is just as empty, and just as quiet, as it was when I made my way over the steep camber. It was a journey made in complete silence.

'Mr Luck says he's not made of money, and he wants to be paid on Friday and that's flat.'

'Oh, dear old Mr Luck, always joking. Of course, he knows my father.'

She would wander off, whistling tunelessly in and out, a cigarette dangling from an undeniably elegant hand. She too believed in the special quality of Simpson blood, and she seemed to think that the Simpsons still dominated Norwood; so that if Mr Luck really decided to insist that she should pay her bills, all she would have to do was invoke her father's influence. A chance, as my father used to say, would be a fine thing.

My grandmother was a woman forced to the farthest extreme of her mental balance by family duty and a bad husband. Yet even at her lowest point she had a kind of grandeur which intimidated outsiders as much as it irritated the people closest to her. Her profile was as stunning now, in her sixties, as it had been when she was on the receiving end of so much admiration in Paris. Her carriage was excellent, and she still behaved as though she was beautiful, in spite of the housecoat and the floating, untamed grey hair. When something made her angry, as it quite often did, her grey-blue eyes would flash, and you would see why policemen and the drivers of over-laden horses would be scared of her.

Later in life I began to collect Edwardian novels, which were often illustrated with pictures of proud, beautiful young women indignantly repelling the advances of brutal villains, or facing up to crowds of rebellious natives, or sitting at the dinner table by candlelight, listening to the plans of handsome, slender young men, and I understood that this was the life my grandmother had been cut out for: a life of incident and glamour and emotion. Instead, she was as much a prisoner of 111 Marlow Road as I was of 41 Lullington Road: no villains, no natives, no handsome young men, merely a husband who had deserted her and a serious lifelong shortage of money. Those things, her whole existence seemed to say, destroy a woman's spirit far more effectively than anything else.

Her house was in a bad state, and the garden even worse. I would play there for most of the afternoon, trying to keep out of the reach of the brambles which grew over everything.

Somewhere underneath them was an Anderson Shelter, which hadn't been seen since 1945, but I managed eventually to tunnel my way through to the door: I was a Red Indian, a bear, an escapee, a Mountie tracking down a villain. I scared myself witless by these games.

From time to time as I played I would hear my grandmother's voice, singing or arguing with a visitor or simply talking to herself. I stayed away when I heard these things, because they obscurely upset me. I was frightened, I suppose, by anything which seemed off-balance, crazy. My grandmother was greatly exercised by strange issues: the rights and wrongs of the abdication of Edward VIII, the question of whether French singers like Maurice Chevalier and Edith Piaf had been collaborators because they had continued to perform under the German Occupation. Her French was now largely non-existent, thrown overboard like so much from her life in order to keep the vessel afloat; but her pronunciation was still perfect, and her loyalty total. She spoke of Chevalier as though he were a close personal friend whom she alone had supported in his darkest hour. When I was very young I thought he might even be a member of the family, like all the cousins and aunts she talked about and I hadn't met, but I slowly began to identify him with the man in the straw hat whose pictures she cut out of magazines.

Sometimes, late in the afternoon, her daughter Daphne would come to see her. Daphne was the gentlest and most sensitive of people, yet while my father had inherited the Simpson ectomorphic frame, with its long hands and bony features, she looked like the Fidlers, jolly and comfortable and rounded with a handsome Roman nose, and was mercifully free of any tendency to be soulful. She had a pleasant if loud and slightly throaty voice, with a depth of expression which always seem to melt you instantly. To hear Daphne say 'hello' after you hadn't seen her for a long time was like being taken in her arms and held there comfortably. She was more motherly to me than anyone else; more even than my own mother, who increasingly seemed to regard me as having been taken over, like a small and unprofitable company, by my father and his influences.

'Well, you do look nice,' Daphne would tell me, or 'I say, that's really interesting,' or 'Well, I never thought of that; you're a very clever boy, you know.'

She had been in the ATS during the war, and something of the old comradely jollity still clung to her: the swing of her hips as she walked, the slanginess of her speech, the way she would throw herself down on the old leather armchair when she came into my grandmother's house.

'Oh, E., don't tell me you haven't given Johnny his tea yet. Crikey O'Reilly, mother, he'll collapse with hunger and then they'll cart you off to prison.'

And she would laugh her pleasant comfortable mezzo-soprano laugh and immediately go and put the kettle on the gas-stove, starting the inevitable search of all the surrounding surfaces for the tea-caddy.

A faint but utterly characteristic scent hung around 111 Marlow Road: the remnants of some excellent perfume which my uncle Alan had brought back with him from the Continent when he was on leave a year or so earlier, combined with the disinfectant TCP. My grandmother might be muddled in her thinking and deeply untidy in her habits, but she was obsessively clean. Nothing dirty was allowed into the house, and that included me. If I wandered back into the house from my exploits in the garden she was perfectly capable of seizing me and scrubbing my hands or knees, whistling to herself to mask the noise of my complaints or blowing Craven 'A' smoke into my face. The smoke, and the threat of a cleaning, were the reasons why I stayed outdoors for as long as I possibly could.

My grandmother had a black cat called Amber, which she credited with remarkable powers. Some of them were undoubtedly genuine – I myself saw it sit on the lavatory seat to do its business, though the notion that it was also capable of pulling the chain seemed more far-fetched – and some were a matter of opinion. My grandmother believed that Amber could read your thoughts, and knew who was good and who was bad.

'She jumped on to Mr Hutton's lap and immediately jumped off it. He said she scratched him, though I don't believe a word of that.'

My father, who treasured eccentricity like a collector might treasure a fine T'ang dynasty clay horse, loved to draw her out on these things.

'What did Amber do after she jumped off his lap?'

'She went into the corner and started washing herself.'

'And what happened to Hutton?'

'Oh, he soon went off with his nose in the air, foolish little man.'

I knew that my father was storing all these things up for later. Often, if he couldn't get a better audience, he would tell me. He would add just enough embroidery to make the story really funny, but the essence of it was always accurate.

'Oh, Roy, don't. It's not fair on poor old E.,' Daphne would say, if she was the audience; but she would laugh and laugh all the same, and my father knew she didn't really mean he was supposed to stop.

In the autumn evenings my grandmother and I would settle round the gas fire. I can remember the crisp sound of the ceramic plates at the back of the fire as they settled down in the heat, and the sour smell of the gas itself, and Amber sitting on a hearthrug as black as herself, her eyes half-closed with the pleasure of the warmth, and my grandmother trying to decide whether or not we should toast the last couple of slices of bread in the house – 'Because I haven't any coupons left, and God alone knows what we'll have to eat tomorrow. We could easily starve, and no one would ever find us here.' Which seemed somehow to cheer her up, as did the thought that she might have to go and charm grumpy, susceptible old Mr Luck out of part of a loaf tomorrow.

At first I tended to believe these disturbing notions; perhaps not quite literally, because even I could see that someone would be likely to come and see what had happened to us, but as a rough guide to the awfulness of her position, and therefore of mine. Soon, though, I realized that my grandmother was essentially a tragedienne, and that this was all part of the script. She liked the sound of these melancholy words, because they matched the feeling if not the facts of her own existence. It was mood music; and once I realized that, as my father and Alan and Daphne had all realized it, decades before, I felt perfectly comfortable with it all. We wouldn't die of hunger, but we might not have enough bread to toast in front of the fire this evening. That was all.

When we did, she would impale a bit of roughly cut white bread on a brass toasting-fork in the shape of a curlicued trident, another piece of the flotsam left over from the Art Nouveau contents of her first house, and prop it, usually too closely, in front of the gas-flame. I looked forward intensely to these times, and did my best to engineer them if it looked as though she wanted to do something else, because I knew that once we were sitting there she would start telling me stories about the past, and singing me songs.

In a way, it was a little like having a Victorian upbringing myself. She told me how I should behave, and how self-sacrifice and honour were the most important principles. She taught me to be patriotic, but not noisily so. She was deeply Francophile – the result, I suppose, of all the compliments which Frenchmen had paid her when she modelled my grandfather's clothes in Paris – and equally Germanophobe.

'The Germans,' she assured me, 'are either at your throat or at your feet.'

Americans were attractive and pleasant, but excessively bumptious and needed to be taken down a peg or two. The

Empire was the greatest force for good that there had ever
been, and its inhabitants (with one or two exceptions) utterly
loyal and affectionate; particularly the Indians and the Africans.
The Chinese I should beware of. The Japanese were simply
inhuman.

It was a pretty accurate run-down of the beliefs of the
average, not terribly well-informed middle-class Briton of about
1908. In a way, then, I suppose these things had their effect on
me; though I have long since come to regard both Germany
and Japan with real affection, and have developed a deep love
of Chinese culture.

Sitting there with our toast and margarine, she would often
go off into song – a random selection of late Victorian and
Edwardian music-hall melodies. She had a fine contralto voice,
affected only a little by the years of cigarette-smoke, and I
would join in, with my feeble little voice warbling away.

> Josh-u-a, Josh-u-a,
>> Why don't you come and meet Mama?
> She'll be pleased to know
>> You are my best beau.
> Josh-u-a, Gosh you are
>> Better than orange squash you are.
> Oh, by gosh, you are,
>> Josh-u-osh-u-a.

She loved Scottish songs, like 'Can Ye Sew Cushions?' and
'Corn Rigs Are Bonny', and would sing little couplets from
them, often adapting them to her own circumstances:

> Back hame in dear old Norwood
> With my ain folk.

I had difficulties understanding all her songs, and was nervous
about one of them in particular:

> When a body meets a body,
>   Comin' thro' the rye,
> When a body meets a body,
>   Should a body cry?

I could imagine the sheeted dead, passing each other through the fields, nodding and weeping and wailing at one another in the most terrifying fashion. Once I asked her about this.

'Why must they all be dead, Auntie?'

'Dead? Who's dead?'

'The bodies.'

She laughed and laughed, and told Daphne who was in the kitchen, and she laughed too. And when my father came to collect me that evening, he laughed the loudest of all. But they never quite got round to explaining to me that it was much the same as saying 'everybody', or 'somebody'; and even now, when I hear it, the song has a sinister tone to it, like a ghost story by M. R. James, or Michael Jackson's video *Thriller*.

My grandmother came from a generation which jokingly imitated Scottish speech patterns, much as people in the 20s imitated cockneys and people in the 60s imitated Americans:

'How are you feeling today, Auntie?'

'I'm awfu' bad, I'm afraid, darling.'

Sometimes she would break into a famous music-hall song in a rather effective cockney accent, adding in the names of local pubs where required:

> We're all living at The Cloisters,
> That's what we call our 'ome.
> We're cloister the Bull,
> We're cloister the Plough,
> We're cloister the Mitre and the Old Brown Cow.
>
> We're cloister, cloister the brewery,
> And we all know what they brew,
> And it doesn't really matter when the rent-day comes,
> 'Cos we're cloister the workhouse too.

She had a sentimental, almost literary, appreciation for beggars and outcasts, though if any actually came to the door – Uncle Harold, for instance, who was both a beggar and an outcast – she would drive them away angrily; in Harold's case because he was capable of becoming violent towards her. But she would sing 'Underneath the Arches' with great feeling, even so.

> Underneath the arches,
> > On cobblestones we lay,
> Underneath the arches,
> > We dream our dreams away.
> Every night you'll find us,
> > Tired out and worn,
> Waitin' till the daylight comes creepin',
> > Heraldin' the dawn.
> Sleepin' when it's rainin',
> > Sleepin' when it's fine,
> Trains rumbling by above.
> > Pavement is my pillow,
> No matter where I stray,
> > Underneath the arches
> I dream my dreams away.

I would cry when she sang this, and she would cry too, perhaps thinking about Harold, bottle in hand, sleeping under the arches of Waterloo station.

There were, of course, endless patriotic songs. My grandmother loved the armed forces and their uniforms, and she always had an 1890s air about her, as though she was just about to celebrate Queen Victoria's Jubilee, with the brilliant uniforms of the imperial soldiery parading past here down the street. When she sang, you could imagine the scarlet tunics and the smart pillbox hats:

> The soldiers of the Queen, my lads,
> They've been, my lads,

> They've seen, my lads,
> In the fight for England's glory, lads,
> When we had to show them what we mean.

> And when they say we've always won,
> And when they ask us how it's done,
> We proudly point to every one
> Of England's Soldiers of the Queen.

It never occurred to her, and it only occurred to me much later, how arrogant and unpleasant all that really was. Why should we have to show them what we meant? And did we always win, anyway? My grandmother, like Kipling and thousands of other Empire-builders, had a special affection for all those who made sure we didn't always win, like the Zulus and the Boers and the Afghans and the Fuzzy-Wuzzies; as long, of course, as we sent a larger, far more heavily armed force to avenge our losses later, and massacred them in their thousands.

If the weather turned nasty, with the rain beating against the window and the wind howling down the dreariness of Marlow Road, she would say, 'God help sailors on a night like this,' and I would think of the poor sailors, drenched and faced with drowning; and I would imagine the road outside Number 111 as the open sea, with the waves crashing against the houses as though they were the sides of ships. But my grandmother's moods switched with extraordinary swiftness, and often she had no sooner wiped away her tears for Harold or the sailors than she would start singing something much jollier; perhaps a little song that everyone of her generation would have called 'roguish', which had something to do with a girl called Nellie, who wore a huge 1890s hat with an entire bird on it. Butter wouldn't melt in Nellie's mouth, but she was naughty in a particularly *fin de siècle* way. The only bit of the song I can now remember my grandmother singing is the chorus:

> 'But you don't know Nellie like I do,'
> Said the saucy little bird on Nellie's hat.

The songs she sang were forty or fifty years old, and belonged to a period which was impossibly distant and antique. The curious thing today is that songs from four or five decades ago are still part of our lives: Elvis Presley, the Beatles, the Rolling Stones, all as popular as ever. The difference is that in the late 1940s two World Wars had changed everything beyond any kind of recognition, smashing social hierarchies, overthrowing the monuments of past taste and past habits; whereas by the first decade of the twenty-first century we can look back on sixty years of peace at home, where change – though it has been real enough – has come about logically and naturally and reasonably slowly. My grandmother's generation took the brunt of it, and by the age of sixty she was regarded as the survivor of a past which was almost as foreign as the Middle Ages.

She had a particular interest in the early pioneers of flight, and although she didn't like my mother very much she did like Colonel Cody, and was proud of the tenuous link with him. Most of all, though, she admired Claude Grahame-White, partly because he was handsome and well-spoken, but also because his plane had once crash-landed near her and when she helped him out of the wreckage he presented her with his steering-wheel. Whenever she talked about him she would go and search for it, and bring it to show me. And that would make her start singing a song about flying:

> I'm an airman, I'm an airman,
>   And I fly, fly, fly, fly, fly,
> Up in the sky, ever so high.
>   The birdies cannot catch me,
> No matter how they try.
>   I'm an airman, I'm an airman,
> And I fly, fly, fly, fly, fly.
>
> I've got a house way down in Kent,
>   I live in peace, don't pay no rent,

The reason is for this, you see,
    That when the landlord calls on me –

I'm an airman (etc., etc.)

'And don't I wish I could do just that, darling, and gang awa' from all these wretched people who come round wanting money?'

We would fantasize about where she would keep the plane, and how she would escape and jump into it, and whether I should be allowed to come too or would have to stay behind and explain that there was no use pestering her for money because the little dot way up in the blue was her in her plane, and we would end up in fits of laughter; and then she would sing something a little more melancholy, and I would realize that this was for herself, and I should stay quiet and listen.

Just a song at twilight,
    When the lights are low,
And the flick'ring shadows
    Softly come and go.
Though your heart be weary,
    Sad the day, and long,
Still to us at twilight
    Comes love's sweet song.
    Comes love's old, sweet song.

And afterwards, when she had finished, she would sit quietly and watch the blueish red flames of the gas fire, and think perhaps how different her life would have been if only she had been allowed to marry Rex Bailey, the man she'd really loved.

Often she would tell me stories about the family. There was her grandfather George Simpson, weak-chested and gentle, arriving in London from rural Suffolk with his ferocious red-haired wife Charlotte, George anxious only for a quiet life and

Charlotte burning to start a business which would dominate the entire neighbourhood: as indeed it did.

There was George's and Charlotte's son Alfred, dreamy and literary, walking out of All Saints' church in Norwood with his bride Annie on his arm, and being accosted by some gipsy woman who may or may not have put a curse on him and his whole family.

'I always think she did, darling, and that's why we are all in such a mess and so poor, so that I can't even afford to get anyone to look at my poor old arthritic fingers. And that could be why we're all so mad, too. Completely crazy!'

And she would laugh and laugh, and I would laugh with her and wonder if I was as crazy as she and all the others obviously were.

There was Harold, the son of Alfred and Annie, a paragon of intelligence and good looks, playing cricket so chivalrously that he would start walking back to the pavilion while the umpire was still trying to work out if he really had been bowled out, leg before wicket.

There was Bobbie, my grandmother's younger sister, who had volunteered to be a nurse in the First World War and had endured such great hardships and seen such terrible sights in the hospitals behind the line on the Western Front that she could never be induced to speak about them.

This, I later found, was almost entirely true. Bobbie was prepared to see my father and me when it became clear that we were no longer poor and déclassé, and once she even looked after me for a week or so at her house on the South Coast. She was stranger and less anchored even than my grandmother was, and would always claim that because her house looked the same as all the others in the street she could never be certain which one it was. Coming home with me from a drive she would invariably park outside the wrong house and try unsuccessfully to open the front door with her key.

Yet Bobbie, too, had been a heroine. In 1915 she had joined the Voluntary Aid Detachment, and had been given some fairly rudimentary training to enable her to work as an assistant to nurses in military hospitals behind the front lines. It was a terrible experience for the VAD girls, as they were called; they were close to the front line, with the guns going off close by and stray shells often landing near them. Bobbie never put anything down on paper about her time in France, but several VAD nurses did. One was Enid Bagnold, who wrote a book called *A Diary Without Dates*, published just before the war ended in 1918. She writes about the wounded soldiers she nursed with a strange emotion which sometimes seems almost like envy of the terrible things they had gone through; and yet at the same time she treats them almost like children:

> Living so near the edge of death, they are more aware of life than we are . . . They are new-born; they have as yet no standards and do not look for any. Ah, to have had that experience too!

Bobby, in later life, seemed to take refuge from her memories in a kind of outer-suburban silliness, as though nothing more serious had ever happened to her than forgetting the house-maid's name. And yet when she was young she went through some terrifying experiences, and showed remarkable coolness.

During the Battle of Somme, she had been within a few miles of Uncle Harold's regiment and had had to help with some of the most appalling casualties from the front line. Her hospital suddenly found itself in the path of a ferocious German counter-attack. The matron, a tough old bird who had served in the Eastern Cape during the Boer War, asked the nurses if any of them had weapons to defend themselves; there were stories going the rounds that captured nurses had been raped by German soldiers, and after the initial German advance in

August 1914, when Germany breached Belgium's neutrality and took over its territory, there were several well-documented cases of nurses being raped and sometimes shot. Bobbie had been given an absurd toy-like .22 pistol with a pearl handle by her father, so she put her hand up. The matron ordered her to take the German patients, thirty of them, back to the main hospital to the rear of the lines.

Bobbie had become used to driving ambulances when she was farther back behind the lines, and she was also used to sitting in the back with injured soldiers. But this time it was different. The German prisoners all knew their army was advancing, and many of them were not particularly badly wounded. Bobbie sat there nervously, watching the Germans as they watched her. There was no way of contacting the corporal in the driving cab.

The lorry lurched over the potholed tracks, jerking the men's heads backwards and forwards. One of the prisoners started giving some whispered instructions to the rest. Bobbie strained her eyes to see who it was, but could make out nothing.

'Silence!' she shouted, her voice sounding young and shrill and unconvincing.

Soon one voice, from the darker part at the back of the lorry, said something menacing in German. The heads turned in her direction, dark eyes stared at her. Back here, she was entirely alone. No one could help her now.

Outside, the noise of the battle was getting louder. A shell exploded not far away. From the depths of the lorry the unseen leader shouted a single word, and the men closest to her reached out to grab her.

Until now Bobbie had forgotten about the little revolver she was holding. It was so small and absurd that it scarcely showed even in her hand. But for all her silliness, and in spite of the fact that she was only twenty-two, she had had to cope with injuries which would have disturbed a soldier twice her age. There was something firm and decisive in her character which showed itself now. She held the little gun out in front of herself and let them see it for the first time.

The man nearest her looked at it contemptuously, and opened his mouth in a wolfish grin. Bobbie stared him in the eyes, pointed the gun an inch above his head, and fired. The little bullet missed everyone in the lorry, and passed through the cabin and out just above the windscreen. Then she fired a second shot, to make sure everyone got the point.

The lorry's brakes jammed on, the cabin door opened, and the corporal ran round to the back.

'Everything all right in here, miss?'

Bobbie looked at the prisoners. They had passed from aggression to fear when the little gun went off, and had now sunk back into the usual dull passivity of wounded prisoners.

'I had to fire a couple of warning shots,' she said, trying to make sure her voice didn't shake. 'They seem to be pretty quiet now.'

'And you think you can manage them for another hour or so?'

'Oh yes,' Bobbie answered, 'I'm sure I can.'

She pointed the revolver directly at the face of the wolfish man, and grinned. The corporal grinned back.

'That's the spirit. You're a plucked 'un, all right.'

The lady in late middle age whom I remember, unable to remember exactly which one of an identical series of front doors was hers, the flame-coloured hair which she had inherited from her tough grandmother Charlotte starting to turn pale and thin, hadn't always been vague and silly. Once, when it mattered, she had shown a toughness of spirit that any front-line soldier would have been proud of.

They gave her a testimonial and a scroll to mark her moment of courage, since nurses couldn't be awarded medals, and they sent her straight back to front-line nursing. When her brother Harold was wounded a second time at the Battle of Passchendaele, she was quite close by again. She must have seen more injuries from high explosive, more amputated limbs, more men screaming with the horror of shell-shock, than existed in most people's nightmares.

And then she went directly back from the Western Front to her quiet, dull existence in Norwood; one day she was in France, and the next she was at Sunny Bank with her family. They called her Elsie, but in 1919 she had her hair cut in a bob, after the new fashion, and after that everyone else called her Bobbie. It was as though in cutting her hair she had cut herself off entirely from the young woman who saw the injured of the Somme and Passchendaele, and quelled a rebellion by thirty German prisoners.

Soon afterwards she married a bank manager twenty years her senior. Uncle Cookie had had some mildly ignoble physical problem which had kept him out of the war, and he had never seen a wound or heard a gun fired in his life. At the start of their marriage, according to my grandmother, he asked Bobbie never to describe her front-line experiences to him, since he would find them too upsetting. No one else wanted to hear about them, either. Her two elder sisters, neither of whom had seen anything of the war at all, still believed it had been a noble and necessary business. Her younger sister was too interested in jazz and dances and boys with motorbikes to be interested. Harold, her brother, had enough nightmares of his own and didn't need anyone else's. And so Bobbie was left alone with the screams echoing in her head, and the terrible sights rising up occasionally in her mind.

She and her husband never had children; Uncle Cookie felt he was too old and set in his ways, and Auntie Bobbie once said in my hearing that this was too cruel a world to bring little boys or girls into – and supposing there was another war as bad as the one she had known? She escaped from her memories into a quiet kind of silliness. No one took her seriously, and she didn't take herself seriously.

She kept her little revolver hidden away in a drawer for

years, until I went to stay with her. Then she gave it to me. I used to play with it as though it was a toy. And it was – an absurd thing four inches long with chasing on the silver barrel and two foolish mother-of-pearl handles, looking as though it had never been used in its life for anything remotely serious. It only fired a couple of shots; then it became a toy again, for ever more.

My grandmother would have made a great wife for an Empire-builder; and in a later era, when women had more power, she might well have carved out an empire of her own. Unlike her sisters – May, who was gentle and motherly, Bobbie, who was light and silly, and Vera, who was the youngest and, growing up in the 20s, a bit of a tearaway – Eva was a true Victorian, with proper seriousness of mind and purpose. As we sat toasting our bread in front of the gas fire and trying to keep warm in the cold room, she told me stories of people sacrificing their lives for each other, or behaving decently when everyone else was panicking. As I stared at the blue and red flames of the gas fire she told me at great length about the troopship *Birkenhead*, which sank off the coast of South Africa in the 1870s. There weren't enough lifeboats for the 400 soldiers and their wives and children, so the commanding officer decided that the men should be drawn up on deck at attention while their families got into the boats; that way there would be no panic, no chaos to endanger the escape of the women and children.

Plenty of these stories could be found in a couple of books called *Our Island Story* and *Our Empire Story*, which I came across a few years later. When I look at them now, they often seem like the most simplistic type of propaganda; and when I had children of my own they were just about the only books among my childhood favourites which I didn't pass on to them. All the same, when I look at them now, I can see why my grandmother took such pride in stories like the wreck of the *Birkenhead*:

Amid the sobs of women, who were leaving their husbands and sons behind, and the cries of frightened children who knew not what was happening, the boats were filled. But the ship was sinking fast. There was not the slightest hope that the boats would reach the shore and return in time to save the men. Yet not a soldier stirred. Calmly and quietly they awaited certain death. It was harder, this, than facing cannon, harder than charging a savage foe. To die fighting, that were easy! But to have this courage to be still, to stand shoulder to shoulder, in the cold grey light of dawn, to feel beneath their feet the boards heave and sink, to see the cruel waves creep upward – that was hard.

And so four hundred heroes stood to meet their death. The boats with the women and children were scarcely at a safe distance when the ship went to pieces and every man went down.

The tears flowed plentifully, of course, as she described all this to me. I hoped that I, too, would have the courage to sacrifice my life for others, and assured her that I would always try to help those who were weaker than I because that was the duty of a gentleman. And I really wanted to be a gentleman.

Long ago, the copies of *Our Island Story* and *Our Empire Story* which she gave me vanished. I was embarrassed to have them around, because they represented an attitude which had ceased to be fashionable. Yet they had meant a good deal to me. I had learned at least a version of history from them, deeply inaccurate and questionable though it often was, and the stories and illustrations had been fixed in my memory like data on burned onto a CD. And so when I started to think about writing this book I felt I needed to check them all out again. I found copies of both of them on the Internet, and re-read them after more than fifty years.

As I had thought, the history was suspect. Britain's motives were always of the highest, and those who stood against the British were wicked, conniving, and wrong-headed, yet were always treated decently and fairly by us – and in the end they always came to love the Motherland which had taken them to herself. Flicking through the pages, I found all the illustrations which I had once examined with minute care, and had made up stories to myself about the individual soldiers or natives or settlers who were depicted there. The pictures seemed like the oldest of friends: King John grimly signing Magna Carta, noblemen plucking red or white roses in the Temple gardens and thereby starting the Wars of the Roses, pale-faced Nelson lying on the deck of the *Victory*, Jessie the sergeant's wife who, at the lowest point of the Siege of Lucknow during the Indian Mutiny (a term I'd nowadays think about before using), is lying on her sickbed when she hears the distant pipes of the Campbells as General Havelock and his Highlanders arrive to save them.

Then, suddenly springing up and turning her startled eyes on her mistress, she cried, 'Dinna ye hear them? Dinna ye hear them?'

The lady thought that Jessie had gone mad. 'Jessie, dear, lie down,' she said, 'you are not well.'

'No, no,' cried Jessie, 'I'm well, I'm well, it's the Campbells I'm hearin'. Dinna ye hear them? Dinna ye hear them?'

It was indeed the sound of the pipes.

If only history were simply a long record of heroism and decency and reconciliation, my job for the past forty years would have been a far more uplifting one.

My grandmother, I am certain, believed that this was precisely the nature of history. And not only my grandmother. On the flyleaf of my new copy of *Our Island Story* there is a bold inscription in black ink:

To my dear brother John
With loving birthday wishes
from
Meriel
Jan: 6th 1927.

'A glorious charter deny it who can
Is contained in the words,
I'm an Englishman.'

Above this, someone has pasted a paper sticker, like a bookplate:

This Book is from the collection of
V. C. C. Brooke, R.A.F., V.R.
who gave his life on Active Service
8th September, 1940.

That was during the Battle of Britain: another myth compounded of honour and duty and self-sacrifice, fully in the tradition of *Our Island Story*. Some parts of it were true, others not; probably the decisive moment of the Battle was when Hitler and Goering, in their anger against an isolated raid by the RAF on Berlin – something that Goering had sworn would never happen – decided to switch from the disturbingly effective destruction of RAF airfields in the east and south of England, and started bombing London instead.

But we need our myths; and the courage of young, often newly-trained pilots like V. C. C. Brooke, who once owned my copy of *Our Island Story*, is an important part of the British myth; just like the wreck of the *Birkenhead*, or faithful Jessie hearing the pipes. It's often quite easy to show that there are inconsistencies and falsities in the myth, that the good guys weren't always as good as the guys we have always regarded as bad, that whatever was done to us was no worse than what we did to them. But we all need something to keep us going.

Nowadays it seems pretty clear to many people that the whole idea of empire and power over others is a bad one. It does little good to the masters, and no good at all to the subjects. But the British Empire is an historical fact which we can't wish away, even if we would like to, and we might as well be honest about it, and about the people who created it. It was begun by a host of buccaneering characters who seized vast amounts of territory, continued by decent, honourable but often deeply unimaginative administrators, and finished awkwardly, and sometimes brutally.

India may have been run for a century by one of the most upright and effective administrations in human history, but we now know that the British dealt with the Mau-Mau uprising in Kenya during the 1950s in appalling fashion. Colleagues of my uncle Alan, when he was a senior intelligence officer in Malaya during the Communist Emergency, probably used torture on some of their suspects; though he never told me about it.

Yet for the most part the British Empire was wound up in quiet agreement rather than anger and hatred; Pandit Nehru would not have ordered that 'God Save the King' should be played before the Indian national anthem after independence if he and his political allies had loathed everything about the British presence. Sometimes there is a certain amount of willing self-deception about the end of Empire. In Zambia, for instance, you can see a monument to the national martyrs; but if you ask who they were, you will find they were a small crowd of demonstrators who were tear-gassed by a nervous young policeman. Understandably, perhaps, not everyone is comfortable with the thought that they might have received their freedom as a gift, rather seizing it for themselves.

The British Empire was an important historical fact in the lives of a sizeable proportion of the human race for more than 100 years. It existed – to the detriment of some, and the benefit of others. Nowadays, if you go to Iraq, and see how the American soldiers often behave to the local population, you can understand a little of what it must have felt like when the British Army patrolled the streets. Still, the entire Empire, a quarter of the earth's surface, was controlled by an army of fewer than 250,000 soldiers, many of whom were not themselves British. It was administered by a few tens of thousands of British officials, who had to govern their vast areas more by persuasion than by force. Most of them, no doubt, were brought up as I was, with stories of courage and self-sacrifice ringing in their ears. And, like the rest of us, they probably only did a very middling job of it. But with the best of motives, of course.

AT THE VERY TIME my grandmother was telling me what a decent and noble country Britain was, and how its power reached right around the world, British power in the world was effectively starting to collapse. Though it would be twenty years or more before many of Britain's other Imperial possessions were granted their independence, the heart had gone out of it. As Winston Churchill realized, India effectively *was* the British Empire. Once that was gone, it was time to shut up the shop – slowly, but irrevocably.

The Second World War had shown that Britain couldn't protect its Empire in the Far East, and that the fundamental necessity of any empire – the ability to protect itself with force, if required – was now missing; and the war had done serious damage to Britain's already declining economic power. So the British would never be able to cut the same figure internationally again. It's surprising how little this was realized at the time, either by the British themselves or by the rest of the world.

The withdrawal from Palestine was a clear indication that the British had lost the will to continue battling for control over its possessions. Few people come particularly well out of the story of the establishment of the state of Israel in the territory of Palestine, and there is even a revisionist school of thought among Israeli historians which – in the light of what was to come later – finds a certain amount of sympathy for the British in what had become an impossible position. They may be too generous. The British authorities in Palestine were never able to decide whether to favour the Palestinians or the Jews, and ended up damaging both sides. They permitted tens of thousands of Jews to die in the Nazi concentration camps, because they would not accept them as immigrants in Palestine; they allowed thousands more to spend weeks, sometimes months, on coffin ships like the *Struma*, which sank off Istanbul after two months of waiting, with the deaths of 763 people. And yet in the end the Palestinians were driven off their land anyway.

Both Churchill himself and the Labour Party were in favour of allowing Jews to enter Palestine in large numbers. The creation of 'a Jewish National Home' was an important plank in Labour's 1945 election manifesto. What changed British attitudes was the campaign of violence and murder by Jewish extremists. The Stern Gang killed Lord Moyne, the British minister in Cairo, in 1944, and the UN mediator, Count Bernadotte, four years later. One member of the Gang even hid a bomb in the British House of Commons with the aim of murdering Ernest Bevin, the foreign secretary, and it remained there for a month without going off.

The bombing of the King David Hotel in Jerusalem, which housed much of the British Mandatory Administration and was the Army headquarters, killed nearly 100 people, including British officials, Jews and Arabs. David Ben-Gurion, the far-sighted and generous-spirited man who was later to be Israel's first Prime Minister, called it 'a dastardly crime committed by a gang of desperados'; but it was planned by another future Prime Minister of Israel, Menahem Begin. Today, a plaque in the foyer of the hotel refers to the attack in surprisingly positive terms, given the dreadful losses Israelis themselves have suffered from bomb attacks: don't they understand that there is no such thing as a benign or noble explosion? Later, the murder of two British sergeants at the hands of another future Israeli Prime Minister, Yizhak Shamir, added to the anger and shock felt by the British. There were the inevitable calls to teach people a lesson – in recent times, American commanders were ordered to do the same in Iraq – and General Sir Evelyn Barker, the British military commander in Palestine, fell into the trap:

> The Jewish community in Palestine cannot be absolved from the long series of outrages culminating in the blowing up of a large part of the Government offices in the King David Hotel ...
>
> I am determined that they shall suffer punishment and be made aware of the contempt and loathing with which we regard their conduct.

In other words, instead of building on the natural revulsion which many, perhaps most, Jews felt for the extremists' atrocities, and isolating the bombers as criminals, Barker managed to lump them all together, the moderates with the extremists, and antagonized even those who might have stayed friendly by his distinctly anti-Semitic opinions. It was a tactic which had led to Irish independence after the Easter Rising in 1916; now another irreflective British general was doing the same in Palestine. Barker's letter was so useful to the extremists' cause that the *Irgun* group printed it on posters and put them up everywhere.

There were further vicious crimes in Palestine, and an outbreak of almost Nazi-like anti-semitism in Britain: thanks largely to Barker, the extremists had achieved precisely what they wanted. In the United States anti-British feeling reached new heights. The Hollywood scriptwriter Ben Hecht, who wrote *The Front Page*, said there was a song in his heart each time a British soldier was killed in Palestine. It was all getting thoroughly out of hand. Ernest Bevin, the bulky, bullying, quick-tempered former union leader who turned out to be one of the Foreign Office's most popular bosses of the century, despite his aitchlessness and his occasional blunders, infuriated President Truman by suggesting that an American intervention on behalf of the Jews was just an election ploy; which it probably was.

But British actions against the Jews in Palestine were often heavy-handed and sometimes downright wrong, and this was faithfully reported in the American press. The New York dockers refused to handle Bevin's luggage the next time he went to the United States (as a former docker and a dockers' leader himself, it was quite painful for him), and several people in the Truman administration accused him privately of being anti-Jewish. Perhaps he was; by 1948 he certainly seemed to hope that the Arabs would sweep the newborn state of Israel into the sea. They didn't, of course, and two wars and two insurrections later they still haven't.

The only answer to the problem, Bevin saw, was to get out of Palestine as quickly as possible. He decided to recommend handing the whole mess over to the United Nations and clearing out. It was an admission of total defeat, and a considerable humiliation, but it was also the most sensible thing to do.

Over a period of three days in February 1947, when there was no heating and sometimes no electricity in the cold, gloomy Foreign Office in Whitehall, Ernest Bevin sorted out the three main problems that faced Britain abroad. One was to leave Palestine. The second was to give India its independence. The third was just as important, and its effects would turn out to be just as long-lasting: to withdraw British troops and British funding from Greece. The other decisions were pretty inevitable, but on Greece Bevin might just have delayed for a while if he had been prepared to fight the British Treasury harder. He chose not to; and by doing so signalled to the entire world that Britain had been forced to admit it was no longer a first-class power.

For more than 200 years the British had been the arbiters of what went on in the eastern Mediterranean; just as they were in the Middle East. But Hugh Dalton, the Chancellor of the Exchequer, was clear that Britain could no longer pay the £60 million necessary to shore up the shaky Greek Government, strongly threatened by the Soviet Union and its own Communist Party. British troops were based in Greece, and it was ruinously expensive to keep them there. Money was needed to supply the Turkish Government and Army, too: Soviet pressure on Turkey was growing. But the British no longer had the money or the resources, or perhaps the will, for any of this. To Dalton's surprise, and the surprise of the Foreign Office officials who warned him it would be disastrous, Bevin agreed. He would ask the Americans to take over Britain's job instead. It was a seminal moment.

Congress, which was dominated by the Republican Party, was in resentful and complaining mood. There was still little understanding in Washington that the US would soon have to face up to the threat posed by the frightening rate of Soviet expansion in Europe; that was Britain's job, many Americans argued, and now the British were shirking it. On 12 March President Truman came to Congress to announce that the United States must 'support free peoples who are resisting attempted subjugation by armed minorities or outside pressures' – still, at this stage, no real sense of the ideological conflict looming between the Western democracies and Stalin's Russia. One senator, sounding the true note of American isolationism, complained:

> I am for giving aid to the people of Greece, but as to money for maintaining British soldiers in Greece, I would say nix. It is poppycock, this fear that Russia would move in. There are a lot of nations crying wolf against the Russians to get us in.

Plenty of other people in America felt the same – as though it was all scare-tactics by the British, intended simply to get America to pay for things they could no longer afford. After a good deal of fuss, though, Truman's bill passed through Congress on 22 May 1947: the precise moment, perhaps, when the

United States can be said to have become a super-power. British reactions were mixed: some resentment, yet a good deal of relief that the Americans weren't going to retreat into isolationism again, as they had after the First World War.

Ernest Bevin seemed to believe that Britain could carry on after this and still be a great power in its own right – not as rich or as powerful as the US, perhaps, but certainly on a par with Russia. Maybe it was his success as Foreign Secretary to hide the fact that the game was essentially over for the British. But from now on they would no longer be independent players; their only real future would be as loyal supporters of the Americans. And when, seven years later over Suez, the British made the mistake of not being loyal enough, the Americans would make sure they paid the price.

THAT DAY, THERE WAS a sign that Britain was determinedly heading off down another and different blind alley.

The Organization for European Economic Co-operation, based in Paris, had called for greater integration between the countries of Western Europe. M. Hoffman, one of the driving forces behind the OEEC, had recently proposed that they should create a single market of 270 million people – greater even than the United States. France, in the person of its foreign minister Maurice Schumann, had already agreed to the plan, in spite of its complex foreign obligations. Even the West Germans would be allowed in; a meeting of the Council of Europe at the Quai d'Orsay the following morning would vote to admit them.

In all of this, Britain stood aloof and slightly supercilious. Sir Stafford Cripps gave the British response to M. Hoffman's invitation. The United Kingdom could not, he said, integrate her economy into that of Europe in any way that would prejudice her responsibilities as the centre of the world's largest multilateral trading area, or her special relationship with the Commonwealth and the sterling area.

It was remarkably short-sighted. Within ten years Britain's trading position was fading fast, the countries of the Commonwealth were mostly going their own way, and the sterling area had effectively evaporated. The British, still believing that the rest of the free world owed them something for not caving in during the war, found that no one cared very much about them after all: the Commonwealth countries, which understood that they would now have to make their own way in the world, least of all.

In that day's *Times*, a 'special correspondent' begins a deeply self-deluding account of Britain's position in the world which lay behind the response of Sir Stafford Cripps.

> In the past hundred years there have grown from the Mother of Parliaments, at Westminster, not far short of fifty daughter Parliaments within the family circle of the British Commonwealth.

This relationship, the correspondent argues, is much closer than the one that would link the countries of Western Europe. It is based on a common system, a common language, and allegiance to the same Crown. Now, the first piece of machinery has been set in place to bring the countries of the Commonwealth even closer: a Commonwealth Parliamentary Council, which would have annual meetings. A special relationship was also being forged between this Council and the United States. A grand English-speaking, democratic association was being formed; why would the British need to join the European grouping? The *Times* correspondent puts it in a slightly more feline way:

> The significance of Commonwealth parliamentary unity for the Strasbourg experiment is not yet clear.

In other words, the Commonwealth system is well in place, and is working; the OEEC proposal is nothing more than an abstract idea, which is liable to fail.

> Commonwealth unity and closer European unity are not or should not be incompatible, but while the European Assembly sets out to become itself a 'parliament', in which national differences are abolished, rather than a conference in which they are perpetuated, the Commonwealth, further advanced than Europe in its basic unity, has not thought of

building a common Parliament. The aim has been rather to create a community of Parliamentarians.

In its reading of the past and its vision of the future, this stodgy, self-satisfied approach could hardly be more wrong.

We are one people, Mr R. G. Menzies, a former prime minister of Australia, has said; or as the Speaker of the Parliament of Ceylon put it last October at the Guildhall, 'We shall be in one mind, one brotherhood with the Mother Country that taught us and nurtured us.'

All very charming, and precisely what the British people, bruised and tired and anxious, wanted to hear. But it was also entirely delusional.

The dead end was coming closer and closer.

Another of the Labour Government's failures, the groundnut scheme, was exposed on this day. The scheme itself was sensible enough: to grow peanuts and other nutritious types of nut in the empty wastes of Tanganyika, and so raise the standard of living in British East Africa while improving the diet of the British. The big problem was that the land was much less suitable than the planners had anticipated, and the groundnuts proved to be uneconomical to plant, grow and harvest on newly cleared land. Unprecedented frosts had made the problem worse.

The Overseas Food Corporation, which had become responsible for the groundnut scheme in March 1948, issued its first annual report. This showed that in the scheme's first year of operation, only 49,620 acres had actually been sown with groundnuts out of the 150,000 originally envisaged, and that the overall cost was a monumental £23,975,000. Since the average yield per acre was 850 pounds of nuts, this meant that the cost per pound was a little over £1 15s. 0d; and a pound of peanuts in the British shops cost about 4d. Worse, it was clear that proper accounting methods had not been used. Now the

Corporation was considering growing sunflowers rather than groundnuts; but for twenty years afterwards those with longer memories taunted the Labour Party with this failure, and a heckler called out 'Groundnuts!' at Harold Wilson during the 1970 election campaign.

'Ah,' he said, 'an elderly Young Conservative.'

He lost the election, all the same.

SCOTLAND YARD ISSUED an appeal on this day for information connected with the murder of the racketeer and spiv Stanley Setty. His torso had been discovered in marshland near the River Blackwater at Tillingham, wrapped, said the Yard, 'in a piece of good quality brown-dyed grey wool art felt, machine stitched, six feet six inches by four feet six inches'. It was a fifth of an inch thick, and was thought to have been manufactured in the North of England. This, or a larger piece from which it was cut, may have been sold to someone before 5 October in north London, and they wanted anyone who might know something about it to contact them.

Setty had spent the war making money on the black market. He was famous by the mid-1940s for his expensive silk shirts, his well-made suits, and his garish ties, and for pulling out a fat roll of fivers to pay for his double whiskies. He dealt in stolen cars and stolen petrol. But his business affairs started to go downhill, and he got mixed up with one or two robberies and rackets that went wrong.

Among his associates was a small-time spiv and smuggler, Donald Hume. Hume would steal the cars that Setty then sold at a big mark-up. On 4 October 1949, not long after his forty-fourth birthday, Setty went to Hume's flat in the Finchley Road with £1,000 in fivers in his pocket – a huge sum of money – and never left it alive. He didn't even leave it in one piece. He was killed with a German SS knife, his body was cut up, and the head was put in a carton marked 'Crosse & Blackwell Baked

Beans'. Then the various bundles were dropped out of a plane over the North Sea.

The case was a sensational one, and as a result of the publicity the United Services Flying Club at Southend told the police that Hume, who was a member of the club, had hired a plane on 5 October 1949 and had been seen to load a large parcel into it. When the plane returned to Southend there was no parcel in it, and the window of the plane had been damaged. The police also discovered that after he had landed Hume paid for a taxi from a roll of £5 notes. He was arrested, but he told the police he had been contacted by a smuggler who told him the parcels contained forged petrol coupons and asked him to throw them out over the sea. The smuggler had paid him in £5 notes. When the police searched Hume's flat they found blood under the floorboards of the hall and living-room. Hume had an answer for that, too: he said he had found the blood and cleaned it up because he assumed that the smugglers had murdered Setty.

When the case came to court, the prosecution decided to limit the charges to being an accessory to murder. Hume pleaded guilty to this and was given a life sentence. After twelve years he was released, and sold his story to the newspapers. I remember seeing the banner headlines everywhere: 'I Killed Setty – Hume Confesses'.

On the morning of Thursday 1 November the sloop HMS *Amethyst*, after an epic escape from under the noses of the Chinese Communist Army, sailed into Plymouth harbour and was welcomed by the Board of the Admiralty. In the last stages of the fighting in China between the People's Liberation Army and the Nationalist Kuomintang, the Royal Navy stationed a vessel at Nanking on the Yangtze River to look after British interests. On 19 April 1949, *Amethyst* was dispatched to relieve HMS *Consort*, and anchored the first night at Chiang-yin. At around eight-thirty the next morning, the PLA opened fire on *Amethyst* with machine-guns and artillery, and an hour later, as a result of a direct hit on the wheelhouse, she was grounded on Rose Island. A second shell mortally wounded her captain. Her lieutenant took over, but was injured too.

That left only a junior officer, John Kerans, to command her. By the time the shelling stopped, twenty-two men were dead and thirty-one wounded. Kerans sent about seventy of his ratings, including the wounded, ashore with orders to make for the Nationalist lines. *Consort* was forced back under heavy fire, and the next day the cruiser HMS *London* suffered three killed and fourteen seriously injured before withdrawing. In spite of intense diplomatic efforts to free *Amethyst*, she was detained on the river for another ten weeks. Then on the moonless night of 30 July, she slipped her anchor and headed downstream in the wake of a freighter. She was fired on by a battery at Kiang-yin, and had to get past another one at Woo-sung, but early the next morning she was free.

She was given a hero's welcome in Plymouth. The signal lights of HMS *Vanguard*, off Devonport, read 'Welcome, well done', the Royal Marine band of HMS *Drake* played 'Rule Britannia', and the crew of an American store ship cheered her as she went past. Sixteen of her men who had been injured and brought back to Britain for treatment were there to welcome her in. The reporters who were allowed on board kept remarking on the smallness of the ship and the youthfulness of her crew – including her captain, John Kerans, now promoted to lieutenant-commander.

'*Amethyst*, well done. Up to standard,' said the C-in-Plymouth, in best stiff-upper-lip fashion.

Then Kerans and the rest of his crew were given a civic luncheon in the ballroom of the Duke of Cornwall Hotel. The speeches were so long that it lasted nearly three hours, and very few of the *Amethyst*'s men returned to the ship entirely sober.

Saturday 16 September 1950

Sun rises, 6.33 a.m.; sets, 7.17 p.m.
Lighting-up time: 8.17 p.m.
Maximum temperature: 59°F; minimum: 52°F.
Rainfall: 0.26 inches.
Sunshine: nil.
Fresh or strong southerly winds, veering west in the afternoon. Mainly fair at first, followed by occasional light rain clearing during the evening. Rather cool.

I GLOW WITH COLOUR: an electric, rather unattractive purple. To me, it is a matter for pride, and I can't help looking at my reflection with great self-satisfaction. We are sitting on top of a 49 bus in the left-hand front seat, and the purple burns so brightly that I can see myself reflected in the shop windows as we pass: as bright as the red of the bus itself, bright enough to shine out of the bus's shadowy interior. I am wearing a purple cap with a large white Gothic 'C' on it, a white shirt, a tie with lateral purple and silver stripes, and a purple blazer so new that it almost creaks when I move. It has another Gothic 'C' on the breast pocket. I am also wearing grey shorts, and purple socks that come up to my knees. I look like an exotic and slightly indigestible fruit on a fruiterer's barrow, but I am very, very happy.

My year's prison sentence is over. Suddenly, I can show myself in public without fear of being arrested. I started at my first real school on Thursday, and although this is Saturday and therefore a day off, I still insist on wearing my brand-new uniform. My father isn't happy about it; on the contrary, I have the strong impression that he is rather embarrassed. But he can't say no to me, and of course he is equally glad that my year of living in hiding has finished.

There is only one real subject of dissension between us. Beneath my shirt and shorts I have been forced to wear a dreadful thing which combines vest and underpants, and are known as combinations. My father calls them 'coms', to rhyme with 'bombs'. He has a disturbing liking for such oddities:

coms, and pressure-cookers, and gadgets like the dreadful duck-shaped glass container which he fills with slightly salted warm water when my nose is blocked with a cold, and pours it into my nostrils. He believes in the efficacy of gadgets, and there are times when I think that he even sees Christian Science as a kind of gadget for warding off illness and making himself happy and financially comfortable.

My coms are scratchy, and hard to put on and take off. When, in later years, I read about religious devotees like Sir Thomas More wearing a hair-shirt, I feel I know exactly how it feels. But there is a real sense of shame attached to the coms as well. They are not what other boys wear, for one thing, and for another they are slow and difficult to take off or put on, so any kind of communal changing will be a matter of embarrassment for me. Even going to the department store in Penge and being fitted with my school uniform is a humiliation, not just because of the coms themselves but because of the state they're in. Since getting into or out of them is a difficult, gymnastic business, I have managed to tear them in more than one place. Great gaping holes stretch under my arms and, even worse, between my legs.

My father has various methods for dealing with the problem which my coms present.

There is, for instance, the attempt to shame: 'Oh, you're much too sensitive. You think everyone's looking at you all the time, but I promise you they aren't.'

There is his instinctive salesman's pitch: 'Just wear them for now, and we'll see if we can't get you some new ones directly I can afford to.'

There is the appeal to reason: 'Look, old Johnny-boy, I just don't have the money to buy you any more at the moment, and coms are much cheaper than buying you vests *and* pants.'

There is the outright assault: 'For God's sake just put the bloody things on and stop whining about them. And don't tear them any more, or I'll be really cross with you.'

And then the final threat, which he knows I won't be able to withstand: 'Right, well, directly we get home I'll ask Mrs Rayner to mend them for you.'

That will be worse than anything, and when he says it I agree to stop nagging him. He would be perfectly willingly to mend them himself, I know: he quite enjoys doing tasks like that for me, and has already attacked the coms once or twice. But his time with the P & O taught him only the roughest cobbling as a way of darning, and the big, rough patches he makes are almost as bad and as shameful as the holes themselves.

'One day there'll be more holes than coms,' I say, with an early attempt at surreal humour.

My father laughs, and the coms crisis is over for the time being – very much on his terms, of course. It is true that I am much too easily humiliated and embarrassed, but that comes from a growing sense of being different from everyone else around me. My year spent under house arrest may have lifted my reading and comprehension to considerable heights, but it has done nothing for my social skills.

I have no friends of my own age, and I am aware that the relationship between my father and mother is an odd and very divided one. The coms seem to illustrate that perfectly. A mother, I reason, wouldn't let her son go around in these weird, unmaintained things; only a father who likes gadgets and isn't good at practical things like sewing would force them on to me. Read the signs right, and you can see my mother isn't around. I am convinced that just about everybody can read the signs right.

In fact, my mother *is* around at the moment. She is living at Lullington Road, and we are going back to see her now. Things are no better between my parents, but I am happy she is there.

'Are you going back to Epsom soon?' is the first question I usually ask when I see her; and when she says 'No' I always let out a sigh of relief and put my arms round her. If it were up to me to choose, I would much rather they were together, arguing, than apart.

But for now I have no real thought in my mind except an inordinate and thoroughly misplaced pride in my uniform. I am officially a schoolboy, enrolled in the Crispin School, Penge, and about to start my education. It is a small but decisive step to becoming like everyone else. I am sick of being different from the herd.

This is not how my father sees life. He is a quintessential individualist: that, really, is why he became an anarchist in the 1930s. He loathes the ordinary, the normal, the crowd. For him, the best moment is when he steps out from it and becomes his own man again. And, of course, he feels he has to inculcate these ideas in me.

We are making our way home by bus from the Everyman cinema in Hampstead. Each year at around this time the Everyman has a Marx Brothers season, when it shows all the films one by one. Today we have seen two: *A Day at the Races* and *Horse Feathers*. My father thinks that exposing me to the Marx Brothers and explaining their humour is one of the most important ways of educating me; and decades later I agree with him entirely.

The bus drives through the greyness of London, with its half-empty shops, its inevitable queues, and the bombed sites where the wild flowers and brambles have been spreading for years now, the stumps of old brick walls showing through the undergrowth like ancient monuments awaiting the archaeologists. As we go, he runs through what we have seen together. My father has an easy way of imparting ideas, and finding ways of expressing them which ensure I will remember and appreciate them for the rest of my life.

'You see, those two films were very different. *Horse Feathers* is early Marx Brothers, when nobody minded what they said and the scriptwriters let them be as crazy as they wanted. *A Day at the Races* is just a bit later, when Hollywood didn't like the craziness so much. They wanted the Marx Brothers to be cuter and nicer and not so crazy, because that was the way the audiences liked it.

'So you get Chico being sweet and affectionate, when he used to be just as crazy as the others, and everybody thinks he's cuddly; especially the girls. These big studios, you see, just want as many people as possible to watch their films, and the cuter the films, the more people will watch them. The studios didn't care how good the early films were. The only thing they cared about was that they made a lot more money from *A Day at the Races* than they did from *Horse Feathers*, but even so *Horse Feathers* is a hell of a lot better. And *Duck Soup* is the best of all. We're seeing that early next week.'

And then we started telling each other about the bits we liked, and I suppose I moulded my views on his. I still do.

Earlier that afternoon, as we sat companionably side by side in the mostly empty cinema, looking up at the huge figures on the screen, he would nudge me heavily and make his loud comments. Since there wasn't anyone sitting near us, I didn't mind it so much, but it could be a real torment if the cinema was full.

Margaret Dumont, large-bosomed and long-suffering, comes down the sanatorium stairs and announces that she's going to leave because the doctor has told her that her complaint is imaginary.

'Of course,' my father hisses. 'For once the doctor's right. Only her mind can heal her. It's all in the stupid cow's imagination.'

As a faithful Christian Scientist now, I nod.

But although my father feels he is a different man, thanks to Mary Baker Eddy, the old Adam hasn't entirely been chased out of him: at least in terms of making jokes.

'Who does the old girl remind you of?'

I look at Margaret Dumont, and know that there is someone; I just can't think who.

'Auntie Mollie,' he says, and goes off into hoots of laughter, which have nothing to do with the action on the screen. People look round at us: one of the worst things that can happen to me at this age.

'Shh, Daddy,' I whisper. I feel, as ever, that I have to look after him, keep him in line, or— Or what? This is never clear to me. Perhaps it is simply that children are instinctive conformists, even more so than most adults, and cannot bear to behave differently from the crowd.

Yet as I look at Margaret Dumont, and at the bosom, and listen to the grand, rounded voice, I can see what he means, and I find it guiltily funny as well. I would no more criticize Auntie Mollie than I would Mary Baker Eddy herself; but there is unquestionably a certain resemblance. It's the grandeur and the sense of authority, I suppose. Also the bosom. *A Day at the Races* comes to an end, and I wriggle round on the Everyman's red plush seats, trying to get comfortable. An usherette, fifty years old but still wearing the traditional little short skirt and with a tray of ice creams hanging on thick red tapes round her neck, walks slowly backwards down from step to step in the gangway. My father, without asking me, gives me sixpence, but by the time I reach the head of the queue the tray is empty.

'Sorry, dear – rationing.'

It doesn't matter: post-war ice cream tastes pretty chemical anyway. I settle down beside my father, who is reading the *Evening News* and shaking his head at the political reporting. He is getting involved in politics, as a Liberal activist. It would be hard to think of anything less likely to be successful, but when my mother tells him so he snorts, and tells her she mustn't believe the distorted news the other political parties put out.

I still wonder what he meant about the film. I liked it,

and can't really understand my father's criticisms. What's wrong with being cute, anyway? I like Chico all the more for it: it makes me feel as though he's a kid too, just like me, only bigger. It will be years before I understand what my father meant, and appreciate it. Of course he's right. The Marx Brothers sold out to the duller sensibilities of Hollywood, after their first four unpredictable, anarchic, outrageous films.

'You'll see,' my father says as the red curtains billow open again, and the painful wait for the big feature is over.

Horse Feathers, says the square black and white certificate, and I settle back with pleasure. I'm still laughing at the way Groucho, as Professor Wagstaffe, walks on to the stage of Huxley College auditorium, with all the ancient teachers in gowns, mortar-boards and beards behind him, when my father nudges me hard.

'Listen,' he hisses. 'This is the important bit. Listen.'

I listen – as much as I can for laughing, that is.

Outgoing head of faculty: Professor Wagstaffe, now that
    you've stepped into my shoes—
Wagstaffe: Oh, is that what I've stepped in? I wondered
    what it was. If these are your shoes the least you can
    do is have them cleaned.
Head: The trustees have a few suggestions they would like
    to put to you.
Wagstaffe: I think you know what the trustees can do with
    their suggestions.

Then he blows a mouth-organ and starts singing.

> I don't know what they have to say,
> It makes no difference anyway,
> Whatever it is, I'm against it.
> No matter what it is or who commenced it,
> I'm against it.

> Your proposition may be good,
> But let's have one thing understood,
> Whatever it is, I'm against it.
> And even when you've changed it or condensed it,
> I'm against it.

There is more singing, and I look round at my father. He has been laughing till the tears came, and nudging me as is his way when he finds something intolerably funny; but now he nudges me and whispers loudly in my ear:

'That's exactly how you should be.'

I find some parts of the film wonderful and some a bit boring, especially when none of the three main Marx Brothers is on. But afterwards, as I am sitting beside him on the top of the 49 bus in all my Crispin School glory, it occurs to me to ask him why he said that about the song. Why should I be against everything?

'I didn't quite mean you be against everything, dear old boy. I just want you to grow up without being worried too much what other people say.'

He looks out at the grey bombed city. Scarcely a stretch of road here in Battersea doesn't have its bombed sites.

'You know, everyone wants you to do what they think you ought to do, and it's very hard to have your own ideas and just follow them. Not easy at all.'

His voices trails off a little, and he looks away again. I realize he is talking about himself, but I can't tell what he really means. And why isn't it easy to have your own ideas?

'You must always be a nonconformist. Promise me you will.'

'I don't know what it means,' I say quietly, embarrassed.

It sounds like something to do with corduroy.

He explains.

'All right, I'll be a non-what you said. I promise.'

'Good boy. It really is the only way, you know. No good following the herd.'

Not following the herd was to take my father into all sorts of difficult directions. But he lived at a time when conventionality was important. Someone who didn't wear a proper suit and tie would find it hard to get a job, or a bank loan. My father rather liked dressing well, and he was always treated much better when he did; but he was vague and eccentric all his life, and sometimes it got him into trouble.

Once, years later, he told me that he bought a boxful of glasses in a junk shop, hoping to find a pair that would suit him. He had a particular dislike of opticians, which had nothing to do with Christian Science; he just felt they were unnecessary, con artists. By now, anyway, he had pretty much given up Christian Science, but he still felt he ought to be able to see better merely by thinking about it. He tried them on, one after the other, at home, and when he found a pair that suited him he wandered round, getting ready to go out.

In the street he noticed that people either smiled at him in a particularly superior kind of way, or else moved away sharply from him altogether. Eventually he caught sight of himself in a shop window, and realized why. The pair that suited him so well were exaggeratedly pink, with twirly bits of diamante on their frames: the kind of glasses Dame Edna Everage might wear. My father was awkward and difficult sometimes, and not at all an easy man to live with; but he was never boring.

On our way home to Upper Norwood, the bus bucks like an animal, so that I have to grip the handle in front of me in order to keep my seat. I have been reading about sailing-ships, and it seems to me that climbing the stairs of the bus while it is racing along is a little like going up to take in the sails: one false step could be my last. The journey is a long one, and even at this age I can see that we are well outside the inner circle of things. We are nobodies, out-of-towners. The dome of St Paul's is visible from Upper Norwood, but it is a good seven miles away. London for us is like Moscow was for Chekhov's three sisters: a place where wonderful, magical things take place, and from which we are always excluded. I feel exiled from a place I have scarcely even been to.

The route the buses take to central London from Norwood runs down Church Road; the church being the one where my Simpson great-grandparents were married in 1879. The road is half a mile long, and in the summer the end of it is lost in a blue mistiness which I found both exciting and deeply romantic. When I heard people like my aunt Daphne talk about 'going to town', it was down into this blue, magical formlessness that I imagined them heading. For a while I thought that London itself, 'town', lay at the end of Church Road and was quite close. It was only later that I found you had to travel through mile after mile of dreary suburban red and grey brick, entire suburbs built by the local equivalents of A. F. Simpson & Co., before you reached the true, exciting heart of things.

Somehow, I managed to fit my father's stories of his travels into this strange, microcosmic view. It wasn't merely London which lay in the mistiness at the end of Church Road, it was the rest of his world as he described it to me, too: Le Havre, where the people hated the British and tried to cheat them; the Mediterranean, where the sun always shone and people wore scarcely any clothes; the Suez Canal, which was like being at sea in a desert, with Bedouin and camels racing alongside your ship on the desert sands: that magical phrase again; Aden, where it was so hot that everything melted and your head ached with the brightness of the sun; India, where you could ride on elephants and see snakes rising out of baskets to the sound of a flute, and watch little boys as they dived into the harbour for coins and clustered round you, shouting 'Give it *pice*', *pice* being the small divisions of an *anna*, and an *anna* being a fourteenth of a rupee, coins which my father would then bring out of a velvet bag and show me; Australia, where the people were the same as us except that for some inexplicable reason they didn't want to be and didn't like us very much. My father told me how beautiful Sydney Harbour was, and how you only had to take a short bus-ride, like the 49 we were on, and be out in the bush where kangaroos loped along in their dozens, or rose up on their hind legs and attacked each other like boxers.

And then he would tell me about the unpleasant side of being at sea, when the waves were higher than the top of the ship's mast and crashed down on the decks, and the passengers fell down the companionways and broke their wrists and ankles, and no one wanted any food but you had to prepare it and take it to them anyway, because that was all included in the fare. There would be disgusting stories, like one of the cooks throwing up into a big pot of mashed potatoes, and being so depressed and resentful that he allowed it to be dished out anyway; or the time when my father was trying to balance three plates on a tray in heavy seas, and the rissole on one of them rolled off the plate and along the deck where, with a wonderful, depressing inevitability, a blind passenger put his boot on it. My father merely reshaped the rissole and put it back on the plate. And there was the story about the Duchess of York, later Queen Elizabeth, the wife of George VI, when she travelled on one of the P&O liners. The officers, so my father was told, rigged up a net in the S-bend of her lavatory, caught a turd, and had it varnished and mounted.

'It's still there, on the wardroom mantelpiece,' he said, roaring with his open, infectious laughter, while my mother clucked her teeth and said it was disgraceful, and then laughed herself; which meant that I could laugh too, without getting into trouble. But I felt it was all a bit disrespectful, and wondered that the ship's officers didn't get into trouble.

My FATHER HAD run away to sea at the age of sixteen, travelling I suppose down Church Road to do so. At the time his mother, Eva, had been furious with him, and it was largely because of her neurotic scenes that he felt he had to leave home. That would have been in 1930, when his brother Alan was eleven and his sister Daphne only six, and they lived in a rented house in Anerley, also built by the family business. But Eva soon got over her rage, and realized it was easier to make do with two children rather than three on the tiny allowance my great-grandfather grudgingly paid her (he believed that Eva had been responsible for the breakdown of her marriage to Herbert Fidler – the marriage the Simpsons had made her go through with, against her wishes). The money my father sent back from his pay as an assistant steward for P&O cannot have been much either, but it clearly helped a little.

In his papers there is a letter to him from Eva in her firm, round handwriting. The envelope is stamped 'Anerley S. E. 20, 7.15 pm 12 NOV 1936', and the penny-ha'penny stamp bears the head of Edward VIII, who was just about to give up the throne for Mrs Simpson. ('Such an outrage, that woman,' said my great-grandfather, 'and using our name, too.' As though Wallis Simpson were somehow trying to win respectability by wrapping herself up in the respectability of the Simpsons of Norwood.) It is addressed to

Mr. R. S. Fidler
Asst. Steward,

"S.S. Moldavia"
P. & O. Agents
Aden.

Another hand has crossed out the last two words and readdressed the letter to 'Tilbury Docks Essex'.

The *Moldavia* was a small and not particularly sought-after liner which plied the Australia route, and carried 840 passengers. There was only one class: tourist. For my father, that meant relatively few tips and inferior food. Being an assistant steward on the *Moldavia* was not regarded as a particularly good job. Nor was she a good or particularly comfortable sailer, only 573 feet long and weighing 16,543 tons. By the time my father sailed on her she was reaching the end of her relatively short life: built in 1922, she was broken up in 1938.

My father's other ship was the *Viceroy of India*, an altogether bigger and better P&O liner on the Indian service. She was 612 feet long, and weighed 19,648 tons, and carried 415 first class and 258 second class passengers. She had been built in 1929, and was eventually torpedoed and sunk off the coast of Oran in November 1942.

His mother's letter read as follows:

12.11.36

6 Oak Grove
Anerley S.E. 20

Hullo! My very darling.

It will be really hullo, this time *next* month, 'In person' & how? Sometimes Dec. 11th seems such a long terrible wait, and then I feel after all, it will not be very long before I see the beloved old Robbles again . . .

How I would love to be with you. I remember as a kiddie I often contemplated running away, and fondly imagined myself as a little stowaway, and the Captain of the ship would be a kind man and let me see all the wonderful sights of other countries . . .

Darling I wonder if you will remember to write, and tell me *about* what time you will arrive, and forgive me but I forget how I get to you. Anyhow only illness or worse will stop D[aphne] and I from coming to meet you, our loved one. The doctor (Dr. Pringle) said that was rheumatism, (crystals between the joints) that made my hand so painful and swollen, and the dear old chairman of the committee at Penge said he knew this house was terribly damp, and today Alan's bedroom is in a terrible state the rain through the roof has flooded the walls & floor. I told the landlord about it ages ago when I was doing the kitchen floor, but still nothing has been done so I suppose I must get very angry and go and see him again. I hate doing it, and am only existing until *we*, you, Alan, Daphne and I can get somewhere better to live. Now darling I think it will be wonderful if you manage to stick it out for as long as you can to get some money together. I am sure *this is our worst time*, & we have had some awfu' bad ones . . .

The shifts from gaiety to depression and back again were characteristic of my grandmother. A year later, prompted by his gentler, much kinder wife, my great-grandfather relented and gave Eva the use of one of his houses, 111 Marlow Road. It was much better, and scarcely damp at all. Perhaps he realized that she had not entirely been to blame for the fact that her husband had left her; or perhaps it was just the recognition that he had never been kind enough to her. When she died my father found an empty envelope from a letter he had written to her; on the envelope the old man had put, 'To the only one who was, once.'

As we sit on the upper deck of the 49 bus, where every adult except my father is smoking, he tells me random stories that occur to him about the past. How, for instance, the upper decks of London buses used not to have a roof, and there were large leather aprons attached to the seat in front which you could pull over yourself and your companion in the cold or rain;

and what fun it was if you were with someone you really liked. Or the story of how Uncle Jack Geale found his son on the beach at Dunkirk in 1940.

Hearing stories like these or reading them in books, my mind is inclined to play a curious trick, and interweaves the details of the story with the look of the place where I am when I hear it or read it. Sometimes this has the most ludicrous effects. To this day when I think of my father and mother lying in bed and being bombed shortly before I was born, my mind doesn't set it in a small, comfortable bedroom in Croydon; the bed is somehow set in the street near the Crispin School, just where the Anerley Road curves down to the Robin Hood pub.

By the same principle, when I think of the events of the Indian Mutiny of 1857 they do not take place at Kanpur, or Cawnpore, nor in the old city of Delhi, which I have visited and followed the course of the battle when the British and the Sikhs stormed it, but in the quiet suburban street outside my prep school in Dulwich, where I first read John Masters's novel about the Mutiny. The same is true of the siege of Constantinople in 1453. I have walked around the walls of the old city, examining the places where it all happened; yet when I think about it, St Sophia's Cathedral shrinks to a little Greek church beside my 68 bus route to Herne Hill railway station, where as a boy I first read Steven Runciman's account of the fall of the city.

Exactly this strange metamorphosis has occurred to the story of Jack and Alistair Geale at Dunkirk: the whole thing takes place, not on the windswept beaches with the marshes behind them and the grey sea stretching out to the horizon, but, ludicrously enough, at the point where the 49 bus runs through Clapham Common. I have only to think about Dunkirk, and I am there again, on top of the bus in my garish new school uniform, on our long way back home after seeing *Horse Feathers* at the Everyman, Hampstead.

I saw Uncle Jack Geale just once in my life: a big, gloomy

man with a fleshy nose and dark eyes that looked angry. I shook his large hand, and he looked briefly at me and then ignored me. That must have been when I was five; the incident at Dunkirk had happened nine years earlier. He was a lawyer, and a successful one, and he was fanatical about music. He became a leading figure in the management of the Albert Hall, and for years he had two seats dedicated to his use – with his name on them on a brass plate, my grandmother used to say with a certain pride. His wife Florence was the sister of my grandfather, Herbert Fidler, and she and Jack Geale had an only son, Alistair.

Alistair was seven years younger than my father, and much richer; but they were friendly and used to go out on the town together when my father was on leave from the P&O. Alistair took after his mother, but had a jollity and a boisterousness to him which didn't come from her or from his father. His favourite possession was his motorbike, a hugely powerful Norton, which he persuaded his parents to give him when he was seventeen.

'I always knew when Alistair was around,' my father says as I look out across the Common, 'because I could hear that infernal machine roaring from streets away.'

'Go on,' I say. My greatest fear is that my father will lose interest in the story, or fall asleep from tiredness; he was very given to that. 'Go on, Daddy. What happened next?'

'We used to go racing round everywhere on his wretched bike. To be honest, I was always scared of falling off, but he loved it. We'd head off to Henley or Brighton on it, and have a superb time.'

'Was Alistair nice?'

'Oh, he was a lovely boy – charming and funny and kind. Everyone always felt better when he was around.'

The war came the following year, and Alistair, now eighteen, insisted on joining the Army as a dispatch rider. He wasn't allowed to take his Norton when he went to France at the beginning of 1940, but the Army gave him an even more glamorous one, painted matt black and equipped with a sidecar which he could attach to it whenever he had to ferry a passenger around as well as his dispatches and signals. Alistair, young and dashing and handsome in a dark, stocky way, was in his element.

The Phoney War became a real one, and things quickly turned out badly for the British Army. The German advance through Northern France and Belgium was fast, and the French will to resist collapsed. Britain's will might have collapsed as well if the Cabinet had chosen Lord Halifax to replace Neville Chamberlain as Prime Minister, rather than the erratic, often unreliable but unremittingly bellicose Winston Churchill. One of the new Cabinet's first duties was to ensure that as many of the British soldiers retreating to Dunkirk could be brought back to England as possible.

The pleasure-boats and fishing-boats and yachts and life-boats went out in their hundreds to pick them up. By a series of small miracles the German planes which bombed the beaches and the rescue boats mercilessly never quite managed to destroy the main pier from which the soldiers were evacuated, so the operation as a whole continued until everyone was taken off. Almost everyone, anyway.

In their expensive, dark, rather forbidding house in Penge, Jack Geale woke up during the first night of the evacuation in a great sweat, and shook Florence awake beside him.

'It's Alistair,' he told her. 'I've seen him. He's injured, and no one's doing anything to help him.'

Florence tried to calm him down, telling him that it was only a dream and that Alistair would soon be back and everything was all right. Maybe she didn't believe it, but she felt there was nothing they could do anyway, and they might as well try to keep calm and hopeful. But Jack Geale wouldn't be quiet, and he wouldn't be hopeful.

'They'll leave him on the beach unless I can get to him,' he shouted.

'Get to him?'

'I've to go over there and bring him back.'

'But—'

An hour later, pale and lowering and angry, Jack Geale was sitting behind the wheel of his expensive car, wearing a dark double-breasted suit. Florence handed him a packet of sandwiches, and another package containing a change of shirts and some underwear.

'Oh, for heaven's sake, woman,' Geale said, but he took them from her all the same, and permitted her to kiss him goodbye. She and the housekeeper stood side by side in the darkness, waving as the car headed off.

How he reached Southend and persuaded the master of a little motor-launch to take him on board as it was leaving for Dunkirk isn't clear; but by ten the next morning they were lying off the coast, with the planes flying low overhead and machine-gunning the soldiers in their dugouts on the beach, and the bombs sending up columns of smoke that reached high up into the still air.

Orderly lines of soldiers queued up to get on to the long wooden jetty, and others marched along it to take their turn to climb down into the boats. They would take a dozen, or thirty, or fifty, according to their capacity, then head out into the Channel with them, going as fast as they could. And every now and then there would be the scream of a dive-bomber, and another boat would explode in a burst of fire and start to sink.

'You're on your own from now on,' said the skipper of Jack Geale's boat, pocketing the fifty pounds Geale had given him.

Geale said nothing. He put his leg over the side of the little boat and jumped down into the water, which came up to his chest and ruined his suit instantly. He didn't even look round or acknowledge the skipper's goodbye.

It took him a long time to wade to the shore, and when he did he found that the sense of orderliness which he thought he had observed from a distance collapsed in the face of the excitement and fear on the beach. There was a lot of shouting and arguing, and once or twice he saw fights breaking out among the soldiers; and especially between the British and the French, who were also hoping to be taken off the beach.

Jack Geale took no notice. He could see now that his dream wouldn't be much use to him in finding Alistair: the men were scattered over a huge area, and the clumps of reeds he had seen in the dream were everywhere inland – no guidance at all. But he knew his son, and how much he loved motorcycles; and it occurred to him that Alistair wouldn't leave his machine unless he was absolutely forced to.

That meant Geale would have to make his way to the road that lay behind the beach: he could see that many vehicles had stopped there. Some were still arriving, even now.

He had to throw himself down on to the sand several times, as German planes came over and strafed the beach. Once a bomb dropped quite close to him, but he quickly got up again and went on, his ears ringing with the sound of the explosion.

It was slow progress, making his way through the dazed and nervous soldiers on the beach, and it took him more than an hour to reach the road. Things were just as disorganized and dangerous there. A truck exploded a few hundred yards from him as he walked down the road. He took no notice; he was looking for a motorcycle with his son sitting beside it, waiting for orders. That was what Jack Geale's dream had shown him.

And the absurd thing was that, with a quarter of a million men on the beach and with all the bombing and strafing going on, he found Alistair quite quickly. He could see him from some way off, lying asleep by his bike, his dark hair blowing in the slight breeze. He ran towards him, shouting, hoping Alistair would wake up; but in all the noise he couldn't make him hear. He wasn't even surprised to have found him, but his gloomy heart gave way to a great feeling of joy and gratitude.

'Thank God you're safe, my dearest boy,' he shouted as he came up to him.

And then he saw and understood the awkward angle of Alistair's legs, the dark stain on the grass underneath him, the hair still blowing in the light breeze.

After that Jack Geale had no interest in leaving the beach, but someone saw him and realized what must have happened, and shepherded him down to one of the hundreds of groups of soldiers who were waiting to be rescued. He sat there on the sand, still gripping the bloodstained documents he had found in Alistair's pockets, not hearing the questions people put to him, not taking shelter even when the planes came right down overhead. On the boat he was the only one who didn't drink the hot, milky tea the crew had prepared, the only one who didn't cheer when they saw the English coast, the only one who didn't shake the sailors' hands and thank them for their courage and their kindness, and wish them good luck as they prepared to go back to Dunkirk and pick up more soldiers. The others knew by now what had happened, so they left him alone.

He was still wearing his dark double-breasted suit and his white shirt. But afterwards, when he got home and told Florence what had happened, the housekeeper threw them away because of the bloodstains all down the front.

Florence died the following year, though she was only in her forties and had always been so healthy. Jack Geale, awkward, rude, brutally unhappy, didn't die for several years to come. He didn't even have that comfort.

THE 49 BUS TRUNDLES ALONG its way, and these things fix themselves in my mind for ever, interacting with the scenes of suburban ordinariness we are passing through like some kind of mental fixative. When my father finishes telling me about Alistair I cry a bit, the tears running down my cheeks and falling on the lapels of my absurdly colourful blazer, and my father sits silently, thinking it all over. But he is too ebullient to stay sad for long.

'I tell you what, when we get to Crystal Palace let's go and ask Daphne to take some pictures of you in your nice new outfit.'

It is always 'Daphne', and never 'Auntie Daphne', even though she is the only genuine aunt I have, and all the others are aunts of convenience. Perhaps it's because she is ten years younger than he is, and he finds it hard to think of her as a grown-up. She is twenty-six now, and she runs a little photographic studio in Upper Norwood called Polyfoto.

The bell rings, but there is no one behind the counter.

'I'll be out in a mo',' calls the familiar, slightly throaty voice: very pleasant to listen to.

Then: 'Oh, Roy, why didn't you give me a tinkle and let me know you were coming. And look at you, Johnny! Don't you look lovely in your new uniform!'

She swarms round the side of the counter and gives me a crushing hug. Daphne is a big, strong girl, with emotions that flow quickly and readily. She isn't pretty; her features are too strong for that. But she is fine-looking and quite striking, and she makes you think of tennis-courts and afternoon tea. You can see her gentle, demonstrative character in her face. Of all my relatives, she is the least complicated. There is nothing even faintly neurotic about her, and she is never moody. She simply accepts what life gives her without complaint, and gets on with things.

Now she starts getting on with taking my picture.

'What about a sheet of twenty-four?'

'Poor old Johnny, I don't suppose he's got twenty-four expressions.'

'We can give him different things to do. I say, that's quite a strong colour the school makes him wear, isn't it?'

'Ghastly,' my father says, then apologizes quickly to me. 'I just meant it's quite striking.'

'The Crispin School,' I say under my breath to myself. I must have done it five or six times during the day, delighted to feel that I belong somewhere at last.

Daphne is getting the set ready, and preparing the camera.

'So what's your new school like?'

'It's really fun. The teachers are all ladies, you know.'

I sense that my father is pulling a face.

'And we have girls and boys. They all seem quite nice to me.'

This business of the feminine aspect of the school is something my father dislikes. He hadn't quite realized before we went there that there wouldn't be any male teachers. 'A dame school', he calls it; I can tell this is a disparaging term. And although I feel great loyalty to it already, even I was shocked when we went to the school concert at the end of the previous term and saw how inherently female the whole thing was.

Oddly, given that so much else has vanished, the programme from the concert has survived among my father's papers. 'The Crispin School', it says in purple letters on the top of a cover of poor-quality greyish paper. Underneath is the usual large Gothic 'C', and the words 'Programme 6d'.

Inside, the lettering is also in purple. So, in a sense, are the contents. The concert throbs with patriotism.

PART I

GOD SAVE THE KING

Recital

King Henry V's Speech at Agincourt

Welcome Song

Recitations

'What they like' Kindergarten
Cousin Peter "
Excerpt from The Importance of Being Earnest
The Lost Sheep The fives and sixes
The Butcher, the Baker & Candlestick Maker

Musical Play by the Kindergarten.
"BOBBY SHAFTOE"

Interval
(10 minutes)

All the children taking part in the Concert
with one exception are 12 years old or under.

PART II

The Revd. Leslie R. King M.A.
From The British and Foreign Bible Society

Excerpt from: "The Merchant of Venice"
(Awarded honours at the Addiscombe Festival)

Recitations

How'd you like to be a Baby Girl? K.G.
Apple Dumplings
The Witch and the Wizard Class I & II
All in the April Evening Girls
"Too clever"
Alice in Wonderland
Daisy Post
Beautiful Flowers

Presentations distributed by Mrs King.

What disturbed me when we went to hear this was the fact that the Kindergarten was singing 'How'd You Like to Be a Baby Girl', and I was going to be in the Kindergarten. Like most children, I already had a clearly delineated sense of my own and other children's sexuality. Apart from *Alice in Wonderland* and *Through the Looking-Glass*, I avoided books about girls, and once got annoyed with my father because he read me a bedtime story which was narrated by a girl, and tried unsuccessfully to transpose it all into a boy's experience as he told it to me.

'Don't they sing any songs about boys here?' I whispered anxiously as the children's squeaky voices sang about being the problems of being a baby girl.

'Look, there are some boys.'

But I was shocked to see that they were singing the words as enthusiastically as the girls were. Something bad had happened here, I felt. It was like one of those science fiction films where the hero slowly begins to realize that all the human beings who are wandering around, behaving strangely, have been taken over by aliens.

'Oh, I'm sure they'll sing a song about boys in a minute,' he whispered back, reassuringly.

But they didn't. In spite of her intense patriotism and her liking for Henry V, whom she no doubt thought of as Laurence Olivier with his hair blonded, jumping on and off horses and making stirring speeches about England, Mrs Isabel Jones, the headmistress of the Crispin School, was deeply attached to the feminine principle. She was rather nice and maternal, and had a bosom to rival Margaret Dumont's and Auntie Mollie's, but it was quite clear that little boys were lower down her scale of humanity than little girls. Hence the songs. Hence the purple.

My father didn't like that kind of thing any more than I did, but he was trapped. By the time we went to see the concert he had paid the deposit for my school fees – £2 17s. 6d. a term – and couldn't afford to sacrifice either the money or the time to find another school. Anyway, after the war middle-class outposts in Penge and Anerley had become pretty rare and quite embattled, like medieval castles besieged by the peasantry, and the Crispin School was one of the few. I suspect my father decided that he himself would have to provide me with all the masculine influences I would need, and hope for the best.

My mother, who came to the concert with us, hated everything about it.

'I can't believe you want to put him into that awful place with that woman.'

For once my father was rather abashed.

'I know what you mean, but I don't think we've got any alternative.'

Anerley Primary School was the alternative, she said, and it wouldn't cost us anything.

'I can't go there,' I started to say.

I wanted to tell her about the rough kids who went to Anerley Primary. There was a tribe of fierce, dark-haired children there who terrified me.

'No, he can't. Think what my family would say.'

'Oh, your family: those terrible snobs who won't do anything to help you when you need it.'

'Look, forget about my family. Your family hasn't exactly been . . .'

And they were off. It didn't worry me, as I wandered away to read a book. As long as they disagreed, I would go to the Crispin School; it was only if they agreed that I would be in trouble.

'Still, your uniform is a bit bright, you know.'

Daphne sits me down at a table and hands me a book to read.

'Well, I like it,' I say. 'It's a lot better than sitting around at home, anyway.'

I know this is a clincher. Any reference to the crime of keeping me out of school for a year always is. Both Daphne and my father stay quiet for a moment.

'Do you know what, darling, I think it'd look better if you took your blazer off.'

As it happens, I agree. The material is stiff, and her little studio is hot, with the lights on so harshly.

'Pick the book up and start reading it. I know it's not very interesting, but it's all I've got here.'

I immerse myself in an account of photographing the Scottish landscape, and the best lenses to use. This may explain a certain vegetable quality in my expression, since I cannot understand a single word of what I am reading.

Daphne goes off behind the curtain, and brings out a large camera on a tripod. Much of it seems to be made of brass.

'Where on earth did you get that? The Boer War?'

'Oh, shut up, Roy.' She snorts with laughter, in a particularly attractive way. 'The lens is absolutely fine. That's why they gave it to me.'

My father makes a derisive sound; her boss is famous for his meanness, especially towards Daphne.

'And it does take lovely photos. You wait and see.'

'Yes, wait twelve hours while they're developed. In silver nitrate, I suppose.'

'What's silver nitrate?'

'Shh, dear old boy, don't talk now. It's supposed to be a joke, anyway. Daphne needs to take your photo.'

It requires a good deal of time. Twenty-four poses, even pretty rudimentary ones, can't be struck altogether quickly. But there they are, on a sheet of paper: a definitive portrait of myself at the age of six, two days after my education has begun. Sometimes I am looking down at the book, sometimes I am looking to the side, sometimes I am looking straight at the camera. I don't in any way resemble the large, sprawling figure I was to become, but there are little details of similarity: our big ears, our red lips.

The thing this six-year-old and I have most in common, though, is that he and I see almost everything alike. The same things frighten us, and the same things incline us to take the same kind of risk. The same emotions sway us, and bring tears to our eyes. We both hate the kind of scenes that my father and mother seem to have most of the time, and we both try to escape from them. I know more than the six-year-old does, and can intimidate people better than he can, and have endured things he would never have survived. I would shock him, I suppose, with my worldliness, and my occasional brutality, and my willingness to put up with things that are second best.

But we each know how the other's mind works, because it is essentially the same mind, whereas our legs and faces and hands are not the same at all, merely similar. I know what stories he likes, and he knows what stories I like. He would recognize the thread of romanticism and of pity that is common to us both, and the carelessness and thoughtlessness too. He is me psychologically, in a way he is not physically. I like him; I just hope he would like me, and can't be absolutely sure he would.

'There we are, darling, all over now. You were a very good

boy. I'm sorry it was so hot. You can put your blazer back on now, if you like. Roy, wasn't he good?'

None of us knows how our lives will turn out. Daphne's was a difficult one, which she got through as best she could by being jolly and courageous, and whistling tunelessly like her mother when things got too bad. She wasn't a complainer, nor did she hint, as her mother invariably did, that life was terrible and that only someone with her fortitude could bear it. Daphne would write me cheerful little notes from time to time, and would always try to watch the programmes I made for television. She was proud of me, and talked about me to everyone she knew; and although that sometimes made me feel awkward it mostly gave me a sense of pleasure that I could make her happy. She had a difficult husband, and a charming, thoughtful, careful son who sometimes reminded me of myself a little: uncomfortable with rows, keen to overcome his natural timidity by being jolly and bluff and positive, inclined to look on the bright side long after the true scale of the problem had become clear.

Finally, Daphne went into a decline, and fifty years almost to the month after she had taken the photos of me I found myself sitting beside her in hospital, telling her things I had never really told anyone else. What would the little boy in his white shirt and purple tie have thought of that? What would she have thought of it? I suppose she would have laughed and said it was no use worrying about the future, and would have whistled for a while and offered everyone a cup of tea; and within five minutes we would all have forgotten what we were talking about. But the mistake is to think the outer calm and jollity reflects what is going on inside.

By the previous year, 1949, the Labour Government had shown itself to be exhausted. Ernest Bevin was dead, and so was Ellen Wilkinson; Sir Stafford Cripps would soon have to resign his seat because of a terminal illness. The sheer grind of running the country under such difficult conditions was simply too much. The Attlee Government had run out of ideas, out of steam, out of any heartfelt public support. The winter of 1949–50 was another hard one, and death was in the air. A little over a week after the election was announced, George Orwell died. He was only forty-seven.

Election day, 23 February 1950, was windy and wet, and the temperature in many places was only a degree above freezing. The turn-out was less than Labour's own strongest supporters had hoped, and the cold, together with the general sense of disillusion with the great experiment of 1945, told against the Government. They finished the 1945 Parliament with 384 seats to the Conservatives' 203 and the Liberals' ten. Independents held eighteen seats, and the Communists two.

The voters changed all that. When the votes were counted, Labour's majority was cut from 181 to 20. All the independents, and both the Communists, lost their seats. Three hundred of the 479 Liberal candidates scored so few votes that they lost their deposits. Labour's votes totalled 13 million, the Conservatives 11 million, and the Liberals 2½ million.

The spirit of contrariness ('Whatever it is, I'm against it') had persuaded my father to support and work for the one party which was plainly never going to win. In the bag containing my father's papers is a letter with a heading in Liberal green.

General Election, 1950, Peckham Division

Liberal Candidate
Kenneth Gunnell.

Agent: Telephone: Central Committee Rooms
NORMAN STEWART RODney 2427
160 Camberwell Road, S.E.5

23rd February, 1950.

Dear Mr. Simpson,

May I express my appreciation of all you have done on my behalf during this campaign.

Your energetic and persuasive canvassing has undoubtedly helped many people to see the light.

Wishing you every success in your future career, again thanking you for all you have done.

Yours very sincerely,

Kenneth Gunnell.

In fact my father's efforts to help him were scarcely very effective. The Labour candidate, Mrs Corbett, received 32,623 votes, E. H. Lee, the Tory, 13,323, and poor Mr Gunnell only 2,267. Much of that night and through into the following day my father sat in our little kitchen up in the roof at Lullington Road, with the radio on the table and me on a small chair beside him, listening to the election results. Somehow he reminded me of the White Knight, whose ideas and inventions all come to nothing.

'The Liberal candidate loses his deposit,' the newsreader's voice would intone again and again, as he read out the details of each constituency's vote. Each time my father would groan painfully. Mr Gunnell's deposit was well and truly lost too – one of 300 the Liberals forfeited that night. Everyone thought it was the end of the party of Gladstone and Lloyd George, and that the future belonged solely to the Tories and Labour.

I felt sorry for my father, because I could see that, like me, he espoused causes strongly and identified with them whole-heartedly. My mother was sitting in the next room, smoking and reading; she didn't like politics at all, and the only politician she liked was Winston Churchill.

At the polling-station the previous day my father, who didn't live in Mr Gunnell's constituency, had nearly been arrested because as he and my mother walked into the polling-booth, he called out to her, 'Don't forget to vote for McCarthy,' or whatever the Liberal candidate's name was; in those days the ballot-papers only carried the candidates' names, not the parties they belonged to. The policeman on duty thought my father was trying to influence the vote, and it was only when my mother produced some sort of evidence to show they were married, and assured him she had a bad memory for names and needed reminding, that he let my father go.

But if it hadn't been for that, my mother would have voted Tory.

'I know they're only for rich people, but they do understand how to govern the country,' she said.

All my father's left-wing past would rise up in him.

'Just a load of blood-suckers,' he would shout, his ideas starting to flail around without any control or discrimination. 'What have the Tories ever done for anyone, except fail to rearm when Hitler was around? They'll always go where the money is. There's Eva, who always votes Tory because she thinks they're gentlemen, and says "They're our sort of people"' (he did a very good and rather unkind imitation of her voice, and my mother and I both grin) 'when she doesn't realize what a shower they are.'

'Shower' was short for 'shower of shit', so my mother frowned and put her finger to her lips even though the actual word hadn't been used.

'She ought to vote Labour,' my father continued, loudly. 'Labour are the only ones who care about the old and the widows and the unemployed.'

'So why aren't you helping Labour?'

He had no real answer for that, though I can see now that it was because he would never really have wanted to work for a party which had a chance of winning. But even he certainly hadn't want it to lose so badly.

He shared my mother's and grandmother's admiration for Winston Churchill. A few weeks before the 1950 election he took me down to South Norwood, where we stood in the street outside the local Conservative Party headquarters for nearly an hour, waiting for Churchill to turn up. My feet and fingers were entirely numb by the time he arrived, and I was too cold to care very much. My father didn't cheer – that would have been disloyal to his Liberal faith – but he pushed me through the crowd to the front to make sure I had a decent view. All I saw, though, was a large brown fur coat with an old man's head sticking out of it in a Homburg, and an enormous cigar stuck in his mouth. He waved his walking-stick at the small crowd of us and gave us his famous V-sign.

'Wonderful old chap,' my father said as we walked away. 'Saved us in the war. But he's getting too old for it now.'

His feelings were, I suppose, something like those of the Labour minister Ellen Wilkinson, who, on the first day Parliament sat after Labour's historic win in 1945, enthusiastically joined in when the Tory MPs greeted Churchill by singing 'For He's a Jolly Good Fellow'.

'Well, he is,' she said firmly when some of her colleagues complained about it, 'and that's why I joined in.' Poor Ellen Wilkinson died of overwork only two years later. Generosity of spirit has not been characteristic of many of the politicians I have known since.

My father's politics veered from one extreme to the other; he was, in his way, a natural extremist. The young man who volunteered to fight for the Anarchists in Spain and took part in anti-Fascist demonstrations in London in the 1930s and worked for the Liberals in the early 1950s had swung round by the early 1960s to become a noisy supporter of Enoch Powell, of Rhodesian independence, and of apartheid in South Africa. Yet although he shared many of the most racist attitudes of his time, he was never entirely immune to reason.

In 1977 I became the BBC correspondent in South Africa, and he came to visit me in Johannesburg. One Thursday night I took him round to our local supermarket and got him to stand near the shelves where the pet supplies were sold. Then I explained to him that the black women who were there, queuing up to buy cans of dog food, would be giving it to their children that night, not to their dogs; they had run out of money, because the next day was payday. After that he no longer used to support South Africa quite so vocally, and he gave up asking goading little questions such as, 'If South Africa is so terrible, why do so many Africans from the nearby countries want to go there?'

In the end he found a party and a political leader who suited him down to the ground. Margaret Thatcher was everything he loved. She was tough, she was middle class, she looked good, and she seemed to share all his opinions; at least, he thought she did. The only thing he missed in her was the faintest indication of a sense of humour. One day in 1980, shortly before he died, he was telling me yet again how wonderful she was, when I reminded him of Groucho's song from *Horse Feathers*. By that stage I was the BBC's political affairs editor, and he was extremely proud of me.

'You're not against things any more like you used to be, are you? Don't you think you should be?'

He grinned at me.

'But you don't realize that that's what Thatcher is. She's against everyone, and I'm on her side.'

THE THING THAT SURPRISED everyone in 1950 was the way the Conservatives had recovered from their disaster at the polls five years earlier. Yet it was clear enough when the turning-point had been. In 1945 the Conservatives seemed to have been destroyed – so much so, that some wondered if the party shouldn't simply disband itself and begin again under a different name and with different leaders. Less than two years later, during the appalling winter of 1947, when Britain seemed at the lowest ebb in its entire history, the pollsters who stood shivering on the country's doorsteps found that almost as many people now said they would vote Conservative as would vote Labour.

Through no real fault of its own, the Attlee Government had become associated in people's minds with shortages and rationing and hardship and cold, and Sir Stafford Cripps, with his long, ascetic, humourless face, his glittering *pince-nez*, his braying voice and his apparent enjoyment of austerity and pain, seemed to embody the spirit of Labour and its policies. If Clement Attlee had been more of a national leader and less of a quiet, colourless backroom manager, it might have taken some of the attention away from Cripps. As it was, the gloomy spirit of Sir Stafford Cripps was all that anyone really saw of the 1945 Labour Government.

In 1945 people were prepared to make sacrifices for a better and more equitable Britain. The old ways of the 1920s and 30s weren't good enough; the great majority now accepted that decent social policies, the Welfare State and the nationalization of big industries represented the only sensible way forward. Yet the price was very high, and after the sacrifices of the war most people in Britain felt a longing for some kind of respite, an end to rationing and official snooping and high taxes and shortages. The country was developing a sweet tooth again, and wanted a little sugar with its never-ending medicine. The Attlee Government sensed all this, but was incapable of doing anything about it. Britain simply wasn't in a position to break out of the habits of austerity. The only way to improve the conditions of daily life was to produce more; and nationalization seemed the best means of achieving that.

We see everything very differently nowadays, of course. After a quarter of a century during which Britain has thrived as a result of denationalizing the industries taken into public ownership by the 1945 Labour Government, it is hard to remember that at the time even some leading Conservatives accepted that nationalization was the chief answer to Britain's economic problems. The disadvantages only became clear later: the lack of enterprise, the sense that idling and petty thieving didn't really matter, the shoulder-shrugging. In 1945 it genuinely seemed as though the people were taking control of the industries which affected their lives, and that they would make a better job of it than the greedy entrepreneurs who had run them for private profit.

The steel industry had long been an important target for the nationalizers. Not everyone, even inside the Labour movement, was in favour: some of the union leaders most involved, for instance. But a year or so into the Labour Government's time in office it began to look like the necessary next stage, the way of demonstrating that the Government meant what it said. The nationalization of steel was overseen by the elegant, handsome, wealthy, public-school-educated George Strauss, who was on the left of the Party and had once been a great admirer of the Soviet Union. On 9 November the Iron and Steel Nationalization Bill was published.

The debates on the subject acted like a blood transfusion on the Conservatives in the House of Commons. Suddenly, they understood again what they existed for: not just to watch the Labour Government force through everything it chose by virtue of its huge majority, but to oppose – and, what was more, to oppose something which, when they looked into it, they decided would be disastrous. It bound the Tory Party together again in a way nothing else could. And they had help, inevitably, from Sir Stafford Cripps. During one debate he managed not just to irritate everybody with his fussy grasp of detail (he usually did that), but also make his Government sound unnecessarily extreme: the very thing the Conservatives believed it was. He maintained that the Tories opposed the bill because it was an attack on their property. This attitude represented an attack on democracy itself, he said. 'Democracy must assert its rights. The ugly alternative would then be that any such change that is to occur must be brought about by other and more violent means.'

'By gunpowder?' a Tory MP shouted, and there was general laughter. But Cripps had gone too far. Talk about 'violent means' on an issue like this frightened people, especially middle-class people, and gave the Conservatives some useful ammunition. In the House of Lords the Marquess of Salisbury, who led the Tory peers, called the steel bill 'a definite step towards Communism'.

It was passed, of course: given Labour's majority, it couldn't fail. But the business of opposing it had polished up the Conservatives' political skills, which had been inclined to rust until now. Labour had previously made all the running in Parliament, and the Tories had been forced to sit and watch, grateful that they had managed to hold on to their seats in the 1945 landslide. Now things were starting to change. A Conservative recovery was under way. Soon, the Tories would be in a position to take power and keep firm hold of it for thirteen years; and the young, active Conservatives who took the lead in the debates on steel would dominate the new order, replacing 1940s Austerity with a very different and much more welcome creed: 1950s Affluence.

ON THE MORNING OF Saturday 16 September the United States forces in Korea captured Kimpo airfield, fifteen miles south-west of Seoul, and by evening they had penetrated the city suburbs. Seoul was still in Communist hands, but it was clear that the authorities there were panicking. The radio station stayed off the air for eight hours, then came back on with a programme of noisy patriotic music. No mention was made of the American advance. Very soon now Seoul would fall.

The United States and its British allies had received a serious fright from the Communist onslaught in Korea, but that was now effectively over. The big offensive by the North Korean forces, backed by China, had started to evaporate, and the Americans had hit back hard. A couple of days earlier the US 10th Army Corps and elements of the 1st Marine Division, the strongest landing force since D-Day, had stormed ashore from American, British and Allied ships at Inchon, the port of Seoul, which was still in North Korean hands. The landing was 150 miles behind the North Koreans' battlefront, and took them entirely by surprise. The troops went ashore at 6 a.m., and by 6.30 the area was almost entirely in American hands, with minimal losses. It was General Douglas MacArthur's master-stroke: his own idea, his own plan; and it would help to bring this savage, only half-remembered war to an end the following year.

The American forces didn't have numerical superiority, but they didn't need it: they had complete air superiority, and more and better tanks than the North Koreans. But the Communist forces had a ferocity of purpose which reminded the Americans uncomfortably of the Japanese. Even when US planes dropped large quantities of napalm on North Korean troops dug in on Mount Kasan, they stubbornly refused to surrender.

THE LONDON BUS STRIKE was getting worse, though routes like the number 49 weren't affected. Twenty-three out of fifty-two garages were closed. On Friday the Labour Government had told the House of Commons that Communist agitators were behind the strike, and although many of the bus employees were angered by that, the Government was able to show it was true. Some had just returned from a conference in Warsaw. There were fears that the strike would spread to the ports. 'Other agitators,' the Minister of Labour said, 'are active in the ports of London, Liverpool, Newcastle and Hull.' In Smithfield meat market, too, he added, and in several road haulage centres.

It soon became commonplace for governments, both Labour and Conservative, to blame Communist agitators for stirring up strikes in different areas of the British economy, and during the 1950s, 60s and 70s it was equally commonplace to regard that as a tiresome form of Cold War rhetoric. Yet after the collapse of the Soviet Union in 1991 the KGB's records, made public for the first time, showed that Moscow had indeed been highly effective in sabotaging British industry.

On Saturday 16 September delegates from British unions who had made an official visit to the Soviet Union published a report on their findings there. 'Russia with Our Own Eyes' concluded that the picture which most of the British press gave of Soviet society was completely false. Members of the delegation said they had been free to phone or write home, to walk round the streets without being followed, and to talk to anyone they wanted. The Soviet system was working well, they reported. People they spoke to in the streets wanted peace, but were worried about Western preparations for war. The delegates conceded that Russians had to work longer than Westerners to earn the money needed to buy bread, milk, butter and meat, but worked out that they had to work less long for clothes, books and entertainment. Cars and radio sets were cheaper in Russia than in Britain, they reported with a certain glee.

The body of the former South African prime minister, Jan Christian Smuts, lay in Johannesburg overnight awaiting cremation after his state funeral in Pretoria. Smuts, who had fought the British in the Boer War and had afterwards declared himself Britain's friend and ally, and had brought South Africa into both the First and Second World Wars on Britain's side, had been comprehensively defeated by the National Party in 1948 and thrown out of office. He had, people said, committed political suicide by joining Britain in the war against Germany; but Smuts himself couldn't understand that his people had deserted him, and went into a decline soon afterwards.

The Nationalists, some of whom had openly supported Germany, proceeded to introduce the apartheid system, separating blacks, whites and 'coloureds'. Even by 1950, some of the worst aspects of apartheid were already in place; though in some cases they simply built on laws which were already in existence under Smuts' United Party Government.

The Nationalists had hated him as a traitor to the Afrikaner people for his friendship with the British, but they gave him a magnificent state funeral. Two days earlier, his funeral procession had made its way through Pretoria for two miles. The coffin was drawn on a gun-carriage, and followed by a black charger with boots reversed in the stirrups and three men carrying his decorations, including the Order of Merit which George VI had only recently awarded him, on black velvet cushions. Covered by the flag of the Union of South Africa, it then lay before the pulpit in the Groote Kerk, with his field marshal's insignia on it. There was also a wreath from his wife, made up of purple, white and scarlet grasses, with the words 'Tot siens, Pappa' on it; meaning 'Au revoir'. Smuts had made an intense, academic study of the grasses of the South African veld. (Once, when he was standing in a field, joking with his close friend Winston Churchill, he told him, 'You don't even know what kind of grass you're standing on,' and for once Churchill was lost for words.)

Pretoria station, where his coffin was placed on a train for Johannesburg, was draped in purple and black, and a nineteen-gun salute boomed out as the train started on its journey. A flight of SAAF Spitfires raced by overhead, dipping their wings in salute. The train passed the village of Irene, where he had lived for much of his life, and where his ashes were due to be scattered two days later. As it did so, the choir from the 'native' school sang 'Nkosi Sikele Afrika', God Save Africa, which, fifty years later, would be the national anthem of the new South Africa. At a separate service in Pretoria, kept away from the ceremony in the Groote Kerk by the new laws, a coloured clergyman, the Revd J. Reynecke, raised his hand and cried out in Afrikaans, 'We bid you farewell, Oubaas.' The death of Smuts was, he said, a sign that the hand of God was challenging South Africa to halt the sudden worsening of race relations.

'The relationship between black and white is becoming more and more bitter,' he said. 'God's voice calls; will we respond?'

In Britain, a flypast by British and American aircraft to commemorate the tenth anniversary of the Battle of Britain had to be scrapped because of bad weather. Stirling Moss won the RAC Tourist Trophy race at Dundrod, near Belfast, driving a Jaguar. The British Transport Commission announced higher fares for the London Underground. The penny-ha'penny minimum rate would remain the same, but the tuppence-ha'penny fare was raised to threepence. In Kensington, Moore & Co., estate agents, were offering for sale

> a charming little Regency Cottage, beautifully decorated, three double bedrooms, two recs, labour-saving kitchen and one bathroom.

For a quick sale, they said, the owner was prepared to accept £5,750.

Sunday 15 July 1951

AND SO MY FATHER AND I, having been to church together, and without my mother, are walking over Waterloo Bridge towards the Festival of Britain. We have to go all the way around it on the outside in order to get to the Chicheley Street Gate, off York Road, because everyone has told us that this is where the whole thing really starts. Looming above us, to our left, is the huge Dome of Discovery, with the Skylon visible above it, beside the river, and the Shot Tower far down towards Waterloo Bridge next to the Royal Festival Hall; and although I still feel anxious and gloomy about the row between my parents that morning, the excitement of coming to the Festival is already overlaying all this in my mind. It is the most important thing that has ever happened to me, and I am ready to be enthralled.

There is very little I don't know about the Festival of Britain. It isn't simply that it has been a major subject of conversation for everyone I know for months now; *Children's Hour*, on the Home Service of the BBC, has told me everything about it during the past few months.

There is nothing at the start of the twenty-first century to compare even remotely with *Children's Hour*. Of course it was insufferably middle-class, and probably, by today's standards, unbearably prim and proper. No one swore, and only the really bad characters were rude to their parents. Absolutely no one, not even the baddies, said anything against the Royal Family, or religion, or the Prime Minister. There was no sex of even the faintest, most desiccated description. Yet even without these things the programme stimulated the imaginations of entire generations of children, by showing them glimpses of worlds that were altogether different from their own. And you didn't see it with your eyes, you had to sit there and imagine it for yourself: the faces and characters of the announcers, the stories, the places where they took place, were all summed up in your own mind.

At five o'clock every afternoon I turn on my father's large brown Bakelite radio with all those strange names on it – Prague, Luxembourg, Athlone – and savour the strange chemical smell as it warms up, and tune in to the BBC Home Service, sitting there and watching the dial on the face of the radio as though I might be able to see the presenters and actors inside the latticework, telling me what's going to be on the programme later.

But the first fifteen minutes are for little kids, so when their programmes come on I lie on the carpet which my father bought years and years ago in India, when he was with P&O – another smell there, of wool and dye and dust – looking at the pattern on it and absently working the songs and stories into it, like building imaginary castles in a coal fire. If I had any friends at this stage I would be forced to tell them that I find this kids' stuff stupid and boring. But I am alone, and no one can look down on me for listening and sometimes discreetly joining in the singing.

The parade of stories and characters on *Children's Hour* still winds its way through my sixty-year-old head: Worzel Gummidge, the scarecrow, saying 'Stands to reason' in his bad-tempered, rustling voice – I feel I can hear the straw his body was stuffed with – or Peter Scott talking about birds, or L. Hugh Newman about butterflies, or the rounded voice of Uncle Mac, which I never quite manage to like, or the delectably smooth voice of David Davis, which I like immensely. There are women presenters whom I like a good deal too – I have an impression of youthfulness and dark hair and lipstick, which attracts me even at the age of six – and elderly men like C. Gordon Glover, whose accounts of the countryside in the different seasons captivate my suburban mind and show me in word-pictures what landscape really is.

The programme is intended to interest older and older children as the hour wears on (actually rather less than an hour, I notice with pedantic annoyance), but there is no reason to stop listening to stories far beyond your age; so I give the greatest attention to stories about boys at boarding-school, or Biggles flying his plane (apparently you couldn't take off without shouting 'Contact' to the engineer, so I always say 'Contact' when I play with my toy aeroplanes), or young Romans or Greeks, or Robin Hood, or pirates on the Spanish Main; and anything I can't understand I imagine for myself. Phrases and titles from *Children's Hour* still lie heaped up in the corners of my memory: 'Orlando the Marmalade Cat', 'The Riddle of the Painted Box', 'Johnny Appleseed', 'The Magic Bedknob'. They have lain there for most of my life, half-glimpsed, half-heard, like an old jingle or a photograph you used to know well but have set aside and forgotten.

The Britain of 1951 is still wholly controlled by the upper-middle class; it will be the last decade that this is so, and *Children's Hour* is part of the propaganda that goes with that control. Thus, say all these charming, inventive Uncles and Aunts, you are, and thus you shall behave. Everyone you hear, except the comic lowlife characters, speaks like my grandmother and my other, more wealthy relatives, as though they all have an outsized cherrystone in their mouths. Some will spit it out, some will merely pretend to, as the years go by. And I, though I only became upper-middle class by adoption – after all, I was born the son of a factory storekeeper – have kept the cherry-stone in my own mouth because, I suppose, I feel you remain true to what you are. Which, now I come to think of it, is a phrase my grandmother used to me again and again in her damp, cold house in lower-middle class Marlow Road.

After all this time, it is clear that the Festival of Britain too is an upper-middle-class construct, something handed out to the rest of the country to make them feel better for all their wartime efforts, like a particularly generous Christmas box to the staff, or a tip for the taxi-driver for jumping the traffic lights. Like *Children's Hour*, it is full of useful educative information, pleasantly coated to make it edible for the entire nation.

The novelist and playwright Michael Frayn likened the supporters of the Festival to 'Herbivores, or gentle ruminants', the readers of the *News Chronicle*, the *Guardian*, and the *Observer*, the backbone of the BBC. They 'look out from the lush pastures which are their natural station in life with eyes full of sorrow for their fellow creatures, guiltily conscious of their advantages, though not usually ceasing to eat the grass'.

Opposing them, he wrote, were 'the Carnivores – the readers of the *Daily Express*; the Evelyn Waughs; the cast of the Directory of Directors – the members of the upper and middle classes who believe that if God had not wished them to prey on all smaller and weaker creatures without scruple he would not have made them as they are'.

I think that even at the age of six I have a faint sense that I am a Herbivore, a little homunculus who will one day grow into *homo BBCensis*. Somehow, the concept of balance has been bred into my genes: it is my version, perhaps, of Groucho Marx's philosophy about being against everything. There is no doubt that, as a child, I feel well-intentioned to people, and believe that even the most appalling characters must have something fundamentally decent about them. This is an unmistakably Herbivorean credo.

My father, as I trot alongside him towards the Festival of Britain, trying to keep up with the fast pace he always sets, with his feet turned out, looking sharply and humorously about him, is unquestionably a Carnivore. He is already in the process of leaving the *News Chronicle* and the Liberal Party behind, and he rarely trusts anyone until he has evidence that they are worthy of it – which he doesn't often receive.

He is a man without a political party, for now. He can't bring himself to support the Conservatives, after everything he has said about them. He will have to wait for an entire generation to pass before he finds his true meat; something a little stronger, a little gamier. His true political leader is only now getting ready to contest her first seat in the House of Commons, in a few months' time. My father is a Thatcherite even before she has become a politician.

Yet he likes the Festival. Maybe that is the old liberalism still at work in him. He loves the notion of lifting up the country's morale by showing that, even in our difficult times, short of dollars and shorn of power, we can show that we still mean something in the world, and are proud of it. The Festival is the last great action of the 1945 Labour Party, created in the image and likeness of men like Herbert Morrison. That side of it my father doesn't like, of course. But although he glories in Evelyn Waugh's savage vision of the world, he doesn't agree with what Waugh has written about this particular subject:

> In 1951, to celebrate the opening of a happier decade, the Government decreed a Festival. Monstrous constructions appeared on the south bank of the Thames, the foundation stone was solemnly laid for a National Theatre, but there was little popular exuberance among the straitened people, and dollar-bearing tourists curtailed their visits and sped to the countries of the Continent, where, however precarious their condition, they ordered things better.

Not so, says my sixty-year-old self, and my six-year-old self instinctively agrees.

'Are those people over there Americans, Daddy?'

'They could be, but you've got to listen to their accents pretty carefully to make sure. They could be Canadians, and Canadians get cross if you get them mixed up.'

There follows an interesting disquisition on the differences between Americans and Canadians; and I, as the patriot my grandmother has made me, duly sympathize with the Canadians. They, after all, fought for us in the war when the Americans were perfectly prepared to let us sink. My father, on the other hand, prefers Americans, on the grounds that they are likely to have more money than Canadians, and certainly have more attractive film actresses. And they have Christian Science, of course.

Plenty of people had suggested celebrating the centenary of the 1851 Exhibition, but the real project started with, inevitably, the *News Chronicle*. Its editor, Gerald Barry, wrote to Sir Stafford Cripps about it just after the war had ended, in September 1945, and Cripps, newly in office, rather took to the idea. Herbert Morrison championed it strongly, and most people in Britain, and most newspapers, assumed it was his baby; but that wasn't altogether the case.

There was trouble about finding a site, but by chance the London County Council (Herbert Morrison's old power base) wanted to build a concert-hall on the mostly derelict and bombed-out South Bank, across the river from Shell-Mex House and the glories of the Strand. It seemed a sensible idea to associate the idea of the Festival with this plan, and Barry was given the job of presiding over the whole thing.

It was a charming, thoughtful, well-intentioned, decent, inclusive sort of project: just what you would expect of such a man, and such a school of thought. Nowadays, I suppose we might find a lot of it intolerably whimsical: Rowland Emmet, the engineer and artist who specialized in depicting vague Victorian inventors and absurd contraptions, played too great a part in it, and the spirit of the White Knight was certainly there in good measure. Barry himself hinted at this side of it:

It was made in mayoral parlours, on fog-bound airfields, in dingy studios, on visits to experimental building stations, in lecture halls, youth centres, and standing on street corners for a bus. I sometimes think that those who jostled us in a queue might have detected a special smell, for all that time we breathed, thought, imagined, willed, inhaled, and exuded – Festival.

More than a touch too redolent of everything that many English people find too cosy and irritating about their fellow-English, perhaps: too cosy, too cold-showery, too public-school, too 'let's go for a nice long run', too bloody well prepared to put up with rotten conditions.

Lord Beaverbrook, Churchill's old Minister for Aircraft Production, a Canadian and almost a caricature of a Carnivore, loathed the idea and set his dogs on it in the form of the newspapers he owned: the *Evening Standard* and the *Daily Express*; which, though superior to the newspapers which bear these titles nowadays, couldn't work out the difference between information and comment, and existed to promote their owner's own ferocious views. The leader-writers and the chief sub-editors who composed the headlines were no more honest about the Festival than the cartoonists. Low, the *Standard*'s cartoonist, showed Barry telling the press 'We've now cut expenses down to twenty-five quid – and we hope to knock off another ten by not having gates so that visitors can't get in.'

From a newspaper which simultaneously trumpeted that the whole business was a huge and absurd waste of public money, there might seem to be a certain logical disconnect here; but the *Standard* and the *Express* and Beaverbrook's own private office didn't care, just so long as something damaging to the Festival appeared every day.

Yet the Festival sailed on, a Rowland Emmet-style steamship operating a ludicrous conveyor-belt system to get its fuel to the boiler. And slowly, because the Festival had the support of ordinary people as well as of the moribund Labour Government, Beaverbrook's hostile campaign started to fade away;

though even on the day the Festival was opened by the King and Queen, Saturday 3 May 1951, a *Standard* reporter managed to write:

> In one corner stood an object which may be thought symbolical of Mr Morrison and his planners. It was a brand-new twopenny slot machine. The shelves were bare. And on the machine was boldly draped a label reading NOT WORKING.

But even though not everything was quite ready exactly on time, the Festival did work. It worked extraordinarily, triumphantly well, and was a remarkable success with international visitors as well as with the British public. It wasn't true, as Evelyn Waugh had suggested, that foreign visitors bearing dollars headed off to Europe instead; the Festival attracted remarkable numbers of foreign visitors, particularly Americans.

My father and I, as inhabitants of a world far outside the glamorous, urban sphere of London and its politics, have come very late to the party: on this day, 15 July, the Festival has been going for two months. That only makes it more exciting for me, as we approach the turnstiles at the Belvedere Road entrance.

'We're too early,' my father says, looking at the big notice-board with the Festival logo cut out above it, an androgynous Britannia-Mercury head in a Grecian helmet, the head impaled on a red, white and blue cross with a curved line of similarly coloured flags underneath. Below the she-male head are the entrance prices, and it becomes clear that if you go in after 4 p.m. you will only have to pay four shillings each instead of five. As a child, I will cost my father half-a-crown (two shillings and sixpence) or, after 4, a florin (two shillings). Seven and six, £15 in today's money, is quite a lot for a man who currently makes his living walking up and down suburban streets asking housewives if they prefer Tide or Persil.

'Oh, we'll miss so much if we have to rush around,' I say

querulously, knowing this will be my only chance of coming here.

My father's heart is softened. After all, he has saved a few pence in bus fares because we walked over the bridge.

'All right, but we can't have tea. Is that all right?'

I would say yes to almost anything, of course; being so close to the Festival now and having to walk away from it is unthinkable.

The cost of afternoon tea at the Fairway Café, just on the other side of the entrance, has, I know, been a matter of some controversy. It started out at 5s. – the same as the price of admission – but after the howling of the press, which this time had some justification, the Fairway cut its prices by a shilling. There are in fact thirteen cafés and restaurants where we can get a cup of tea or a soft drink later, and many of them cater to people like us, people without much cash.

'Well, it's just gone one. We might as well head in.'

It seems to me that my father feels, as I do, that we are somehow on national business, taking part in a ritual of significance to Britain and the British as a whole: like voting, perhaps, or having a bet on the Derby.

There is a queue, a longish one, and it takes us a while to reach the lady at the box office.

'Hello, dear,' she says to me, in pleasantly matey fashion, 'got a day off from school?'

I freeze, from old habit, but remember I am wearing my school shirt and tie. I nod.

'That'll be seven and six, dear, thanking you,' she tells my father. 'And would you like a Guide?' She holds up a buff-coloured booklet as large as a magazine. 'Half-a-crown.'

'Oh, I don't think—' my father says, but I am desperate for the whole experience and want something tangible to remind me of it in time to come.

'All right,' he says, and finds another large silver coin from somewhere.

I nursed our Festival Guide for years, until its cover came off and the pages, only stapled, dropped out. The remains of it, too, are in the plastic bag with my father's papers.

When I look at it now, each page represents a pleasant memory, from the brilliant green peas in a dish on a tablecloth inside the front cover, with an open tin of Benedict Processed Peas beside it (or

Benedict
processed
Peas

as the tin's label has it, processed peas being a reach-me-down, ersatz, almost flavourless wartime invention), to

Don't be Vague

Ask for

Haig

No finer whisky goes into any bottle

on the last page. In between are dozens of old friends, from the macho winged figure of Mr Mercury advertising National Benzole, a long-forgotten brand of petrol, to Sharp's Toffees, Mr Therm, an odd figure in dungarees advertising the Gas Council, two cats and two kittens sitting side by side in front of a blazing coal fire ('COALITE – Smokeless Coal'), and a gorgeous sophisticated brunette with bare shoulders and dangling earrings, holding a cigarette in her hand.

> How careless memory can be. It can mislay years of happiness, and offer up, instead, one brief moment of enjoyment. But this, at least, is yours to keep, and no-one shall take it away. To millions of men and women, Craven 'A' comes readily to mind. Remembering the cool, firm feel of the *natural* cork tip, so kind to their lips, and recalling the rare flavour of the

rich tobacco, so kind to their throats, the significance
of other cigarettes escapes their memory.

Those who smoke Craven 'A' seldom care for
other cigarettes.

'Yes, well, darling,' my grandmother said when I showed
her the advertisement and she had approved the glamorous
model, 'the main reason we seldom care for other cigarettes is
that we can't afford them. And – ' breaking off theatrically to
cough ' – I don't know about Craven 'A' being particularly kind
to our throats.'

But she wouldn't have changed even if she could have
afforded better cigarettes, because she said the black cat on the
packets looked like her black cat, Amber.

Nowadays, what you notice about the advertisement (apart
from its remarkable claims) is the educated use of the comma.
Advertisers don't use literary stylists to write their copy nowadays, and the comma seems to be starting down the same path
to oblivion as the apostrophe. It holds us up; and we prefer
speed to clarity.

When I flick through the Guide and point out the Prestige
advertisement, my father's old loyalty to Easiwork flares up in
him. He doesn't like the fact that Prestige should be advertising
its Commodore Pressure Cooker in what amounts to the
national brochure, and he snorts over its claim that

The 'Prestige' housewares you buy in 1951 will still be
making light work of kitchen tasks long after the
Festival of Britain has become a memory.

'Still be blowing people's and arms and legs off, more likely,'
he says; though when I press him about this he admits there
has been no provable case where a pressure cooker has actually
blown someone's arm or leg off; not even an Easiwork. But,
unwilling to give up his fantasy so easily, he insists there have

been various cases of scalding, and one of a cat which was never seen again.

'They found bits of fur ten feet up on the wall,' he adds darkly.

There is another advertisement which, today, seems to typify the way the Britain of the 1951 Festival saw itself; and it also seems like a fossil record of an impossibly distant era: the time when the British designed and mass-produced their own cars. There is a large coloured picture of the royal coach moving through the street of London, escorted by the Household Cavalry.

> All that's best in Britain . . .
>
> The State opening of Parliament . . . truly a Royal occasion with its colour and pageantry . . . yet symbolising the very essence of our British Democracy . . . all that's best of the Past joining with, and giving authority to, the needs of the Present . . . an occasion as typical of our way of life as the craftsmanship that goes into the products of the Standard Motor Company, representing as they do in every detail of their design 'all that's best in Britain.'

Underneath is a stylized photograph of a black Standard Vanguard, dull and not terribly well designed. Vanguards were mid-market, boring family cars (Clement Attlee drove to Buckingham Palace in his in July 1945), and although they sold well in Britain they were less effective abroad. Standard itself, which also made Triumph cars, had endless labour problems; and although Triumph Heralds did have a certain dash and style (perhaps I say this because my father had a succession of convertible Triumphs, and passed one on to me in 1967, which I loved dearly), they become part of a conglomerate which slowly sank beneath the waves, killed off by rotten labour relations, a short-sighted union movement, and timid, poorly thought-out Government intervention.

We pause for a moment among the crowds on the Fairway, trying to decide where to go first. There is a photography booth where you each stick your head through a hole and have your picture taken as passengers in a balloon. My father and I go in, and the picture still survives.

At a stall nearby a man is filling balloons with gas from a large cylinder before letting them go into the sky. A little line of black specks over our heads, like a join-the-dots game, shows where the wind is taking them.

'It's going to cost me a bob,' my father says protestingly.

A shilling is worth two pounds today, but he knows he won't be able to refuse me.

'The balloon that travels farthest each week wins a fiver,' the man is announcing to the four or five families standing round him.

'I'll give the fiver to you,' I say confidingly, and my father grins.

He hands me the shilling, and the man fills the balloon while I write my name and address twice on a piece of brown-coloured cardboard – 'John Cody Simpson, 41 Lullington Road, London SE 19, England' in big, awkward letters – and he tears the cardboard in half; one half goes into his book, and the other is tied round the balloon together with a promise of a reward in half-a-dozen languages. He squirts in the gas and throws my balloon up into the air, where the wind catches it and takes it to follow the others in line astern.

(Three weeks later the Festival authorities wrote to say that someone living on the Gulf of Finland had found my balloon, and that I had therefore won the week's prize. I did give the fiver to my father, who promised to spend it on something important for me. I had no notion of what that might have been; possibly it was the electricity bill.)

After the balloon and the Fairway, my later memories of that transcendent day are pretty limited. There is so much to see, and so much I can't really understand. I make my father hang around for fifteen or twenty minutes while we watch an Emmet-like machine which pours water from one container into a larger one, which in turn pours into a larger one still, and so on through a dozen or so conversions, until the whole weighs so much that the water collapses spectacularly back into the first container, and the process starts all over again. We slowly wander through the exhibits looking at vast maps which showed where every British-registered ship was in the world, and where every undersea cable kept us in contact with our vast Empire and Commonwealth. I remember long walkways and steep metal steps up and down, and staring up finally from the inside of the Shot Tower, and listening to a range of British accents, of which the last was a cockney voice saying 'Come on, kettle, boil up' – a phrase my father and I used for years afterwards.

Looking at the Guide now, it is clear that we must have gone clockwise through the Upstream Pavilions, starting obediently, as the Guide suggested, with the Land of Britain, its natural wealth, its farming, its raw materials for industry, its ship-building, its pioneering design, and its road, rail air and sea transport. That took us eventually to the Dome of Discovery, where the earth and sea and Polar caps and space exhibits were. And then we started the Downstream Circuit, which began with the People of Britain ('We are a people of mixed ancestry and now a blend of many qualities'), and the Lion and the Unicorn pavilion.

Here, I suppose, the Festival was at its most characteristic. The idea was that the Lion and Unicorn symbolized 'two of the main qualities of the national character: on the one hand, realism and strength, on the other fantasy, independence and imagination'. So we were shown language and literature, with the English Bible, Shakespeare's First Folio, and the great authors:

> the visitor may care to assess for himself how much of lion, how much of unicorn, has gone into the making of such as Defoe, Swift, Sterne, Carlyle, Dickens, or Lewis Carroll.

We had British craftsmanship, with furniture, textiles, china, guns, and tailoring; and this, mysteriously, led us on to the British instinct for liberty.

> Throughout their history, the British have patiently probed for the weak spot in the defences of the contemporary enemies of their freedom, and, once they have found it, they have swiftly broken through.

In other words, we had Magna Carta and imposed a free constitution on the Stuart monarchy, and John Milton spearheaded the freedom of the press. There was religious freedom, and freedom of labour as a result of the sacrifices of the Tolpuddle Martyrs (the Festival was, after all, essentially the work of a Labour Government) and Mrs Pankhurst's suffragettes. And then the essential, underlying tweeness breaks through again.

> If, on leaving the Pavilion, the visitor from overseas concludes that he is still not much the wiser about the British national character, it might console him to know that British people are themselves very much in the dark about it. For them, the British character is as easy to identify, and as difficult to define, as a British nonsense rhyme.

> > The lion and the unicorn
> > Were fighting for the crown;
> > The lion beat the unicorn
> > All round the town.

> > Some gave them white bread
> > And some gave them brown;
> > Some gave them plum cake
> > And sent them out of town.

'Well, that's as clear as mud,' my father says, irritated. He regards this kind of thing as typical of the middle-class sentimentality he most dislikes He groans at the Homes and

Gardens pavilion too, and comically hurries us through the kitchen exhibit:

> More and more, in the past two decades, the housewife has been finding herself relegated to what, in the days when there were servants galore, used to be called 'service quarters'. Designers have therefore been aiming to bring her back where she belongs – into the social life of the house – without interrupting her work in the kitchen.

He doesn't think much of all that.

As we make our way further, it becomes clear how pre-eminent Britain has been in inventing and developing the things that define the twentieth century: radio, television, the computer, the jet engine, civil aviation, nuclear energy and so on. But the South Bank Exhibition isn't an exercise in boasting; on the contrary, the whole thing has a self-deprecating quality which makes it rather charming and pleasant. Overseas visitors, who are here in their hundreds of thousands, may not come away with much understanding of the British national character, but they can see that Britain is still remarkably at ease with itself: there is no sign of the collapse of national self-belief which will follow in the early 1960s, and which will last for a good twenty years. The Festival is an affable, amused, self-applied pat on the back for a country which has been through much that is painful and frightening, and has come out of it with its pride and its traditions and its sense of humour remarkably intact.

There is one last exhibit that makes a major impact on me, and I remember it very clearly.

'Look,' says my father, who is now in a tremendously good humour and has even broken down and taken me into the Unicorn Café for tea and toast and a rock cake. 'Let's go into the Telecinema.'

A film has just started, but the usherette lets us in and puts something into my hand. We stumble down the side of the cinema in the darkness, watching the curious and rather frightening flashes on the vast screen which isn't at all the neat rectangle I am used to, but runs round the whole of the front of the cinema. I am suddenly frightened: every one of the people sitting in the auditorium is wearing an alien set of glasses, with one red and one green lens; and as we find our way to our seats my father hisses at me to put mine on as well: this is what the usherette had given me.

Instantly the meaningless flashes become a clear picture, and the objects on the screen roar out at us in three-dimensional vision, so that I duck instinctively as a light plane shoots towards me, just overhead. Everyone around me does the same, laughing. The sound, which is called Stereophonic, rushes at us as well, and fades as the plane passes us. One day, intones a voice, this quality of vision will be available not simply in our cinemas but also in our own homes, on television. I have never been so excited in my entire life.

We talk about it all the entire way home, revisiting the exhibits we liked the most, and joking together, and we are still laughing and nudging each other and interrupting each other with new memories and new ideas, when we turn into Lullington Road. From this point, for the rest of the evening, everything that happens is imprinted with great thoroughness and clarity in my memory. The most significant day in my life so far isn't yet over.

It is quite chilly now. We walk past the spot where, a year before, I was knocked down and bitten by a boxer dog (I can never pass it without mentioning at some length what happened) and climb the steep steps to the front door with its strange old knocker, a bearded face: perhaps a lion, or a man, or a manticore. I hoist myself up hand over hand, as I always do, with the help of the iron railings, feeling the way they shake uneasily in their cement sockets, ready to fall out one day, like loose teeth. My father digs into his pocket for the key.

'Oh God,' he says, suddenly remembering, 'more rows.'

'No, please not, Daddy.'

'Well, it's not entirely up to me, old chap.'

'Yes it is. It is, Daddy. Please not.'

The heavy black door swings open, and my mother is sitting right there at the foot of the stairs. She is dressed to go out, in a light bottle-green coat and a little hat. A suitcase stands across the stair below her: open, for some reason.

'I've been waiting quite a long time,' she says.

She isn't angry; she never is. She isn't even reproachful. It's just a statement of fact.

'I'm very sorry,' I start to say.

And I am. I've had such a wonderful time, and she plainly hasn't. But my voice is drowned out by my father's.

'I don't know what you're doing here anyway. What's the point of sitting around on the stairs, like Little Orphan Annie? You'll just make everybody else talk about you.'

'There isn't anyone else, except your friend Mrs Rayner. She knows what it's all about anyway – you must have told her ten times over.'

There is a discussion about Mrs Rayner, with lowered voices.

I want them both to go upstairs, so we don't have to stand here in the hall. There might be some way of making my mother stay with us then. But they don't look at me, or listen to me. You don't, when you're trying to concentrate on the next thing to say. I hang around at knee level, looking up at their faces reflected in the big, dust-bloomed old mirror hanging in the hall, my weight first on one tired foot and then on the other. If only they could look round and see each other in the mirror, I feel, they might laugh and stop arguing.

I look in my pockets for something to help me through this time. All I can find are our ticket-stubs from the Festival, a rolled-up programme from the Telecinema, and a little blond teddy-bear two inches high and covered with some kind of sprayed-on fluff, with a tiny red ribbon round his neck. He appeared from somewhere – perhaps someone gave him to me – and I've been carrying him around ever since. I look at him, and put him on my hand to start playing with him.

'Look, you can tell Johnny's perfectly happy. I don't know what you're on about.'

'That's just typical of you. Can't you see how upset he's getting?'

'Are you upset?'

I shake my head: if I say yes, that's going to draw me into this on one side or the other, and I'll hurt someone.

'You see? I don't know what you're talking about. You don't understand the first thing about children.'

'Well, I've got two of my own, so I think I know a great deal better than you do about children and the way they are.'

The row takes a diversion via Epsom, the past, my mother's first husband, husbands in general, the inadequacies of my father, the inadequacies of my mother.

'Please don't argue any more.'

'You're starting to upset him. Go upstairs, Johnny, I'll be with you in a moment.'

'No,' says my mother, with an unusual note of decisiveness in her voice. 'There's no point in his going upstairs. I've got everything he needs here.'

'Whatever are you talking about?'

'Johnny's coming with me. We're going back to Epsom.'

There is a pause: this is something that has never occurred to my father, clearly.

'But you're not taking my son away from me.'

'I am. You're too domineering to look after him properly.'

She reaches down and picks up the suitcase, and then takes me by the hand. We go out on to the large front step, with its steep cement stairs down to the street. Looking down, with all this going round me, it seems horribly vertiginous. I grip my mother's hand tighter.

My father follows us out, and we turn to face him, while the door closes quietly behind his back. The door-knocker, with the strange brass bearded creature on it, comes into place behind his head. From this moment on, every little detail remains as clear in my mind as though it is just happening now.

'You can't just go off with him like that, without talking it over.'

'Why not?'

'Well, don't you think it should be up to the boy to decide where he wants to go and what he wants to do?'

With hindsight, this is probably just a debating tactic on my father's part. He loves me, and wants me to remain here as his son, but he knows it would be almost impossibly difficult for him to look after me on his own. If my mother really wants to take me, he won't be able to stop her.

'All right,' says my mother.

My mother is standing to my right now, and the late sun shines down along the line of the street behind her, lighting up her hair, her hat, her rather charming dress. She may not be beautiful, but she has an excellent figure and a natural elegance; even I can appreciate that. These are the last moments in my life when I will be the child of a couple, and not just of one person; but I don't yet realize it.

'Johnny,' my mother says, her husky voice breaking slightly with the tension of the moment, 'I'm going to have to leave now. Daddy and I just can't get on – he's too impossible. We have to decide what's going to happen with you.'

I look up at her, trying to work out what will be expected of me now, what I should do. Curiously, I'm not considering my own interests here: it hasn't quite occurred to me yet that my casting vote will now decide which of these two people I will never really see again. For a moment or two I assume that the in-and-out progression of my parents' relationship will simply continue, like one of those Swiss clocks where one emerges and the other disappears inside the little house. This, surely, is just another stage in it all.

And then I understand: this time it's different. The clock has stopped, and I will stay with whichever figure is outside now, the man or the woman. It's a disturbing moment, when I realize that the decision is to be mine. So as I stand here on the broad doorstep, with the front steps just below me and the two adults looking down questioningly at me, the important thing I have to decide is, which of them needs me more? There are so many issues here. My parents both love me, even though they don't love each other; that much is clear. I love them equally. My father is better company but has a difficult temper; my mother is sweeter and gentler and quieter. So I am not the issue; they are. I hold the little bear more tightly in my left hand, feeling his hard snout against the inside of my fingers. They are both looking down at me intently, suddenly realizing they have given me the casting vote on their futures. I stand there quietly, uncertainly, staring at the manticore door-knocker while they stare at me, thinking it over.

My mother has two children already, Pat and Michael. They need her, but they also give her a great deal. My father, by contrast, doesn't have any children except for me. The fairest thing to do would be for me to stay with him, to make sure he too has a child in his life. That will make everybody even. King Solomon decreed that a disputed baby should be cut in half and divided between the two women who claimed him, thus flushing out the true mother, who wept and protested. This is a kind of reversal of that: a child's judgement of Solomon.

'Well,' I say, my voice croaking as though I haven't used it for several days, my left hand gripping the bear even more tightly, my eyes fixed on the manticore still, as though I'd never noticed it before, 'I think Daddy hasn't got any children, so I'd better stay with him.'

I can't look at my mother after that, so I have to look up at my father instead. A strange expression comes over his face, which I cannot possibly identify. It is only some years later that I realize it cannot be a look of pleasure or of victory. By choosing him, I have saddled him with the most impossible burden. 1951 is not the age of the single parent; especially not the age of the single male parent without much money. I have no idea what I am getting my father, or myself, into. And now that the decision has been taken, there is no reversing it for either of them.

My mother makes a strange little sound in her throat. She picks up the suitcase without looking at either of us, and goes down the steep steps, holding on to the precarious railings with her left hand. I have, I see now, betrayed her utterly: all her love, all her gentleness, that long look of the deepest affection during the night completely thrown away. But I can't call back my decision now, and I don't know what to say.

None of us speaks. She reaches the bottom of the steps and walks down Lullington Road with the sun blazing in her face, a handsome, elegant, sad figure with a suitcase, the little feather in her green hat catching the last of the sunlight. I can't say anything to her now, because she is too far away. And anyway what is there ever going to be for me to say to her again, except how sorry I am, and how sorry I will always be?

My father never seems to feel guilty about anything. But my mother does, and I do. Our guilt will build up over the years, worse and worse, until it becomes hard for us even to see each other, even to call, even to write. There is no lack of love, no anger, no resentment: the guilt is directed entirely at ourselves – my mother for obliging me to choose, I for choosing against her.

We are condemned never to deal with it, never to talk it over. Our meetings will always be accompanied by the greatest awkwardness. I will tell her many times how much I love her, and she will tell me how much she loves me; yet we both know that at the critical moment we left each other. At six years of age, I turned her out of my life. At forty-three, she walked out on me.

She reaches the corner, and turns right towards the main road. She will never come here again, and I will only see her a few times before her death, thirty years later.

It feels very lonely, standing on the top step with my hand clamped on my bear, and hurting. Going to the Festival seems a pretty poor consolation for all this.

'Come on, old chap,' says my father, with an unusual

gentleness in his voice, 'we'd better get you upstairs and put some food into you. I expect you're hungry.'

He's got a lot of thinking to do tonight. I have too. This is something I will think about for the rest of my life.

Tuesday 14 November 2000

Sun rises, 07.14; sets, 16.31.
Maximum temperature: 12°C; minimum, 9°C.
Rainfall: 0.55 cm.
Sunshine: 5.25 hours.
Strong westerly winds, gusting at times. Bright
periods, occasional brief showers.

AND NOW I AM well into middle age. My father has been dead for twenty years, my mother for seventeen. I have had one marriage, which I walked out of, and one long relationship, and am married again, very happily. I am the father of two handsome daughters, and the grandfather of two girls, with two more boys to come. I have a difficult but exciting job, and am, I suppose, successful enough.

It is a windy autumn morning, and I am at the wheel of my car, driving a little faster than I should through the outer suburbs of South London to attend the funeral of my aunt Daphne, my father's sister: the last remaining member of my close family. The clouds have been ripped apart angrily, and there are twigs and leaves all over the roadway from the night's storm. My tyres crush them greedily.

I can see I am behaving like a resentful child, feeling I have been left behind, abandoned, deserted, betrayed, orphaned. The tidy shops I passed, the young mothers out with their prams, the carefully tended gardens, irritate me. Not even the brilliant sun, flashing and glittering in the puddles, has any effect on my self-pity.

Death is a disturbance in the orderly pattern of things: a chair left unexpectedly empty at the table, an unpleasant reminder that your chair too will one day be empty, that others will be gathering to remember you, just as you are gathering with them now to remember someone else. And if you have known the person who has died for a long time, and loved them, then the pain of acknowledging that you will never see them or hear their voice again is as sharp as a cut with a razor blade.

I am dreading the whole business of Daphne's funeral: meeting the other relatives, each as miserable as I am myself, enduring the gloom of the occasion, forcing myself to be kind and cheerful, and knowing all the time that the last link with my father and mother and their entire generation has been broken. We won't just be marking the death of an elderly lady, as you might close a book when you have finished reading it; in this case we will be closing the entire library, and it will stay closed for ever.

In future there will be no one to ask about the meaning of some puzzling family event, or the identity of a face in a faded sepia photograph. What precisely caused my father to run away to sea and my uncle to join the Air Force when they were boys? Why had my grandparents' marriage broken down? What really happened to my father during the late 1930s? Why should he and my mother, two people so different from each other in every way, have decided to get married? Questions like these are of no real interest to anyone except me; and now that my aunt, the last remaining family member of her generation, is dead, they have become permanently unanswerable.

There is something irredeemably depressing about a crematorium, over and above its function. It's partly the way the architect and builders have tried to pretend that it has nothing to do with pain, death and suffering, and everything to do with lightness and happiness and forgetting. The attempt is invariably a failure, like turning a labour exchange into a job centre with a lick of paint, a few posters on the wall, and a bunch of plastic flowers in a vase. In spite of all the effort that has gone into the disguise, the basic impersonal factory quality of the crematorium shows through, and no amount of roses and carefully planted trees round the building can dispel it.

The music may be Bach, but you know it is recorded; just as you know that the minister will soon be fumbling with a switch and hoping it works as he says the final words and commits the reusable box to the gas flames; just as you cannot forget that it takes, on average, three hours and five minutes to reduce a human body to the requisite level of ash and bone.

At least, I reflect as I follow the signs to the Chapel of Rest, this place is set in the countryside and not in some desolate outer suburb, like most of the other crematoria I have been to; like the one I consigned my father's body to. Who cares, anyhow? Not the body in its reusable box, that's for sure; just those of us who are obliged to gather together in order to be ritually depressed by an empty ceremony.

I am angry as well as gloomy as I drive through the gates; angry with myself because I know I should have done something a bit grander and better when my father died, in 1980. Just cremate me and don't invite anyone, he had said; no point in depressing them all. And tell the man who scatters my ashes to watch which way the wind's blowing. I should have ignored him, instead of arranging that silent, secretive funeral.

The parking area lies ahead of me, and I obediently slot my car into it. Ahead of me, beside his own car, stands my father's long-term friend and one-time business partner, scholarly, gentle, who was inducted into my family and its ways decades before. Things become a little easier when I see him: he helped to shape my childhood, and he is the closest person I have to a father now. Neither of us will do anything more than shake hands as we meet, but I know he shares many of my feelings: Daphne was only a few years older than he was, and she was as fond of him as he was of her. Now we each thank the other for coming.

We walk together between the yew trees to the chapel. Really, I tell myself, this place isn't as bad as I expected. The architecture is tasteful and unobtrusive: a bit like a good undertaker. We turn, and see a woman in her sixties ahead of us: a cousin of mine, the daughter of one of my grandmother's sisters. I haven't seen her for decades; but she still looks as beautiful to me as I remember from my teens. I suppose I was always a little in love with her. Her life has not turned out easily, and her head is bowed, but she still has something of the sparkle I remember from nearly five decades before. These relatives of mine are resilient people, it seems to me. It takes more than loss and unhappiness to crush them. Obscurely, for the first time in my life, I feel a certain pride in being one of them.

An older woman walks slowly into the chapel ahead of us, helped gently and tactfully by a smart, upright man who could be a few years younger; I have never seen him before, but I know her, of course. She is another of my grandmother's nieces, almost the same age as my father would have been, and once upon a time there had been an idea that they might marry. It had come to nothing, perhaps because of my father's wildness, but everything would have been remarkably different if it had happened. This isn't merely a gathering of relatives; it's a collection of past possibilities, of paths not taken.

Inside, with the sun glinting through the reds and blues of the stained glass and colouring the blond, grainy wood which modern chapels always go in for, a bright, jovial, attractive woman stands in the front row, looking round at us newcomers. My uncle Alan's widow is a woman of courage and spirit, having carried on his business and various others and brought up two daughters at the same time. I remember her wedding day in Pont Street: an eruption of glamour in the quiet Simpson existence. I was in my teens at the time, and most of the people at present settling down in the chapel pews were there. And now Diana herself has only a year or so to live.

The clergyman is unobtrusive, with a voice like a polite sheep. He knows, and we know, that officiating at these things is simply a way for a cleric to make a bit of extra money. There is no question of pastoral care at a crematorium; the vast majority of the people who are brought here to be dealt with will have had no interest in, no contact with, religion of any kind. Most will have shied away from it all their lives; and it is only because the survivors who arranged the funeral feel there is something formal and proper about an Anglican service that this is taking place here at all. A touch of ceremony to see off the departed: the equivalent of putting a couple of copper coins on their eyes. Well, I've seen opium addicts dying in ditches, unnoticed by their fellow-addicts around them, slipping into death among the unburied bones of others who had died before; so a little ceremony means something to me. Without it we are nothing more than the beasts of the field.

The clergyman knows that as well. He has to check the name of the deceased from another piece of paper as he reads through the formulaic prayers, and announces the hymns which even the most heathen among us know.

> A thousand ages in Thy sight
> Are like an evening gone.
> Short as the watch that ends the night
> Before the rising sun.

We sing it quite loudly in our anxiety to give Daphne a decent send-off, our voices trailing off at the end of each line in a peculiarly English fashion. 'Short as the watch that ends the night': how terrible that is, how depressingly true. I stand here, a man in my late fifties, soon no doubt to pass through that invisible gateway that leads to old age, decay and dissolution, with my surviving relatives all round me: my watch has passed in the time it takes to snap my fingers. The fuller the life, the quicker it goes; and maybe its fullness is only a kind of defence against time and change anyway – a defence which, in my case, has manifestly failed.

I glance round at the others. There is a definite resemblance: bony frames, strong chins, light-coloured hair. The family comes originally from East Anglia, and every blood relative here is an unmistakable Angle. If you test them, they will probably all have A+ blood in their veins, like the majority of East

Anglians do. How suitable that tribal name is, anyway! Everything about the Simpsons is angular, from their bodies to their sharp sense of humour, their peremptory way with children, with badly behaved animals and with civil servants who get above themselves and try to order them around. The wives or husbands who have married into the clan are rounder, shorter, darker, easier: type O positive, probably. Among them, the Simpsons stand out tall and fairish and assertive, like thriving weeds in an uncared-for garden.

Time, like an ever rolling stream
Bears all its sons away.

The words are intended to be comforting; but all I can think about when I hear them is the owner of the poor shrunken body in the coffin, who had no peace, no comfort, no ease in her last months, when she was desperate to die, and was only kept alive by medical skill and her body's own unconscious strength. God protect me from a death like that, I think, and in my mind I step once again round the curtain in the isolated ward where they put her, and saw her lying there.

She had been a big woman, the ranginess of the Simpson frame hidden by years of frank enjoyment of food and a charming, comfortable quality. She was easy-going and self-sacrificing, and her loud but most attractive voice was scarcely ever raised in anger. Yet there was anger there somewhere, beaten down and usually tamed; and in her last few months of life it showed itself in terrible ways.

'I hope you won't be too shocked,' said the Irish nurse defensively, as she led me towards the curtained area where my aunt lay. 'It's how she's been, you know.'

I wasn't expecting to be shocked, because I have seen plenty of unpleasant sights in my life. But I forgot that I would be looking at my aunt with the eyes of childhood, not the professional detachment gained from years of reporting on horrors. I went round the curtain, drawn on by the sound of stertorous breathing and occasional low moaning, and was very shocked indeed.

She lay on her back, sedated against pain and anger, her large comfortable body wasted away almost to thinness. She had no top teeth left, and the teeth in her lower jaw chewed away agonizingly at her upper lip, which was covered with raw, open wounds. Her eyes turned on me with a kind of silent appeal, as though she was a helpless prisoner in this terrible decaying body and I had the power of release.

I looked round. The nurse, who had certainly seen far worse, was looking at her with a kind of affection. She spoke in that patronizing way which medical people have to adopt if they are not to break down and run from the room in despair.

'Here you are. It's your nephew John come to see you. Do you remember him?'

The figure on the bed nodded; it would have been easier if she hadn't.

'She was a bit naughty at first, throwing things around and shouting, but now she's settled down very calm and quiet. But the trouble is, she's refusing to eat. It makes things very difficult.'

It was as though we were in a zoo, and the animal in the cage couldn't understand our conversation.

'Of course, we have to—. You know.'

I did know: they had had to sedate her massively. Yet it didn't seem to stop that terrible worrying at the upper lip.

'Well, I'll leave you to it. Be careful not to get her excited.'

The curtain swished. I was left alone with the last close member of my family, as frightened as if I were six years old and she was having some kind of incomprehensible, mortal fit.

Her hand, at least, hadn't changed. I remembered it from decades past: strong, well-formed, a more feminine version of my father's tough, reddened, thick-fingered hands. He and his sister used sometimes to measure their hands against one another, comparing them, laughing at themselves and their matched ungainliness, while I watched. Now I was sitting beside her, concentrating on her hand rather than on her face, with its terrible, captured, dumb eyes and its self-inflicted wounds.

'Can you hear me?'

An inclination of the head, a pressure from the fingers. The dark brown eyes strayed to my face.

'And you know who I am?'

She did: another pressure. The roaring breaths came a little more quietly.

I talked to her, and she listened and reacted calmly and, it seemed to me, entirely rationally. I asked her about all our close relatives, her mother and my father and her brother and my half-brother, and her son and his wife and their children, and with each, it seemed to me, she relaxed a little more.

Then I spoke about my own remarriage. She had been uncharacteristically critical of me for leaving my first wife and my two daughters, and it had taken several years for me to overcome my anger about that; anger that allied itself, of course, to my own feelings of guilt. I explained to her, as I had to no one else, that it looked as though Dee and I would be having a baby in seven months' time. I couldn't know – it never occurred to me – that my wife would miscarry. I was certain we would have a bouncing, happy child. Life, after all, must be packed with success and joy. Mustn't it?

'You'd like to see that, I know you would.'

The wild, animal eyes seemed to soften. There was certainly an extra pressure of the fingers.

'But you can't, unless you look after yourself. You've got to eat something. Promise me you'll start to eat again.'

She nodded.

I stayed with her for an hour and a half altogether, talking to her about all the old times, when she was a little girl, and how her mother was, and the birth of her son, and the houses she had lived in, and my father, whom she had loved; and the places she had been to, and the people she had known during her life.

It disturbed me how little I knew of it – her real life, the inwardness which all of us wear as naturally as a dressing-gown, in which every event, every memory has a logic of its own, which is obvious to us and impenetrable to everyone else. The fact was, I had no real idea who this woman was, or why she now wanted her life to end. I just knew her from one angle, like an astronomer staring at one side of the moon all his life. The underlying reality of her life, her true feelings, even her true history – these were things I knew nothing whatever about, and would never be able to understand properly now.

'You're all I've got left,' I told her, gripping her hand harder than ever in my own raw self-pity. 'You mustn't leave me.'

If she had been able to speak, she might have reminded me that she had seen very little of me for years – 'for donkey's years', she would have said; as a child I learned the expression from her. This was a fine time to come and ask her to stay, when it was clear that she had taken the decision to die, and was desperate for the blankness and relief from suffering which death offered.

Her problem was that her tough, big-boned East Anglian body refused to obey her will. What we had here was a deathbed scene, extended only because of my aunt's physical strength; and with all my talk of family and unborn children I was simply delaying the proceedings, weakening her decision to be free of all the pain and the complications attendant on approaching death. I was wasting her time, and my own, and the hospital's; and I was the only one who didn't understand that.

It was self-indulgence on my part, of course, yet I couldn't stop. Life is very strong, and it calls from one of us to another; turning your back on life is a betrayal of everything human beings exist for. Without the strength of the life-force, we would all surrender and die at the first challenge.

'Do you remember when you got married?'

She nodded. It was a quick, unremarkable post-war register office wedding in south London, nothing like the glamorous occasion she must have hoped for; and her husband, though kindly enough, was not the man she would ideally have chosen.

'Do you remember Eva's house at Marlow Road?'

Another nod. My grandmother's character, beautiful and brave, her occasional rages, and her inclination to let her life decay around her, seemed to enter the room with us.

'What about the way Roy and Alan used to walk, side by side, with their feet turned out – do you remember that?'

It was she who had once pointed that out to me, and now I thought I could detect the faintest of smiles in her eyes, even at this farthest extremity of her life.

'And Peter, as a little baby?'

No doubt about it now: at the thought of her son, her eyes filled with tears. This was manipulative of me, but I felt the need to touch her emotions.

Yet her problem, I later came to see, was not to connect herself to her emotions but to cut loose from them – to find the strength within herself to break away from the things which held her back and prevented her from clearing her mind for death. The physical pain she had suffered, the threatened loss of her leg, her diabetes, the growing sores, the decay of everything that made life decent and bearable and respectable – she needed to escape from all these things, not to be recalled to her slavery to them. And in our society, which wrecks so many lives daily yet refuses to allow people to end their suffering when life becomes indecent and unbearable, this form of self-ending is the only legitimate way out.

But you can't fully realize these things when you have your health, your peace and your hopes, and I couldn't realize them now. I held on to her firm, strong hand and tried to instil life and resistance into it.

'You will wait and see my little baby born, won't you?'

The shrunken, tortured form on the hospital bed held my

hand tighter, and the almost unrecognizable head nodded faintly. Only the eyes, intense and brown, were familiar. They held my own with great pleading intensity, as I got up stiffly and pressed the bell for the nurse; they still held mine as I told her for the fiftieth time how much I loved her, and how much she meant to me; all of which was true. And I promised to come and see her again soon. Her eyes stayed on me as I held back the curtain and stepped round it, and walked out of the atmosphere of suffering and death.

I didn't go back, of course; people like me never seem to. She died two weeks later.

AT FIRST, AS THE cheerful sunlight shines down red and blue through the stained glass of the crematorium on so many white heads of hair, we all seem full of gloom and sorrow. But slowly it is noticeable that the singing grows louder, as though it is starting to purge us and replace our feelings with a proper show of affection and respect for the person who has died.

> Thou art our God while Ages last,
> And our eternal home.

The liturgy of the Anglican Church is particularly good for this kind of replacement therapy. We find ourselves chanting the responses and chorusing the 'amens' with growing enthusiasm; and when the coffin has disappeared behind the stagy curtains and the notes from the organ have rumbled away for the last time, we stand up and begin smiling at one another in an unconstrained, friendly way for the first time.

Afterwards, the gathering at my cousin's house turns out to be a considerable relief. The food is good, no one patronizes or snubs anyone else, and we quickly slip into a series of anecdotes and reminiscences of Daphne and of other family members, now dead: my father among them. Even those on the outermost edges of the family join in, and for once no one questions the accuracy of the jokes, many of which are exaggerated, or suggests (as they might have done under other circumstances) that the person telling the story couldn't possibly have got the details right. In the past, a kind of companionable bickering has always characterized my family's get-togethers. Now, perhaps because such a significant figure has been taken away from us, there is only agreement.

I look round at the others, seeing them differently from the way I saw the gloomy, sombre figures at the crematorium earlier. They are no less part of a group, a clan, than they were before, but in the subdued light of a suburban sitting-room I am less aware of the physical similarities between them. The sharp edges seem to have rounded a little, and the faces are more individualistic; it is easier to see that the Simpson looks and characteristics have been thoroughly intermixed with those of other families, other backgrounds, other bloodlines.

These are not Hapsburgs, the product of an interminable history of noble intermarriage; 200 years before, the Simpsons were smallholders, carters and labourers in an obscure collection of villages near the Suffolk town of Bury St Edmunds. When they made the journey to London to settle there and better themselves, they had married into the usual wide variety of other clans: from gypsies and ne'er-do-wells to one of the grandest families in the country (though Countess Kitty had been the Earl's secretary, and probably more than that, before he finally married her in late middle age).

There was the kind of spread that was usual among the upwardly mobile, urban middle class in Britain: people settled at all sorts of different levels, and were looked down on, or up to, as a result. No genuinely blue-blooded duchess, no Qing Dynasty Chinese official, was as aware of the finest social distinctions as the British middle-middle class of the 100 years from 1840, when George Simpson had made the long social journey from Wickhambrook in Suffolk to the London suburb of Norwood. Even now, in the year 2000, when the entire structure of life is beginning to be visibly different, each Simpson around me knows exactly which rung he or she occupies, and exactly which the other members are on.

As the footsteps of the past dissolve faster than ever on the sands of modern existence, the clues become harder for people to understand, and harder still to sympathize with. In some cases they had to do with accents, or dress, or the way they held their cup or their knife, or ate their sandwiches. Nowadays the young mostly speak the same argot, with something of the same kind of accent, and their manners and dress are largely indistinguishable; which is perhaps how things should be. But at our funeral party the arcane distinctions which most of us grew up with are still evident; and as we munch our sausage rolls and our egg and prawn sandwiches we are each fully aware of these things.

Yet we tacitly agree to ignore them. This is a tribal gathering to mark the passing of a leading member, not a point-scoring session. Once again, the similarities begin to show themselves, rather than the elements of difference. The people here have a tone of speech, an attitude of mind, which is mocking and self-mocking, deprecating and self-deprecating.

I have been aware of this tone a thousand times before: from my grandfather, my father, my uncle, my aunt, my cousins, stretching out across the lines of consanguinity. Somehow, at some distant time, someone introduced a thread of it into the complex pattern of the family's discourse, and it became dominant, so that it is the first thing you think about when my family comes to mind: that sharp banter, close to bickering, which falls short of spite only because the speaker so often turns the humour against himself or herself. I can hear them at it around me now, as they sit over the remains of the meal.

'To be honest, I feel nowadays I've got one foot in the grave and another on a banana skin.'

'The silly old thing – she's almost as stupid as I am.'

'Did you meet my new husband? He still flies a plane at the age of seventy-eight, you know. Must be the oldest pilot in the country. I told him he'd better not take me up, or else it'd be the last flight he ever made. Do you think it's possible to back-seat-drive in a plane?'

Sitting there, letting the conversation flow over me, I

remember how this sharp, self-mocking Simpson tone brought me some comfort in the days immediately after my father died suddenly and unexpected, at the age of sixty-five. I had had to go through the miserable chores which follow anyone's death: registering it, paying the bills, cutting off the milk and the newspapers, informing the tax authorities, telling the post office not to deliver any more letters.

I managed to hit the post office on the day they handed out old-age pensions, and a long and depressing line of claimants lay ahead of me. I watched as one particularly ancient character, pallid with age and illness, shuffled forward in the queue; and to my right, as though someone was speaking into my ear, I heard my father's voice, with precisely the right intonation, say words which only he, with his particular version of the family sense of humour, could possibly have said.

'By God, I looked better than that poor old bastard after I'd been dead for three days.'

I don't suppose for one minute that it really was my father's spirit speaking in my ear; it must have been some objective correlative, thrown up by my intense sorrow, and my senses interpreted it as something external to myself, instead of being merely internal. All the same, the words seemed to be spoken in the air outside my head, and it was so clearly his manner, and the kind of words that only he would have used, that I was utterly convinced it had been him; and for days afterwards I was lifted out of the misery of the aftermath of his death by the feeling that he was still around, still speaking to me, and still observing us all with his sharp, satirical, mocking eye. If he had said something compassionate, loving and peaceful I would have been far less convinced.

None of us at the party after Daphne's funeral has quite my father's wit or his ability to please a crowd: certainly not I. He would have relished the conversation, even so. It has the precise family touch to it, and that gives heart to everyone there.

AFTERWARDS, AS I DRIVE back to London, the afternoon is soft and pleasant. I feel much easier in myself, much more at peace. Life has cut us off so from our families, our clans, and has taken away from us the comfort they can provide. Being with my family has somehow restored me. It's strange: I have very little in common with most of them, except our shared descent, and yet it is absolutely clear I belong with them and need them. They aren't particularly remarkable, yet with them I can, perhaps, be more of myself than with any other group of people. Families have to accept you with all your failings and inadequacies, because you are tied to them more closely than you are to a husband or wife. Those you can divorce; your family is, for richer or for poorer, in sickness and in health, in feud or in harmony, always your family.

Just as I recognized the familiar tone of the conversation among these Simpsons and their relatives, so we instantly pick up the tone of our fellow countrymen and women: their accents, their humour, their attitude to success and adversity, their good points and their dreadful points. Often, as with our own families, we are ashamed and appalled by them; yet when we are reunited with them after a period of time, it is usually with a certain sense of pleasurable relief.

The country where I was born and grew up has changed out of all recognition since the 1940s. It is unthinkably richer, yet far more dangerous and crime-ridden. It is obsessed with things that could scarcely be spoken about then. Its exaggerated respect for authority and for doing the right thing has utterly evaporated. So would the British today put up with the shortages, the bombing, the bitter cold, the hunger that the people who have appeared in this book were forced to bear? Would they be prepared to put their lives on the line, if necessary, as they did in 1914 and 1939?

I have seen British people under difficult conditions in many parts of the world. Sometimes they behave well, sometimes not so well. In that, they are no different from any other group of human beings. But two things are noticeable about British people when they get into difficulties. One is that a certain mordant humour appears quite quickly: often a little along the lines of the self-deprecating jokes my own family tend to make about themselves. The other is that, somewhere deep in their consciousness, the old attitudes about doing the right thing and not being downhearted and keeping on to the end of the road and not showing off and giving the other chap a chance are as much present now as they ever were, even if it is unfashionable to speak about such things.

In other words, the British still recognizably belong to the same stock as some of the people we have come across in these pages: the soldiers who looked after my heavily pregnant mother on her way to Blackpool to give birth to me; the housewives who kept things going while the bombs fell; the Chindits who slowly realized they could fight better in the jungle than the Japanese could; the men and women who endured the rationing and the power cuts and the shortages, and made their grumbling jokes about it all. Their responses to all these things were distinctive, and you can see precisely the same responses today. And although the ethnic make-up of Britain is partly different today from what it was sixty years ago, it is noticeable that the second- and third-generation newcomers assume precisely the same attitudes and the same sense of humour as the rest.

So as I drive, I find myself ignoring the music on the car radio and thinking instead about all these links between us, as family members and members of the same nation. This, I suppose, is the real basis for a post-modern patriotism: not that my country is better than yours, or that my family is better than yours, but that it is simply my country, with all its failings and embarrassments; and I might as well accept that, and make the best of it. It is the same with family pride. Today I have seen my family at its best, behaving as a group and behaving rather well. I haven't always liked my family in the past, but having recognized so much of myself and my other relatives, now dead, in them, I can't fail to sense the closeness between us.

And as I start to reach the depressing high streets, the unnaturally bright shops and the rows of small houses and the blocks of flats, which are the real London just as much as the grand squares and avenues are, I begin to think more about my own past, and my family's past, and the country's past. We can't by any means always be proud of the things we have done, and our families have done, and our country has done. Often we prefer to thrust the bad things out of sight into drawers and cupboards, like we do when the house is untidy and an unexpected visitor turns up. But they belong to us all the same; they're just as much a part of us as the neat and presentable things are. As individuals, as families, as a country we can never be entirely free of our past, and it is probably bad for us if we pretend we can.

I am the result of my past: screwed up by it, indeed; who wouldn't be screwed up by having to choose between their father and mother on a front doorstep at the age of less than seven? Yet the process strengthened me too, just as I was strengthened by having to stay hidden at home for an entire year at the age of five, because my father didn't have the money to send me to school. The emotional stress created by my parents' constant rows steadied me, made me feel I had to look after myself in life, and look after other people as well; and being on my own, reading and playing day and night made me deeply self-sufficient.

We are who we are. We are what we are made. We can hate it or we can come to terms with it: the choice is ours. That, anyway, is what I feel as I hit the ugly road that takes me past Croydon Airport, and decide to make a detour through the part of Croydon where my father first met my mother, and they and my unborn self were nearly killed, and where my mother and I first left my father, and on towards the city itself. Of course this area would be easier on the eye if it had been Paris or Rome. Of course it would have been better if my parents had been healthy, wealthy and happy. But it isn't, and they weren't.

Cutting back to the main road after looking briefly at Kidderminster Place, where some of these things happened, I stop at a set of interminable traffic lights on an ugly street corner. Kids in sloppy clothes slouch by, jostling each other and laughing, as though they're looking for a crime to commit. I glare at them balefully from across the generations. Yet who knows what they really think? Who knows the difficulties they face, the choices they will have to make, the harsh experiences that lie ahead of them?

Some words from an old film drift into my mind: forgiveness, acceptance, love. Hackneyed, I suppose, mawkish even; yet these are three of the most important instincts any of us possesses.

The traffic light changes, and as I drive off I am still thinking it over. Forgiveness, acceptance, love. Maybe I should write a book about that.